GAVIN BELL is a journalist who has discovered that writing books makes an agreeable change from reporting on wars, coups, and other such absurdities. After working in a bewildering number of countries for Reuters and *The Times*, he set off on his own account to write a book called *In Search of Tusitala*, which won the Thomas Cook/*Daily Telegraph* Travel Book of the Year Award. *Somewhere over the Rainbow* is his second book. When last heard of he was living in his native Scotland, although this has probably changed by now.

Also by Gavin Bell

In Search of Tusitala

SOMEWHERE OVER
THE RAINBOW

Travels in South Africa

Gavin Bell

An *Abacus* Book

First published in Great Britain in 2000
by Little, Brown and Company

This edition published by Abacus in 2001
Reprinted 2002

A CIP catalogue record for this book
is available from the British Library.

ISBN 0 349 11261 4

Typeset by Palimpsest Book Production Limited,
Polmont, Stirlingshire
Printed and bound in Great Britain by
Clays Ltd, St Ives plc

Abacus
An imprint of
Time Warner Books UK
Brettenham House
Lancaster Place
London WC2E 7EN

www.TimeWarnerBooks.co.uk

For John Rubython

Acknowledgements

Travelling alone has its rewards. One of them is a finer appreciation of hospitality and kindness extended by those encountered along the way. There are many South Africans who may never read this book to whom I am grateful for help and companionship when both were needed.

Among those who made the miles worth travelling was Davie Cadenhead, chief engineer of the SA *Sederberg*, whose wry humour was a highlight of a splendid voyage; in Cape Town, John Rubython proved the value of old friendship; and in the Jonkershoek valley, Strydom and Hermien van der Merwe generously shared a haven of peace and beauty.

On the edge of the Kalahari, Llewellyn and Mariana Stadler introduced me to life and death in the wild, although they forgot to tell me about the scorpions; in Bloemfontein, Waldie and Maynie Greyvensteyn exemplified Afrikaner hospitality; and in QwaQwa the amiable Fusi Mokubung made me feel at home among the southern Sotho people. In Johannesburg, John Battersby provided a congenial refuge from muggers and flame-throwing motorists, and Steve Crawford kept the show on the road by miraculously repairing my Stone Age laptop.

Godfrey Moloi, the 'Godfather of Soweto', was a star who will be missed; and the company and stories of Willie and Riana Delport around their bush fire in the Marico will linger long in the memory; so will Mashudu Dima's tales of enchanted forests and sacred lakes in the land of the VhaVenda. In Port Elizabeth, Gerda Coetzee banished weariness with bright spirits and home comforts; and at the beginning and the end of my travels, and happily sometimes in between, Connie Greyvensteyn was my personal rainbow. To all of you, thank you in whatever language you use.

Itinerary

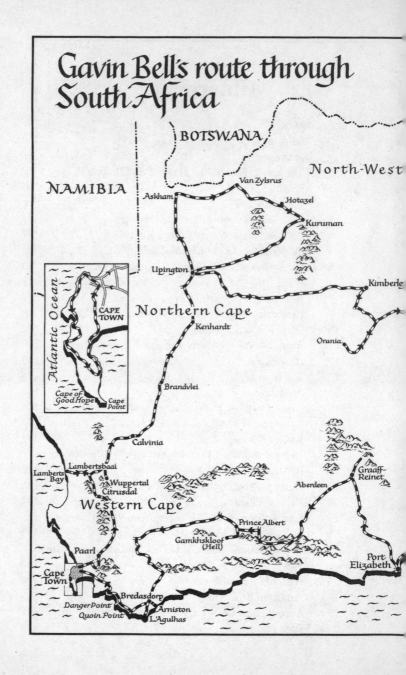

Gavin Bell's route through South Africa

BOTSWANA

NAMIBIA

North-West

Van Zylsrus

Askham

Hotazel

Kuruman

Upington

Kimberle

Northern Cape

CAPE TOWN

Kenhardt

Orania

Atlantic Ocean

Brandvlei

Cape of Good Hope

Cape Point

Calvinia

Lambertsbaai

Lamberts Bay

Wuppertal
Citrusdal

Graaff-Reinet

Aberdeen

Western Cape

Prince Albert

Paarl

Gamkhskloof (Hell)

Port Elizabeth

Cape Town

Bredasdorp

Danger Point

Arniston

Quoin Point

L'Agulhas

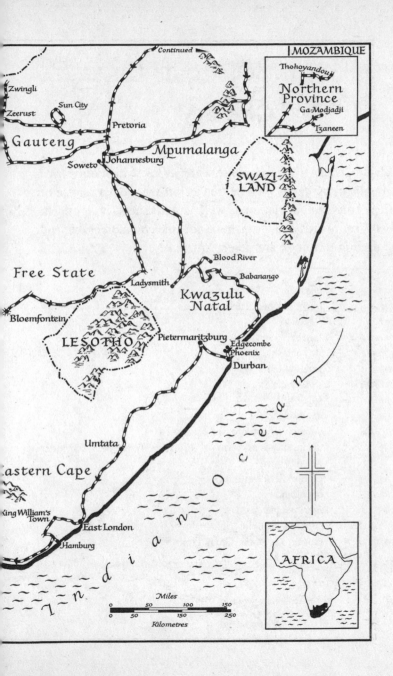

Glossary

It is claimed that Afrikaans is more widely spoken in South Africa than English, and it may well be true as it is the mother tongue of the Cape coloured population as well as Afrikaners. In any event many of their words and terms have become common usage, and those used in this book are hereby translated:

baas	boss
bakkie	open, flat-bed truck
boer	farmer
boerewors	farmers' sausage
braaivleis	barbecue
dorp	small country town
koeksisters	syrupy cakes
koppie	small hill
kraal	enclosure
laager	defensive formation of ox-wagons
Oom	uncle (used as term of affection or respect for older person)
stoep	ground floor veranda
veld	open land
volk	folk, people
volkstaat	people's republic
voortrekker	pioneer (as in the Great Trek)

Look at your hands – different colours representing different people. You are the rainbow people of God.

Archbishop Desmond Tutu

Somewhere over the rainbow, skies are blue
And the dreams that you dare to dream really do come true

Judy Garland (Arlen/Harburg)

The way I see it, if you want the rainbow, you gotta put up with the rain.

Dolly Parton

Prologue

The story goes that when God came to make South Africa, he summoned St Peter to witness his finest creation.

'Mountains that pierce the sky, great forests that shelter all manner of wondrous creatures, endless plains and deserts and grasslands to far horizons. All these things shall this land have,' God said. Peter was impressed. 'Beaches as fine as powdered gold, washed by clear waters and caressed by tropical zephyrs,' God went on. 'And beneath the mountains and the rivers a treasure trove of gold and diamonds, platinum and uranium, riches beyond dreams.' Peter said this was wonderful, but wouldn't South Africans be the envy of every other nation on earth?

'No, they won't,' God said.

'Why not?'

'Wait till you see the government I'm going to give them.'

The story was told to me by a minister in the last white government in Africa, at a cocktail party on a Cape wine farm. Apartheid was collapsing all around him, the dreaded *swart gevaar* (black danger) was loose in the streets and demanding power, and he was joking about a generation of institutionalised racism. South Africa is a surprising country. I first saw it in 1988, when I was posted to Johannesburg as a foreign correspondent. In those days apartheid was still firmly in place, and presided over by a brotherhood of Afrikaners who knew when they were on to a good thing. God in His infinite wisdom had ordained white supremacy, and appointed the Dutch Reformed Church as His spokesman, so all was right with the world.

After decades of repression, I expected black people in South Africa to regard me, as a white, with hostility. At best, I anticipated surliness and resentment. Instead, I found myself among agreeable people more intent on making the best of the little they had than on beating up foreign journalists. In the townships, football matches attracted bigger crowds than political rallies, possibly because they were more entertaining and less dangerous. Shortly after Nelson Mandela was released from prison, I spoke to a truck driver who lived in a shack in a black township near Cape Town. He said: 'I think it is important every person should vote, because if you have a white man in power he will look only on his side, and if you have a black man he will look on his side, so you need the two to look after everybody.' This from a man who had been regarded by whites as inferior for all of his life.

By the time I left in 1993, racism had been abolished from the statute books. The leaders of the main parties were negotiating a power-sharing arrangement, and a threatened right-wing backlash had failed to materialise. I had seen the first cracks appearing in the ivory tower of apartheid, I had seen it crumbling, and I had seen the amazing Mandela stride from its ruins like a latter-day Samson. Now he and his erstwhile jailers were working together to build a democratic society, it was time for me to leave. It was then I realised I had missed out on the mountains that pierce the sky. I had caught glimpses of the great forests and endless grasslands, but I had never explored them. In the rush to report on the collapse of Africa's equivalent of the Berlin Wall, there had been little time to wander off the beaten track and enjoy the natural wonders of the country. In five years in South Africa, I had not been to a game reserve; for all the dramatic events I had witnessed, I had never seen a lion in the wild.

There was something else I had missed. I became aware of it on my return to London, when a friend asked why South Africa was not engulfed by civil war. How is it, he wanted to know, that black and Afrikaner extremists were not at each others' throats, and dragging everybody else into the abyss of a race war? It was a reasonable question, to which I had no clear answer. So why is it a beloved country, and why should anybody cry about it? Desmond Tutu dubbed it hopefully the 'Rainbow Nation', symbolising ethnic diversity and harmony in a country that has eleven official languages, two national anthems, and a parliament that shuttles between two cities. What holds this kaleidoscope of fractious tribes together, and makes people care passionately about it? Clearly there is a spirit, or a sense of identity, in South Africa that binds people of different cultures to the land, and hence, by association, to each other. I had seen it in the eyes of Afrikaner farmers, surveying land that had been in their families for generations, and I had caught echoes of it in the voices of township choirs singing of ancient migrations. Somehow this essence of the country had eluded me, so I decided to go back and look for it.

What I found was a country in the throes of transition – past imperfect, present tense, future conditional. Life in the 'new' South Africa was an emotional roller-coaster, swinging between hope and despair, buoyed by a sense of freedom and haunted by fear of violent crime. Half the population had mobile telephones, the other half had no running water, and all of them were afraid of being mugged. If South Africa was a person it would be a schizophrenic half-caste with a bag of corn in one hand, a cellphone in the other and a gun behind its back. Johannesburg was diligently acquiring a reputation as crime capital of the world, and even the laid-back Western Cape had its share of homicidal lunatics. While I was there, the *Cape Times* noted briefly that eighteen murders and five rapes had been reported in the province over the Christmas period, but police were not unduly concerned. Superintendent Wicus Holtzhausen was quoted as saying: 'If you consider that as many as ten or twelve people are murdered on a normal weekend, then eighteen in half a week is not so bad.'

Writing about this 'Rainbow Nation' posed particular problems. It was impossible to ignore the racial classifications that South Africans still used to define their culture and sense of belonging to a community within the greater whole. When a man stated his race or his tribe, he was telling you where he came from, which language he spoke, where his loyalties lay, and often what his attitudes were on any given subject. The corollary of this was that racism still lurked in all communities at all levels, and the ghosts of apartheid lingered in a land where the distance from the First World to the Third was the breadth of a street. A South African friend reminded me: 'This is a very complex, multi-layered society. No matter how you write about it, you will always get flak from somebody.' So be it, but this book was not intended to be a political or social treatise. My aim was to present snapshots of a country in search of an identity, so that readers might form their own impressions of life after apartheid in a hauntingly beautiful land.

I was also drawn by wanderlust. On the map of Northern Cape Province, near somewhere called Lower Dikgatihong, on a road to nowhere in particular, there is a speck marked Hotazel. I had long been intrigued by the name, imagining a fly-blown shanty town shimmering in the furnace of a vast plain. When I mentioned my wish to go there, a friend who knew about such places said: 'Not for you, Gav. Seriously boring. Place you want up there is Van Zyl's Drift. Wonderful, dusty little frontier town. Suggest you stay with the farmer with the pet cheetah.' It seemed the man owned a sizeable chunk of the Kalahari, where he was breeding Arabian oryx, one of the rarest antelopes on earth. He was doing this mainly because he liked the look of them. The cheetah was a family friend who wandered into the farmhouse at meal times.

It sounded like a good place to look at rainbows.

1

Makes you wonder how the old Clippers ever made it

It was the warning about ships being attacked off West Africa that caught my attention.

The message from a French radio station chattered from a printer on the bridge of the container ship SA *Sederberg*, bound for Port Elizabeth out of Tilbury. Mariners were strongly advised to avoid the ports and territorial waters of Sierra Leone, it said, because of an embargo imposed by neighbouring states following a coup d'état. At the time we were steaming south of the Bay of Biscay towards, among other countries, Sierra Leone. 'Not to worry,' the officer on watch said cheerfully. 'Won't be going anywhere near the place. Wouldn't touch it with a very long barge pole, given the choice.'

A few days later we passed the war zone at night, a respectful 100 miles from the coast. As we did so, I was awakened by a succession of blinding flashes and an intermittent roar like heavy artillery. I looked out my cabin window to see the ship, and the ocean around it, illuminated by the ghostly white lightning of an equatorial storm. The sea was calm, there was hardly a breath of wind, yet for the next hour we were treated to a celestial *son et lumière* of dazzling power and intensity. It was as if a mischievous god was playing around with a galactic light switch.

That is one of the great things about sea travel. When you are in a huge, empty waterworld you gain a new perspective on life and the universe and that sort of thing. The antics of violent men seem absurd and irrelevant on a planet where nature casually demonstrates the power to sweep all of us away.

There is also a blissful sense of release from the pressures and tensions of life ashore. The writer Malcolm Bradbury put it this way: 'My experience of ships is that on them one makes an interesting discovery about the world. One finds one can do without it completely.' I suspect that after a while I would miss trees and flowers and pubs and football, but I take his point about getting away from stuff like traffic jams and the antics of pop stars and politicians.

I admit that my adventurous spirit has limitations. I am not one for bobbing about in big oceans in little boats. Nor does the clamour and contrived gaiety of cruise ships appeal. But give me a berth on a sturdy working vessel, her holds and decks piled with cargo for the other side of the world, and I am a happy man. Throw in the use of the officers' lounge, a decent chef and a few interesting fellow passengers, and my pleasure knows no bounds. Wanderlust and a penchant for creature comforts are fulfilled.

Thus it was with a spring in my step that I boarded the SA *Sederberg*, 52,000 tons, at Tilbury for a ten-day voyage to South Africa via Dutch and French ports. This maritime leviathan was my kind of ship. One of four 'big whites' operated by the South African Marine Corporation, she looked like a recumbent skyscraper. When she left a quay, piled high with containers, the impression was that a substantial part of the docks was sailing away. This was a vessel that inspired confidence in her passengers.

At Tilbury she was an inert giant, oblivious to mobile cranes swarming over her like monstrous spiders, clawing metal boxes from her innards and clanging others in their place. I enjoyed watching this activity from the bridge, feeling like an old sea dog bound for faraway places with strange-sounding names. It beat an airport lounge hands down. 'That's a good one,' one of my fellow passengers remarked. 'There's a 20-ton container coming aboard and the man standing beneath it is wearing a hard hat. Fat lot of good that'll do him.' We observed the manoeuvre with interest, but the strength of the helmet was not put to the test.

There were seven other passengers on board, a motley crew of pensioners, an elderly Austrian millionaire and a young couple setting out on a tour of southern Africa. We all became matey over an excellent buffet dinner, during which one of the officers volunteered an analysis of the 'new' South Africa: 'The blacks are still black, and whites are still white. The blacks want what the whites have and they're not getting it yet, so they're becoming impatient.' This was held by the company to be generally true, the only question being whether the government could give the disadvantaged majority what they wanted before they started taking it.

I had intended staying up to watch the harbour lights disappearing along the Thames estuary, but long before we slipped our moorings I had retired to my cabin and been lulled to sleep by the hypnotic throb of the auxiliary engines.

Dawn in the North Sea was a grey, wintry affair. Clouds and mist and a lumpy sea merged in a monochrome gloom, through which cargo vessels loomed and vanished as if in a dream. A squall lashed the decks, reducing visibility and forming mobile lagoons that swished around the metal plating. We were bound for Rotterdam, across the busiest stretch of water in the world. It was the maritime equivalent of the M25 at rush-hour on a rainy day, and we were all deeply grateful to the chap who invented radar.

Our first port of call materialised as a dark smudge of low-lying land on which the giant propellers of a wind farm were whirling a demented greeting. The port of Rotterdam is not a pretty place, but for admirers of industrial landscapes it is a sprawling masterpiece of docks and oil refineries and chemical plants, reverberating in a cacophony of clanging and banging and hissing. As we edged cautiously into this petrified forest of smokestacks, we towered over barges and ferries and tugs scuttling across the Nieuwe Maas River. Off the bow a flock of birds in a perfect V-formation skimmed low, flashing through a shaft of sunlight that had transformed a patch of dark water into shimmering mercury. The best bit was when tugs nudged us into our berth. It was like parking the Empire State Building.

Ashore for a few hours, I discovered that Rotterdam is a pleasant city. It was agreeable to stroll along tree-lined avenues and canals where cyclists and pedestrians had rights of way over the infernal combustion engine. Wandering through a park by the river, enjoying the woodland scents and the rustle of autumn leaves, I paused on the waterfront to admire the Erasmus Bridge, a bold, modern construction with an array of cables running from a single, mighty pillar. It looked like a giant harp lying on its side, and I wondered if it made music when the wind blew.

It must have been playing something by Wagner the next day. In the Dover Straits we were ploughing into the teeth of a force eight south-westerly gale, gusting to force nine. This is described on the Beaufort scale as: 'High waves; dense streaks of foam along the direction of the wind; crests of waves begin to topple, tumble and roll over; spray may affect visibility.' It is also, for the record, very noisy.

The waves looked fearsome as they rolled towards us, their dark faces scarred with wind-streaks, spray flying from their crests. A coastal freighter to starboard was making heavy weather of it, rearing and plunging violently into walls of water raking her decks. But the *Sederberg* with her 26,000 tons of cargo battered through them with barely a tremor. She might as well have been cruising on Lake Windermere. 'Fairly piddling sea this,' our captain observed laconically. 'Hemmed in by too much land for the waves to really build up.' He recalled rounding Cape Horn in a ship five times smaller in seas three times bigger. It took four days, during which none of the crew slept. 'Interesting passage that,' he recalled. 'Makes you wonder how the old clippers ever made it. Lots of them didn't, of course.'

It is at such times that one appreciates being on a big, modern vessel, where one can observe the sea's changing moods with equanimity from a fairly stable platform 100 feet above it. It is also nice to be able to wander down to a cosy cabin, make a cup of tea, and pick up a Scarlatti sonata on the radio.

Our last view of Europe was of a quay at Le Havre, dimly perceived through gusting curtains of rain on a wild night. The long dark cloak of winter was descending on the northlands, and I was glad to be heading towards the warmth of the tropics. The final tie was broken when BBC Radio 4 faded somewhere off Finisterre and was lost. The last words I heard on it were: *Biscay, south-westerly five to seven, occasionally gale force eight.*

We felt Africa long before we saw it. Its hot breath reached out to us off the coast of Mauritania in the *harmattan*, a dusty desert wind that signalled its approach in a haze creeping over the horizon. Then came the first signs of life, a cluster of big trawlers wallowing in the Atlantic swell. We passed close enough to see that one of them was Russian, her hull and most of her superstructure deeply scarred by rust. She looked as if she was seriously polluting the sea just by being in it. Passing the bulge of West Africa, we entered the doldrums, that dreamy realm of low pressure circling the earth where the air is still and the ocean is flat and lugubrious like a giant oil slick. On the horizon, far out of sight of land, a small open boat with a dozen fishermen in it shimmered like a mirage in the vast, listless seascape.

I stood alone by the fo'c'sle and gazed at these problematic waters, musing on the courage of ancient mariners who ventured across them in rickety wooden ships without the least idea of where they were going or what they would encounter on the way. Among popular beliefs in the fifteenth century was that the southern 'sea of darkness' was boiling hot, and that the sun in these regions turned all men into negroes. Also the world was still flat, which posed the risk of falling off the edge.

We were following in the wakes of the *São Cristovão* and the *São Pantaleão*, caravels of about 100 tons that had left Portugal with a supply ship in August 1487 in search of a sea route to the Spice Islands of the east. Where we were steaming at a steady 21 knots, the little wooden vessels of Captain Bartolomeu Dias had battled against strong southerly winds, forcing them to tack out of sight of land. This was a brave manoeuvre, since the only way Dias could estimate their position was by hugging the coast. His reward came on 3 February 1488, when his ships put into a bay in the Eastern Cape, having unknowingly become the first Europeans to sail around the southern tip of Africa. There then followed the first recorded encounter between whites and natives of southern Africa. It did not go well.

When the Portuguese landed near the present town of Mossel Bay, they were observed by a group of Khoikhoi herdsmen tending cattle. The two groups eyed each other warily, then the visitors made towards a stream to fill their water casks. At this, one of the Khoikhoi hurled a stone, and others joined in. There was a sudden hissing sound, and one of the herders learned to his great surprise about crossbow technology. His companions fled, to spread the word of the terrible strangers who had appeared on their land.

Five centuries later there still appeared to be an ethnic communication problem. One evening over dinner on the *Sederberg*, an elderly woman passenger told a joke. The company had been discussing 'affirmative action', a policy used by the South African government to promote the employment of blacks in jobs previously reserved for whites. This was the joke: 'They used to live in trees and now they are branch managers.' This one-liner was greeted with evident embarrassment. 'There are a lot of these terrible jokes around,' she said. 'But they are funny. You have to laugh at them, don't you?' She was an otherwise intelligent woman, and I felt a twinge of despair.

So I went up to the darkened wheelhouse, where the officer on watch was scanning the dark blue screen of the radar and listening idly to a radio conversation in broken English between Taiwanese and Filipino seamen on passing freighters. They were discussing the attractions of Bangkok, and they sounded like excited schoolboys. Outside, the air was soft and warm. Standing on the bridge of an ocean-going ship on a clear night, watching the moon casting a silver path on the sea and sensing an utter detachment from the rest of the world, is one of life's great experiences.

So is the first time you see dolphins exploding out of the water like smiling torpedoes. They are bigger and faster than you imagine, and when they do their party trick of leaping around the bows they seem to envelop the ship in an aura of happiness. They were among the first to welcome us to the Cape, along with tail-thrashing whales, cavorting seals, and a couple of Arctic skua who hitched a ride on the fo'c'sle. After the grey desert of the North Atlantic, the blue waters off Cape Town seemed like an aquarium teeming with life. The city and its guardian mountain were obscured by clouds, but the skies cleared as we rounded a peninsula that ended in a knife-edged ridge plunging into the sea. On its extremity we could make out the white tower of a lighthouse perched on the slope like a birthday candle. It was the first time I had seen the Cape of Good Hope from the sea. Apart from the lighthouse, it appeared as it would have done to

Dias when he noticed it for the first time on his return voyage to Portugal and christened it *Cabo da Boa Esperança*, meaning hopefully this is the way to India.

Not everyone on board was looking forward to our landfall. Lungele Sunshine, a galley boy with a disposition that matched his name, was looking gloomy. He was the eighteen-year-old father of two children, but when he went home on leave his grandfather would be taking him into bush country to be circumcised, in accordance with tribal customs proclaiming his manhood. Sunny was deeply worried by this, as he had every right to be given the rates of injury, disease and death suffered by initiates at the hands of incompetent practitioners. 'I am not happy for this, but there is no other way,' he said. The purser tried to persuade him there was an alternative, something along the lines of a point-blank refusal, but Sunny knew the ways of his people. 'There is no other way,' he said. So we wished him all the best, and assured him there was nothing to worry about, and privately shuddered.

Months later a doctor in a black township, who was training traditional healers in basic hygiene, explained the purpose and importance of the circumcision rites. During his period of exile in the bush, the youth learned how to provide for his family and to defend them if necessary. 'When our boys come back to us as men we are very proud,' the doctor said. Personally I would not have blamed Sunny for staying on the boat.

I had forgotten about the sharp, clear light of South Africa. It makes everything look as if it has just been cleaned and polished. Even the unprepossessing waterfront of Port Elizabeth was sparkling in the morning sunshine as tugs worried the *Sederberg* into her berth. Beyond a tangled spaghetti of elevated motorways along the shore, I could see the floodlights of a sports stadium rising from the urban sprawl. A steam engine was pulling a string of green and white coaches near the shore and tooting in a friendly way. A strand of white cloud hung virtually motionless in the blue sky, and the warmth of the sun felt good on my back. I was glad to be going ashore, but there was a vague sense of loss. Bonds develop quickly between people and a ship on which, however briefly, their lives depend. It is a barely sensed attachment that one becomes fully aware of only when it is broken. The young couple making their first voyage seemed sad. 'It's like a family breaking up and going out alone into the big bad world again,' the man said. 'Quite scary, really.'

Happily they were not present when a customs officer in the purser's cabin welcomed me to South Africa with the news that a man in a local township had raped a thirteen-year-old girl, stabbed her thirteen times, and then slashed her throat. 'They should bring back the death penalty, it's the only way to stop these killings,' he said. He was an amiable, soft-spoken Afrikaner, and he seemed sad rather than angry. 'Ach, we have troubles in this country, but maybe it will come right,' he said. In the meantime, he hoped I would enjoy my stay in South Africa. Go well, he said.

I had arranged to fly immediately to Cape Town and begin my journey from there, so as to follow in the footsteps of the first European settlers. The other reason I was eager to get to Cape Town was that it is situated in arguably the most splendid setting of any city on earth.

2

The fairest Cape

People who live in and around Cape Town have a big advantage over the rest of us. It is massive, in fact, about 6 miles long and 2 miles wide, and on a clear day it can be seen 125 miles out to sea. It is adorned with more plant species than all of the British Isles, and it is the only geographical feature on earth to have a constellation named after it. This can be seen near the Southern Cross and it is called *Mons Mensa*, which is Latin for Table Mountain.

Personally, I think this 3,000-feet-high wilderness in the middle of a city is without peer. So did Francis Drake evidently, on his jaunt on the *Golden Hind* in 1580, being moved to write in his journal of 'the fairest Cape we saw in the whole circumference of the earth'.

The rugged profile of Table Mountain dominates everything in every direction as far as the eye can see, and from every aspect it is wonderful. Its northern face is unquestionably the most magnificent natural amphitheatre on the planet. Draped in a mantle of white clouds beneath an azure sky, it is like a fantasy kingdom, the work of a creator who decided to complete Africa with an artistic flourish. St Peter must have given it a standing ovation.

Every time I came to Cape Town as a journalist, I used to

gaze gratefully at the green slopes of the mountain sweeping up to grey ramparts etched against the skyline, and I always felt uplifted and a profound sense of peace. In her later years, my grannie was fond of quoting from the 121st Psalm when I took her on car trips through the highlands of Scotland. 'I to the hills will lift mine eyes,' she used to say with a quiet smile. It's a pity she never saw Table Mountain. I think she would have regarded it as a celestial vision.

The airport was bigger and busier than I remembered, and there seemed to be more traffic, but the mountain worked its old magic as an agent of the shipping company drove me to the city. I mentioned that I intended buying or renting a car for a few months, and asked if he had any advice.

'Will you be going to Joburg?'

'Yes.'

'Get one with a machine gun.'

I looked at the mountain, and it said relax, enjoy the sunshine, and worry about that stuff later.

Sentiment took me to an old colonial pile by the sea called Winchester Mansions. It had begun life at the turn of the century as private apartments in the Cape Dutch style, ranged around a courtyard with a fountain, with crimson bougainvillea climbing to open verandas. In the 1930s it was converted to a hotel with self-catering facilities, and over the years it had become worn around the edges like many of its clients. When I first stayed there the furniture had seen better days and room service was a leisurely affair, but the suites smelled of old wood and the sea, and the elderly ladies who ran the place made a fuss of me. I loved the fading elegance of it all.

It was still a handsome whitewashed building framed by palm trees, but it had gone upmarket. The staff were younger and more efficient, and the refurbished apartments had rosewood furniture, and deep pile carpets and big mirrors in gilt frames. My suite had a television in each of its three rooms. It was all very smart, but its charm had gone, like a cosy pub that had been renovated with pseudo Olde Worlde decor. The old dears who used to potter about the palm court were gone, and in their place were business suits chattering into mobile phones. I felt lost.

At least the view was the same. From my window an expanse of grass ran to a promenade bounded by a low wall. Beyond it big blue-grey waves were swelling and heaving and tumbling on to the rocks in a chaos of white spray. Boys were kicking a ball around on the grass, and people were walking their dogs and jogging along the seafront, all of them washed by that clear, bright light. It was balm to the spirit to watch, and even better to slip on running shoes and join them.

Most of the joggers were white, sporting designer athletic wear to enhance images of the body beautiful. The classic racial contrast of South Africa was provided by a few human wrecks sprawled on the grass verges, wizened coloured men and women seeking oblivion in bottles wrapped in brown paper. Then along came a road race, a long file of runners pattering and plodding along the promenade. They were a multi-racial mix, but the first six were black men, loping gracefully like gazelles as if their feet were barely touching the ground. They were a pleasure to behold, and they were way, way ahead of everybody else.

Greenmarket Square is a lively kind of place. The first time I came here riot police were spraying anti-apartheid protesters with purple-dyed water. In a heroic act etched in the memories of Capetonians, one of the demonstrators climbed on to the water cannon, pushed aside its handler, and turned it on the massed ranks of police. It was a moment reminiscent of Czechoslovakia and Tiananmen Square, and in that glorious purple haze, amid a crescendo of cheering, we knew that the tide had turned. The purple people would overcome.

The square in the heart of Cape Town was still buzzing, but this time there were no cops. A deep, insistent beat of drums was throbbing across the plaza, with its flea market of clothes and books and African carvings and aromatherapy oils and whatever else the entrepreneurs of the streets could lay their hands on. In a side street a troupe of barefoot children in blue cotton shorts was performing a song and dance routine, their lithe bodies swaying and stamping and clapping in tune with a choir of their elder sisters. From somewhere drifted the notes of a tenor sax, flitting through a jazz number with nonchalant artistry. The ancient rhythms of Africa and the vitality of the townships had come to the big white city, and everybody seemed relaxed about it.

So you sit at a pavement café and watch the multi-racial crowds strolling in the sunshine, and you think: this is the way it should be, this is Tutu's human rainbow. You are aware that behind the music and the smiles there is deprivation and violence and racism, but you sense that here are people striving to rise above all of that, and you wish them well.

This is a country where you can observe one culture while immersed in another. The musicians in Church Street were African, but the ambience in Café Mozart, with its red and white checked tablecloths and prints of old Vienna, was European. Posters at the counter were advertising a performance of Mozart's *Requiem* in the City Hall (security provided), an illustrated lecture on classical gardens and villas of Italy and a Christmas auction of lead soldiers, dolls and teddy bears on behalf of the Red Cross Children's Hospital Appeal. Outside, people were browsing among bric-a-brac stalls in a pedestrian alley of art galleries and antique shops. It was an agreeable scene, but patrons of the café beneath sun umbrellas were being hassled by beggars, and occasionally harangued by crazies raging at the turmoil in their minds. There was a pursing of lips and hunching of shoulders over the salmon and broccoli quiche, an uneasy sense of a tide of Third World poverty lapping at the shores of Western civilisation.

South Africa is like that. One minute people are optimistic, and the next they are filled with foreboding. The transition to majority rule has been a traumatic experience that has produced a nation of schizophrenics: proud and confident one day, depressed and paranoid the next. The first serious question most visitors face is: 'What do you think will happen to us?' An honest answer depends on the atmosphere or experiences of the day.

To lighten my mood, I went for a stroll along one of my favourite streets. The upper end of Long Street, heading towards the northern face of Table Mountain, had the louche air of a place that remembered when the city was known as the Tavern of the Seas by scurvy-ridden sailors voyaging between Europe and the Spice Islands. The rumbustious bars and brothels were gone, but Victorian buildings with fancy iron balconies preserved a flavour of the past in their second-hand bookstores, junk shops and seedy cafés. I was heading for an old haunt called Cranford's, which I considered the best bookstore in the known universe, a cornucopia of old books in a dozen languages, packed two deep on shelves that you needed a ladder to reach and mysteriously in unmarked cardboard boxes in musty rooms, a labyrinth of literature presided over by an elderly man who looked like a silver-haired gnome. He was usually found behind an ancient wooden desk, framed by piles of books and manuscripts that looked as if they were about to collapse and bury him. The first time I went into the shop I had been looking for an obscure work by Robert Louis Stevenson. The proprietor regarded me with interest, discoursed knowledgably on one of the essays in the book, and offered me a choice of two editions. From then on I was a faithful customer.

Cranford's was no more. It was an empty shell, with a notice on the window saying it was being converted into a restaurant.

A woman in a shop a few doors down said the bookseller had
been in dispute with his landlord and had been evicted. After
a half-hearted attempt to sell the books at cut price, most of
them had been put in black plastic bags and taken in lorries to a
landfill site. 'There were first editions among them,' the woman
said. 'A real shame, isn't it?' I thought of tens of thousands of
books being dumped in the earth, and the shortage of books of
any kind in schools in black townships, and fantasised about
taking out a contract on the landlord with local gangsters. Then
I went to look for another landmark that I was fairly confident
would still be there.

St George's Cathedral is a handsome, neo-Gothic structure
built from Table Mountain sandstone, designed by Sir Herbert
Baker at the turn of the century. Apart from ministering to the
Anglican community of the city, under Archbishop Desmond
Tutu it served as a focus for passive resistance to apartheid, at
once a symbol of defiance and a refuge for those who opposed
the system. A brass plaque had been placed on a small lectern
in a nearby pedestrian mall. It said that on 13 September 1989, a
protest march of 30,000 people had proceeded from the cathedral
to the old City Hall, and it was there that Tutu had first proclaimed
to a multi-racial crowd: 'We are the Rainbow People. We are the
new people of South Africa.' Years later I met Tutu in Scotland,
and I asked him if much had changed. 'Well, now if you go on
a protest march you have to walk all the way,' he said ruefully,
'because the police don't stop you any more.'

There had been other changes. Instead of anti-apartheid rallies,
the noticeboard outside the cathedral was advertising a performance of Bruckner's *Mass in E Minor*. An insurance company
had jumped on the gospel bandwagon by erecting a billboard in
the church precincts declaring that, with their unit trust returns,
'You could say we're blessed.' You could also say that their
marketing was crass.

The last time I was in the cathedral it was packed with frightened people who had been driven from the streets by riot police while staging a demonstration. Outside it was ringed by armoured cars, and framed through a glass door I saw a beefy plain-clothes policeman standing astride the path with a long whip. He looked impatient. A minor cleric came out and roused the congregation to a frenzy with a squeaky imitation of Martin Luther King, declaring that the day of reckoning was nigh and that they would overcome. He was followed by Tutu, who called for silence. He reminded them where they were, then he said: 'We shall overcome, of course, and do you know when that will be? It will be when those chaps out there come in and join us in prayer, because remember they are Christians too.' It was a moving affirmation of Christian beliefs, and it had the desired effect. When the crowd left they did so quietly in an orderly double file, holding hands. The police, bewildered, stood aside.

The cathedral was empty now, its vaulted ceilings echoing to nothing more disturbing than the traffic outside. A couple of young tourists wandered around, speaking in hushed voices, and a verger in a long black cassock strode by with a cup of tea. Looking through the glass door, instead of armoured vehicles I saw a group of children, black, white, and brown, sitting on the grass listening to a lecture by their teacher. A notice by the entrance said the running costs of the church were 1,000 rands a day, and would visitors consider donating ten rands, which represented fifteen minutes' maintenance. For old times' sake, and in appreciation of the improved view through the glass door, I put in enough to keep it going for the next half hour.

The seeds of democracy nurtured in St George's were taking root in a splendid Victorian edifice of red brick and white granite around the corner. The National Assembly, set in botanical gardens laid out in 1652, always had a Lewis Carroll quality about it. With its corinthian columns sparkling in the sunshine, it made me think of a gingerbread palace with icing on top. It was here, beyond the looking-glass of apartheid, that a generation of legislators lived in an elaborate fantasy world of three chambers representing whites, coloureds and Indians while blithely ignoring the majority of the population. The first sign that times had changed was the absence of policemen at the gates. The shady avenue past the parliamentary buildings, once strictly controlled, was now open to anyone who cared to stroll along it.

Also the huge painting of the last National Party cabinet was gone. It used to hang inside the main entrance, a portrait of white supremacy beaming with self-assurance. In its place was a canvas that looked as if the artist had dropped a tin of red paint on it. The work was part of an international exhibition of 'art against apartheid', sponsored by the United Nations, which had transformed the Assembly into a cross between a museum and a modern art gallery. One of the more dramatic works was a huge portrait of a young black man, wearing a bright yellow cape, with his right fist raised in a gesture of either defiance or triumph. It was inscribed 'Biko', after the black consciousness leader murdered by security police. As I passed it, a guide was explaining to a group of tourists: 'Some of the paintings are not really beautiful; they are explosive and aggressive. You know some of our Afrikaner visitors don't like them.'

An interesting contrast between old and new was on display in the main chamber, which was staging the weekly political frolics known as Question Time. On one side of the Assembly were the multi-racial ranks of the African National Congress, which included women in brightly coloured African dresses and a man in a yellow suit. On the other sat the rump of the National Party and its allies, made up largely of middle-aged men in dark suits. One half was an ethnic and sartorial rainbow, the other was as colourful as a pedestrian crossing.

I noted the first question addressed to the deputy president:

'Whether the government is complying with the requirements for good governance in respect of affordability, cost-effectiveness, the size of government, the rendering of services and account-ability; if not, what is the position in this regard; if so, what are the relevant details?' The brief reply, unsurprisingly, was something along the lines of: 'Yes.' After this witty sally, we were treated to a rapier thrust by the leader of the opposition. Why was it, he wanted to know, that violent crime was spiralling out of control, and was it true the government was a bunch of closet commies? Thabo Mbeki, the heir apparent to Nelson Mandela, said basically they were doing their best to tackle crime, and if some of them had communist sympathies it was beside the point.

The exchanges were generally good-humoured and meaning-less, the usual fourth-form scrapping that passes for political discourse in most of the world's democracies. When it was over, I watched with interest erstwhile foes across the racial divide leaving the chamber together, arm in arm in cosy political embraces. They had a long way to go to heal the wounds of the past, but at least this was an improvement on chucking people out of sixth-floor windows of police stations.

Passing the Biko portrait on my way out, I asked an usher what had been hanging there before. He had been working in parliament for twenty-five years, but he couldn't remember. So he asked passers-by, including National Party deputies, and they puzzled and frowned for a while, but they couldn't remember either. Then I asked him, a middle-aged Afrikaner, how the new parliament was for him. 'It's good,' he said. 'The new people here work together well. It's like a jigsaw puzzle coming together, with a tree and a mountain and a river.' I swear, this is what he said.

Musing on this unexpected eloquence, I wandered into the parliamentary shop. The souvenirs on offer included samples of Robben Island quarry rock, of the kind once mined by much of the present government, sold in cardboard boxes decorated with smiling portraits of Mandela against the backdrop of Table Mountain. I tried to figure why anybody would want a piece of Robben Island on their mantelpiece, but I gave up.

Outside, General Louis Botha was still sitting proudly on a prancing horse by the main gate, his bronze uniform glinting in the sunshine. He had many fine qualities, this Boer commander who became the first prime minister of South Africa. As a soldier he fought against British imperialism with distinction, and as a statesman he campaigned for reconciliation and political compromise. But not with blacks. The idea that they should be granted equal rights with whites was a weird notion that only loopy foreigners could dream up. So I wondered how he liked the view. Directly in front of him, the side wall of a building that had once housed offices of the Information Ministry (known to foreign journalists as the Ministry of Truth) had been adorned with a mural. It depicted a multi-racial crowd queuing at a ballot box, and heading towards a promised land symbolised by sunshine, a dove and a rainbow. They were carrying placards that said 'down with apartheid', 'one person one vote' and 'equal education for all'. I would not have been surprised to hear the grinding of bronze teeth.

All of this was fairly cosmetic, of course. It is easy to paint slogans on a building, but millions of South Africans still did not have a decent building to live in. So I went to see how the newly enfranchised majority was enjoying life in the 'Rainbow Nation'.

3

Mandela mustn't be quiet about us

The Cape flats is a dusty, wind-swept plain that stretches south-east of Cape Town to the shores of False Bay, which has, incidentally, one of the highest concentrations of great white sharks in the world. So if you grow tired of life on the flats, there is a solution.

Few white people have been to this conglomeration of black and coloured townships that sprawls around the airport. Most view it only from the air, a sea of dreary suburbs and shanty towns that reek of poverty and danger. They would no more venture there than swim across False Bay. In the bad old days, police and journalists and a handful of teachers and clerics were about the only whites seen in the townships. My most distinct memory of the area was the stench of teargas and burning tyres.

Local entrepreneurs had begun to run tours of the flats, so I decided to join one for a fresh perspective. Our party gathered in a minibus included an elderly Dutchman, a woman tour guide from Washington, two young men from Norway and a real estate developer from New York. South Africans do not generally go on such excursions; it is not their idea of a fun day out. As we drove through Cape Town, we were given an introductory lesson in apartheid by our guide Mohammed, a young man from one of the coloured communities. The idea was that Mohammed would point out a pedestrian and ask us to identify whether the person was black or coloured. The tourists got about half right, which was probably not a bad average on the old race classification board.

Our first stop was a museum in a converted church, devoted to an area called District Six. This was a predominantly coloured ghetto where more than 50,000 people of all races mingled in a community that produced a lot of petty crooks and fine musicians. The streets were alive with the sound of music, and it was usually jazz. Then along came the apartheidniks who classified the area as white in 1966. The bulldozers moved in, and the coloured heart of the city was ripped out. Its people were dumped on the Cape flats, but a planned development of town houses for yuppies barely got off the ground. Most of the area remained a wasteland.

The faces of former residents stare from black and white photographs in the museum, images of a community obliterated as completely as any in wartime. Mr Williams the baker is playing the piano, surrounded by smiling neighbours, and a youth is flexing his muscles for the camera outside a decaying house. You find yourself being drawn into pictures of children dancing in the grounds of a church and a James Dean lookalike posing with his sweetheart by the flashy fender of an American car. One snapshot shows an ornate building with a colonnaded entrance, bearing the sign: 'British Cinema'. You want to walk through these streets, bowl a few balls with the kids playing cricket, pass the time of day with the old men on the corner, listen to some jazz. Then you see a photograph of the demolition of Constitution Street, and it looks like Beirut after a bad night's shelling.

All that remained of District Six on scrubland bounded by freeways were a few churches and mosques. The only developments were a technical college built for whites, later opened to all races, and a small cluster of townhouses cowering in a corner plot behind high gates and razor wire, with signs warning intruders of 'instant armed response'. The district had been officially renamed Zonnebloem, meaning Sunflower, but people still called it by the prosaic name it had before the life went out of it.

The politically correct Newspeak for black communities in South Africa is 'formal' and 'informal' townships. The first refers to planned developments of matchbox houses, the second are the squatter camps of tin and cardboard shacks that have mushroomed around them as people stream from rural areas in search of work. Neither is pretty, but among them there are households that aspire to rise above the squalor.

In Langa, the oldest formal township on the Cape flats, we passed a tiny house with two rooms that boasted a smart brick facade and a new wooden door and windows. The postage-stamp garden was well tended, with a floral border around a vegetable patch. A woman in a red headscarf was clearing weeds, and the New Yorker and the Dutchman got out to take photographs of her. She smiled as she continued with her work, but I felt uncomfortable. I wondered how poor whites would react to a busload of tourists pointing cameras at them. One of the Norwegians felt the same, and he wanted to know why the people were smiling. If strangers came around his house taking photographs he wouldn't like it. Mohammed said: 'Because they know we are bringing business.' Personally I think they were smiling because they were laid-back people who found tourists amusing rather than offensive. It was obvious they had a sense of humour. In an adjacent squatter camp, a dilapidated wooden shack beside a rubbish dump had a neatly painted sign above the door in Afrikaans and English: '*Net Blankes*, Whites Only'.

We entered another shack, empty save for wooden benches on the earthen floor, where men were drinking home-made beer from old oil cans. This was the neighbourhood bar, and we were invited to join in the fun. I had tried this brew before, a milky liquid made from maize, corn and barley, and it tasted foul. Having dutifully purchased a can, I passed it to an old man with a kindly face who had not quite come to grips with the new order. 'Thank you very much, *baas*,' he said.

Outside, the Washington tour guide had lined up a bunch of barefoot kids in dirty shirts and shorts, and she was saying: 'I'm going to say one, two, three, and you're all going to smile, oh pretty please.' And the children, who didn't understand a word she was saying, stared wonderingly at this noisy apparition. They were lovely ragamuffins with big eyes, little dark dolls that you wanted to pick up and hug. 'Most of these kids will fall by the wayside,' Mohammed said. 'They are from the tribal homelands, and they don't speak English, which is the teaching medium in schools. Also to go to school you need a birth certificate, and their births were never registered. Do you see the problem?'

Part of the solution lay in a low, white building nearby. It was dirty, paint was flaking from the walls, and most of the windows were broken. On muddy ground outside, women were washing clothes in concrete basins by a standpipe. This was the Chris Hani Literacy School, named after the assassinated ANC leader and founded by a dumpy woman with a big smile called Maureen who had come from the Xhosa tribal homeland of Transkei. She said: 'I started this school because these children came from Transkei and they had never been to school, and they knew nothing about urban life. They had nothing to do, they were just loitering around, and I thought I must do something for these children.'

What she did was take over an old community hall, acquire a few battered desks dumped by state schools, and start teaching English, Afrikaans and basic mathematics. She also helped the children to obtain birth certificates, to give them a chance of progressing into the state education system. For this she was charging each of her pupils five rands per month, which was less than the cost of a glass of beer. At the last count the one-room school had about 200 children of all ages, sharing fifty desks. They had no homework, because there were no textbooks, but all of them were dressed smartly in home-made uniforms of white shirts and green skirts and shorts. And they could sing and dance. 'Like to hear a song?' Maureen asked. The room filled with melodic voices, and the children swayed and shuffled their feet, and a little soprano piped up with a chorus.

'This is a song about Mandela being quiet about us,' Maureen said. 'He mustn't be quiet about us, he must help us.' It was a refrain that was echoing throughout South Africa. 'The problem is not so much the lack of facilities here,' Mohammed explained, 'it's that there are too few places like this. We need more women like Maureen.'

The longer you spend in a township, the more bemused you become by a kaleidoscope of poverty and pride, violence and kindness, deprivation and optimism. Things are bad but they could be worse, people say. I have no work, but my children are getting an education. When it rains the roof of our shack leaks, but one day maybe we'll have a brick house with curtains in the windows. And they wait patiently, with the fatalism of Africa, without rancour or bitterness, and you wonder how long it will last.

Mohammed was hard on his own community. We were passing through a poor coloured area wracked by murderous strife between gangsters and a vigilante group that called itself Pagad, an acronym for people against gangsterism and drugs. It looked like a seedy inner-city area in Britain, an urban wilderness that exuded menace. 'This is where the cocaine and the crack and the mandrax is,' Mohammed said as we passed a dreary council house estate. 'If a black family moved here they would not have a nice time. They would not be welcome. Coloureds are the most racist group in the country. They would call a black a kaffir to

his face without a tinge of remorse. That's why they still vote
for the National Party, because they don't want blacks to rise to
their level.'

The Washington tour guide and the property developer from
New York were looking confused. The black and white certainties
about South Africa were being clouded by complexities nobody
had told them about. This was not the anti-racist solidarity they
had expected to find in the Rainbow Nation. Our guide's next
little dissertation didn't help: 'Apartheid had victims in all race
groups. Whites who opposed it were considered traitors among
their own people, and they were never fully accepted in black
communities, so they found themselves in a kind of no-man's
land. It suited a lot of coloureds to have privileges denied to
blacks. So you can't just blame whites. It's easy to point fingers,
but it wasn't that simple.'

The Americans were relieved when we turned our attention to
a women's building project in a black squatter camp. Workmen
laid the foundations, and thereafter it was up to the women to
build the houses. They were doing this with ingenuity and skill,
with bricks and wood and whatever other materials came to hand.
Metal shipping containers were popular for corner sections, being
strong, watertight and easy to cut windows in. The women were
having a planning meeting when we arrived. Squatting beneath
sun umbrellas around a tree, they looked strong and happy and
confident. You knew they were enjoying themselves, and feeling
good about what they were doing.

Mohammed ended our tour on an upbeat note. Every year he
took parties of white children to visit Maureen at the Chris Hani
School and the results were spectacular, he said. 'It's amazing
the enthusiasm of the white kids to help. As soon as they get
home they go on fund-raising drives.' We all felt heartened by
this, and goodwill prevailed until the Washington woman began
arguing about the cost of the tour. She was quibbling about the

equivalent of four dollars. As she was leaving she said: 'All of you look me up and I'll show you Washington.' Nobody said anything.

The most dramatic sight in Cape Town is a table cloth. It is white, more than a mile wide, and when it flies off Table Mountain people stand and stare, transfixed by the splendour of it. The phenomenon is caused by south-east winds blowing moisture-laden air from the sea. When the air hits the mountain it rises, cools, and condenses to form thick clouds (the table cloth), which then spill over the amphitheatre of the northern face, evaporating as they descend. It is like a celestial waterfall, a plaything of the gods.

This is another reason for admiring Table Mountain. As if it is not grand enough in itself, it has to do party tricks. There are pretty mountains in Switzerland that have as much character as a chocolate box, and there are brooding bens in Scotland that dare you to set foot on them. But Table Mountain, from all angles and in all weathers, is a kindly rock of ages that seems to shelter and protect the city spread beneath it. It is a great-grandfather of mountains, more than six times older than the Himalayas which are toddlers in geological terms at a mere forty million years. Its crinkly grey visage of layered quartzite is alluring rather than daunting, and it is only a matter of time before visitors feel compelled to hike up it.

The first recorded ascent by a European was in March 1503 by the Portuguese admiral and navigator Antonio de Saldanha, who named it unimaginatively *Taboa do Cabo* (Table of the Cape). He scrambled up Platteklip Gorge, a narrow and extremely steep fault in the northern face that took him directly to the table top, more than half a mile high, from whence he probably saw more of Africa than any white man before him.

My favourite route was a longer but less strenuous stroll up the forested south-east flanks, and then along the undulating spine of the mountain to where Saldanha wandered around admiring the view. For this hike you need a stout pair of boots, waterproof clothing and a friend who knows a delicatessen that makes great Italian sandwiches. Thus equipped, I set off with my friend Connie on a clear day with a spring in my step. Within minutes we were enveloped in the quietness of a pine forest. The tall trees sheltered us from a wind blustering up from False Bay, and we tramped happily through dappled sunlight with only butterflies for company. I like butterflies, with their psychedelic wings and clearly drug-induced aeronautics, but I think we got the name wrong. This occurred to me in Korea when a friend who spoke good but imperfect English once remarked: 'Oh look, a flutterby.'

When the path emerged from the forest, we were confronted by a panorama familiar to sky-divers. To our left, clouds were whirling over a craggy rock face and vanishing in the warmer air. In every other direction, the western Cape rolled to the horizon in a patchwork of leafy suburbs and farms and mountains tumbling into the sea. Far away to the south, beyond a jumble of peaks, rose the distinctive bulk and abrupt cliffs of the Cape of Good Hope.

Then the trail traversed a bluff, turned a corner, and led into another world. Of a sudden the sense of being on the top of a mountain was gone, and instead we were in a rocky, treeless wilderness of boggy ground and low hills reminiscent of the Outer Hebrides of Scotland. There were reservoirs like lochans, their dark waters rippling in the wind, and whitewashed cottages used by workers who serviced the dams, and a narrow road between them with a line of telegraph poles marching into the mist. It had all the sad, mystical beauty of the Western Isles, and when something unseen splashed in one of the reservoirs I christened it *Loch na Beiste*, which translates fairly easily from the Gaelic. Pleased to have found a Table Mountain Monster, we sat in the shelter of a rock to tuck into Italian sausage sandwiches, washed down with hot coffee. Then we climbed up and sat on a dam wall, and watched the wind playing with the water, and listened to sweet birdcalls, and found it hard to believe we were half a mile up in the air.

One of the ubiquitous features of South African life is the museum. The cities have dozens of them, and every little *dorp* with more than a couple of streets has one. As soon as a few houses are built anywhere, up goes a church, then a school, a sports field and a museum. So I was not surprised to find one on Table Mountain with a locomotive in it. The prize exhibit of the Waterworks Museum, in a small stone building by a reservoir, was a steam engine in green and black livery with a brass-tipped funnel. It looked like a splendid toy, the kind that puffs through the pages of children's books. In fact it was a Standard Class Locomotive type 0-4-0, built by Andrew Barclay and Sons at their Caledonia Works in Kilmarnock, Scotland, for the Cape City Council. On its arrival in 1898 it was dismantled, transported in sections to the top of the mountain, and put to work carrying cement for a cableway station and stone blocks for the dams. A black and white photograph on the boiler depicted the works foreman, Mr R. Duncan, standing beside the newly completed Barclay Locomotive No. 826. He was a dark figure in dungarees and cloth cap, looking self-conscious. At least, I thought, in this wild place far from his native Scotland Mr Duncan would be finding the view of misty hills from the window familiar.

Another indispensable item in South Africa is the visitors' book. It stalks guest houses, and restaurants, and museums, and private homes, and anywhere unwary travellers are likely to be waylaid. It is impossible to escape them. In a tumbleweed town on the edge of the Karoo desert, I was invited to sign one in a hamburger joint. I have never understood this compulsion to hoard pages of banal comments by strangers. It makes train-spotting look like fun. So I was pleased to see a flash of wit in the visitors' book in the Waterworks Museum. Among all the very nices and wonderfuls, a man had written: 'Silly buggers didn't tell us they'd just varnished this desk – got varnish on my bum.'

Cheered by this vision of a hiker meeting a sticky end, we struck up a narrow path on to the shoulders of the mountain and into the clouds, where the landscape changed again. This was an eerie world of strange, giant flora, and sandstone sculpted by wind and water into fantastic forms. We were surrounded by gargoyles and dinosaurs looming through tendrils of clouds, Godzillas in the Mist. One formation loomed like the head, shoulders and arms of a man straining to fly from a cliff face, a petrified Superman. On closer inspection the rocks were dotted with orange and dark red lichen like drops of blood, and every tableau of rock and plants was a work of art. It was like being in a botanical garden in the sky. There are species here that occur naturally nowhere else in the world, such as the Table Mountain ghost frog, and a butterfly that feeds only on the nectar of red flowers. We saw neither, but we did see a rock kestrel swooping above a gorge, which is probably the most dramatic wildlife spectacle on the mountain since the lions left.

On the final ascent on to the table top, we skirted a ridge etched against the skyline, which gave an illusion of climbing into the sky. Connie, a woman with a lyrical turn of mind, said: 'You just grab a cloud and fly away, and let your feet drift in the pretty flowers as you go.' Table Mountain has that effect on people. In 1588, the Portuguese explorer Livio Sanuto wrote that the top 'hath formed here a great plain, pleasant in situation, which with the fragrant herbs, variety of flowers, and flourishing verdure of all things, seems a terrestrial paradise'. Personally I have always found the summit bleak, but on a clear day you can see for ever. The Portuguese pioneers would recognise the broad sweep of False Bay to the south, the dark sawtooth peaks of the Hottentots-Holland mountains to the east and the gut-churning precipices above the Atlantic on the western ridge. The grid pattern of diminutive skyscrapers at the foot of the mountain looks like an electronic circuit board, and is not the best feature. On a scary viewing platform projecting from a cliff, I imagined I was standing on the bridge of SS *Africa*, ploughing through the southern seas towards Antarctica. Nice image, wrong direction. The mass of Table Mountain forms a kind of stunted rhino horn, which actually points north and confuses a lot of people.

A few bemused tourists were wandering around the upper cableway station when we strolled up. The old cable cars, which had been operating without mishap for seventy years, had been replaced by two super high-tech revolving cars. They had broken down during the opening ceremony a few weeks before, thus giving the Minister of Tourism plenty of time to admire the view since he was among the dignitaries suspended precariously in mid-air for twenty minutes. It seemed the system was still having teething troubles. A German tour guide was growling into a mobile phone: 'This is ridiculous. You promised us three times there would be a car here at half past four. No, you idiot, the weather here has not changed. This is very embarrassing.' His group was wandering disconsolately around the station, which was still a building site, in a vain search for food and drink. A sign on a hut said: 'Welcome to Table Mountain where there is always Coca Cola'. No there wasn't, because the hut was shut.

So we came down Platteklip Gorge, the route taken by Saldanha centuries before. It can't have changed much in the interim and is one of the most striking features of the mountain, a near vertical funnel of sheer slabs of rock echoing to the cries of birds. The best bit is looking up and imagining that the clouds are stationary, which creates an illusion that the mountain is moving and that the earth itself is spinning through the sky. Which of course it is, although we don't notice it most of the time. Invigorated by the hike, we were in high spirits when we reached the road and hailed a taxi. On the way into the city, the driver welcomed us back to civilisation with a warning about pickpockets: 'They're good these guys, they'll steal the milk out of your tea.'

4

Our life would be unredeemably grim

One of the best views of Table Mountain is from a low smudge of land surrounded by cold, heavy seas 7 miles from Cape Town. It is an unremarkable, oval-shaped island little more than 2 miles by 1, covered with bush and bluegum trees and dotted with coves of white sand that glare fiercely in the sun. Its highest point is barely 100 feet above the Atlantic, and when the big Cape storms sweep in, you wonder how it manages to stay above the waves. To people compelled to live here, it was known simply as *Esiquithini* (the island). It is better known by the name given to it by seventeenth-century Dutchmen who found it inhabited by seals and penguins, and called it by their word for seal, *robbe*.

For almost four centuries Robben Island served as a dumping ground for lepers, lunatics and lawbreakers, and ultimately as a maximum-security prison for the enemies of apartheid. In the late nineteenth-century the historian G.F. Gresley wrote in the *Cape Illustrated Magazine*: 'Few places so small and insignificant looking can boast of having played so important a part in the history of a vast multitude of people.' This was before John Vorster had the bright idea of using it to get rid of Nelson Mandela and other troublemakers. As Justice Minister Vorster introduced the General Laws Amendment Bill, permitting detention without trial in solitary confinement for ninety days, which could be extended *ad infinitum*. The phrase he used was 'to this side of eternity'.

I first visited the island on a press trip shortly after the last political prisoners were released. I found it a melancholy place, haunted by echoes of despair, and I left with a shudder. It had since been declared a heritage site and was becoming the most popular visitor attraction in the country, so I signed up for a tour.

The nondescript, grey brick building in Cape Town harbour had not changed, but now it looked out of place with its barred windows and high wire fence, a sombre relic surrounded by a glitzy new development of restaurants and shopping malls. There was nothing to indicate its purpose and you had to walk around to a wharf lined with rusty cargo ships to see a wooden sign that said: 'Embarkation office. Robben Island prison'.

The first time I saw this building, it was surrounded by people cheering the return of political detainees, quiet men who looked bewildered as they stepped from a ferry, clutching their belongings in plastic bags. Now tourists were queuing for a day-trip to the place these men wondered if they would leave alive.

There are various ways of dealing with the guilt and shame of infamous prisons and concentration camps. You can display them as a warning to future generations, as at Auschwitz, or you can allow them to quietly decay, as in French Guyana, in the hope that people will forget about them. Or you can strive for something more inspiring. Ahmed Kathrada, who was interned with Mandela, wrote: 'We would want Robben Island not to be a monument to our hardship and suffering, but a triumph of the human spirit against the forces of evil.' The authorities were still debating what to do with the island, but that seemed a good *leitmotif*.

The booking clerk behind a grille in the embarkation office

was a little, mild-mannered Afrikaner with greying hair and a small moustache who looked like a startled rabbit. The loudest thing about him was his African shirt. His name was Chris, and he had been one of the prison officers in charge of Mandela. 'If I'd been running the prison service I'd have let him out long ago,' he confided. 'I always thought he was the leader of his people.' Mandela returned the complement when Chris became unemployed by endorsing his application for a job with the new island administration. The erstwhile jailer was grateful, and seemingly oblivious to the irony of his position behind the bars of the booking office.

A motley crew of tourists crowded on the snub-nosed prison ferry *Dias*, and we motored slowly out of the docks, past the tugs and coastal freighters, and a blue-hulled fishing fleet, and seals playing in the outer harbour, until we hit the swell of the South Atlantic. This is not a sea that encourages escape from island prisons. It is fed by a viciously cold current from Antarctica, it tends to be rough and confused, and it is a popular bathing spot for big sharks. Few people have tried to flee across it, and fewer have survived. Carel and Jacob Kruger, a couple of nineteenth-century miscreants, had mixed fortunes after escaping in a boat made of animal hide. They reached the mainland and fled into the interior, where Carel disturbed an elephant that trampled him to death. His brother fared better, living in the wilderness for twenty years until being granted a free pardon. Unfortunately, while travelling to Cape Town to collect his pardon, a lion ate him.

Our first view of this Bastille in the Bay was of low, dun-coloured land with sparse vegetation. A lighthouse appeared, then the white tower of a church, and a cluster of low red-roofed buildings by a jetty. Then came the watchtowers, rising from a grey compound beyond a small harbour. A breakwater of massive concrete spikes bristled as we approached, but the mood on the quay was upbeat with Afro-rock music pounding from

loudspeakers. One of the first things we saw was a welcome
sign on a stone arch, bearing the motto of the prison service:
'We serve with pride'. This seemed a curious boast by an outfit
with a history of sadistic thuggery, and I wondered how long it
would be before somebody removed it.

Our guide was Yasien, a former detainee and activist of the
Pan Africanist Congress, who was tediously long on political
rhetoric and short on prison anecdotes. But he began well with
a story about how factory workers had made a luxury car for
Mandela when he was released, and asked whether he would like
an electronic locking system. 'No more locks, please,' Mandela
replied.

Mandela and the others did not have far to travel when they
arrived on the island. Along a dirt road from the harbour is
the low building faced with blue-grey granite that housed 'B'
section, the detention block for high-ranking political prisoners.
When the big metal doors at the entrance clang behind you, it is
as if they are shutting out not only the sunshine, but life itself.
Awaiting us was a small, wiry figure with a shock of woolly hair,
thick spectacles and a ready smile. Houghton Soci, an erstwhile
regional commander of the ANC armed wing, had spent eleven
years in detention on the island and he had returned as a guide
to earn something extra for his retirement. 'In that room they
would give you your identity card, and from then on you were
a number,' he said.

Prisoner number 466/64 occupied cell No. 5, on the right-hand
side of a long corridor of about fifty identical units painted in
a ubiquitous shade of blue-grey. More of a cage than a cell,
measuring 6 square metres, it barely had room for an iron
bedstead, a small wooden table and a metal bucket that served
as a night toilet. For eighteen years this was the home of Nelson
Mandela. 'Robben Island was without question the harshest, most
iron-fisted outpost in the South African penal system,' he wrote

later. 'We were face to face with the realization that our life would be unredeemably grim . . . time moved glacially.' So I stood and looked at the cramped cell, and wondered at the spirit of a man who could endure such deprivation for so long and emerge with his humanity and ideals intact, and then invite three of the warders to his inauguration as president. I tried to imagine how I would cope in there for a week, and I couldn't.

At least it had a barred window overlooking a courtyard, where prisoners sat in rows breaking stones into gravel for roads for their jailers to walk on. The yard also concealed, among grapevines in a corner, the manuscript of a book being written secretly by Mandela. This was part of the prisoners' code of survival, to remain committed to their goals and to strive to improve themselves. Thus the island became an unofficial university, with the better educated inmates giving courses to their comrades in subjects from history to biology. Despite attempts by warders to stop it, the political theorising in Section B formed the basis of policies the ANC ultimately adopted for governing the country. There was plenty of time to debate them. Kathrada recalled: 'Being life prisoners had one advantage. It is indefinite, so you don't look forward to a date.'

So what was the worst thing about being here, I asked Houghton. 'Memories,' he said. 'I missed my wife and children. In all the years I was here, I never saw my children.' The closest any of the prisoners came to children was the sight of flags flying from a church steeple signalling births in the wardens' village – blue for boys and pink for girls. As we left, somebody asked Houghton if working on the island was therapeutic. 'No it's not,' he said firmly. 'It's disturbing. As soon as my pension comes through I will leave.' Back on the minibus, Yasien took us to see the limestone quarry. This was a shallow depression of searing heat and chalk-white glare that burned the eyes of the prisoners forced to toil there. 'You're lucky to be on the bus,' he said.

There was a forlorn air about the island, littered with decaying relics of human occupation. Ostriches were pecking around the rusting hulks of naval gun batteries, installed during the Second World War to defend Cape Town and the coast. They were never fired in anger, but during a practice session they managed to set fire to their camouflage of bluegum trees and spark an impressive blaze that ravaged the north of the island. At the other end, the skeleton of a Taiwanese tuna boat impaled on rocks bore mute testimony to the hazards of sailing close to the island. At the last count twenty-nine shipwrecks were scattered around it, including the 140-ton *Dageraad* that struck a reef in mist and an unseasonal north-westerly wind in 1694. Seventeen chests of gold went down with her, and only three were recovered. And there were ghosts lurking among the sunken and buried. treasure. During the last war soldiers found a skeleton surrounded by French coins dating from the seventeenth century, and on dark nights warders swore they saw spectral figures with red eyes walking towards them.

Now the prison was closed, the administrators were facing an unusual problem. Crime, virtually unheard of on Robben Island for obvious reasons, was increasing. Shortly before I arrived, the wife of an ANC official was raped in the guest house. A newspaper report identified the victim as black, and her assailant as an Afrikaner 'who had uncomplimentary things to say about the country's transformation process'. A few weeks later the island store was held up by a gun-toting frogman wearing a balaclava, which I thought was worth an entry in the *Guinness Book of Records*.

Yasien's parting shot of political education concerned the 'Rainbow Nation'. This was a foolish name dreamed up by Tutu which had no relevance in the new South Africa, he informed us. People were tired of being divided, and they wanted to be rid of colour tags. 'I don't live in a rainbow, I live in Africa,' he said. As the ferry departed, gulls evoked the ethos of the island with shrill, lonely cries. Preserving it as a monument to the triumph of the human spirit would be a tall order, I thought. It was scarred by centuries of suffering, and its most merciful fate would be to disappear beneath the waters of Table Bay.

'You know we coloureds are bitter people,' the woman was saying. 'A bit of this and a bit of that . . .' We were chatting at the home of a white woman celebrating her eightieth birthday, and the coloured family was explaining its sense of confusion in the new order. The Cape coloured community has always been mixed up in the ethnic sense, being largely the product of liaisons between early European settlers and sailors and black women, with a liberal sprinkling of Malay slave blood. The distinctive mulatto race that emerged is noted for producing artisans, musicians and gangsters, and is incidentally the closest thing in the country to a genuine rainbow people. 'There is a search for identity, particularly now that apartheid has gone,' the wife said. 'We are in the middle, it's as if we don't belong.' Her sister referred to the peculiarity of two national anthems, the retention of the Afrikaner hymn '*Die Stem*' (The Voice) along with the Xhosa gospel song '*Nkosi Sikeleli i'Afrika*' (God Bless Africa) being one of the more bizarre compromises of reconciliation. She said: 'Neither means much to us. The blacks sing one, the whites sing the other, and we just kind of mumble both of them.' She agreed that the coloured community was racist, having enjoyed privileges denied to blacks in the bad old days: 'In that sense apartheid worked, both for us and on us.' The husband said he was concerned about the number of blacks flooding to the Cape townships from rural areas. 'We're not used to it here,' he said.

The next day a white woman told me her father was planning to emigrate because of rising crime. Visibly upset, she said: 'The cream of the whites have left already, it's only the middle-classes and the dregs and the weak that are left. You can't live on sunshine and blue skies. What does it matter how beautiful the weather is if you can't leave your house without being afraid of being attacked? This country is fucked, and it's only going to get worse.' She paused, then said: 'Don't talk to me about how we exploited the blacks. I don't want to hear that shit any more.' This was a common sentiment, shared to varying degrees by whites who felt alienated and threatened by black majority rule. 'I get a funny feeling when foreigners ask me about politics in South Africa,' a businesswoman told me. 'It's like the country doesn't belong to me any more, it's like it's no longer my country.' On to a press club luncheon, addressed by a newspaper editor who said: 'What does press freedom and the public right to know mean in a country where more than half of the people can't read, and where 40 per cent have no jobs? Chasms of misunderstanding still exist in this so-called Rainbow Nation of ours, and we are going to be in serious trouble in a few years if we continue like this.'

For light relief I turned to the sports pages of the local paper, where I read of a rugby match between coloured teams that ended with one player dead, one critically wounded and six with flesh wounds. When the players started brawling, rival spectators threw them guns. Happily the forces of law and order arrived and appraised the situation with their customary brilliance. A detective was quoted as saying: 'It quickly became apparent that the match had been a rather ill-tempered affair.'

Needless to say the police were nowhere to be seen on the day I bought a second-hand car, a Japanese saloon that looked as if it might get me round the country without attracting the attention of smash and grab merchants. I was wrong. That evening I parked in a brightly lit main street outside a cinema and returned to find the rear seats littered with the shards of a smashed window. Luckily I had obeyed the first rule of motoring in South Africa, which is never to leave anything of value in an unattended vehicle, and I took this incident as a good omen. Like a soldier receiving a minor injury in his first battle, I felt that my car had had its baptism of fire and would be safe from now on. Even seasoned travellers are given to bouts of unjustified optimism. At that stage nobody had warned me about rock-throwing baboons.

Before leaving Cape Town, I wanted to see the oldest surviving relic of apartheid. It is about 100 yards long and 20 feet high, and it lies beyond the medicinal plants section in the national botanical garden on the eastern flanks of Table Mountain. It is the remnant of a prickly hedge of *Brabejum stellatifolium*, or wild almond, planted in 1660 as a boundary of the newly established Cape Colony under the command of Jan van Riebeeck of the Dutch East India Company. More to the point, it stretched for several miles as a formidable barrier to Khoi natives given to rustling the cattle of the Dutch settlers. In this manner the first recorded attempt to separate the black and white residents of South Africa was made. By all accounts it was fairly successful as far as it went. The problem was that it became redundant when more Europeans arrived and began grabbing land beyond the hedge. What remains is a straggly but stout thicket, made all the more impenetrable by an interlaced barbed wire of brambles. It would require napalm to clear it, which was not available to the Khoi at the time. This early symbol of racial conflict now serves as a sunshade and a windbreak around a lawn, which is a pleasant place to have a picnic and admire banks of blue flowers. It is not widely known that the fruits of the wild almond contain a cyanide compound, but the Khoi knew how to remove the poison, and roast and grind the nuts into a kind of coffee. So they lost their land, but they got free coffee.

The coastal road heading south towards the Cape of Good Hope passes through a wonderland of high mountains, sparkling seas and very expensive real estate. On one side wooded slopes sweeping up to the crags of Table Mountain are studded with luxurious villas, and on the other apartment buildings with names like *Helianthus* and *La Corniche* are bolted on to cliffs plunging from road level to a succession of sandy coves. During the tourist season, the narrow road winding through this property agency nirvana is a cavalcade of joggers and cyclists and surfers sporting tanned bodies and cool gear. The townships and squatter camps on the other side of the mountain could be on another planet. Everybody seems fairly relaxed. On a concrete wall by the side of the road a wit had inscribed 'Welcome to the Cape of Good Dope', and when I stopped to admire the view, a spaced-out character duly sidled up with a lop-sided grin and an offer of a side-trip: 'Some nice Swazi, man?'

Further south, the road traverses a low plain dominated by two hills, one of which is Cape Point. The geography resembles the boot of Italy, with Cape Point on the toe and the Cape of Good Hope about a mile to the west forming the heel. In between, there were a lot of tourists. In the apartheid era there was hardly anybody here. It was blissfully quiet, a place to listen to the wind and the sea, and imagine pennants fluttering from the masts of Dutch East Indiamen battling round what they called the Cape of Storms. Now it was swarming with a polyglot crowd of tourists, and the burger bar and the curio shop selling Zulu bead dolls and painted ostrich eggs were doing a brisk trade. I skirted the mob, and began climbing a steep path to inspect a monumental maritime blunder.

It seemed like a good idea at the time. Because of the high toll of ships bashing into reefs, it was decided in 1816 to build a lighthouse on Cape Point. About forty years later a prefabricated cast-iron tower was shipped from London and transported by pack horses and mules to the highest peak on the point, 816 feet above sea level. The lighthouse was 29 feet high, painted white with a red top. Shortly before it came into operation on

1 May 1860, *The Cape of Good Hope Gazette* reported that it 'shows its most brilliant beam once in a minute for the space of 12 seconds of time, and is visible in clear weather from a deck 16 feet high at a distance of 36 miles'. The problem, as mariners had known for 300 years, was that clear weather was a rarity at the Cape. Even when visibility at sea level was good, the peak and its lighthouse were frequently shrouded in cloud, and it was hard to see the brilliant beam at 36 yards, never mind 36 miles.

The inevitable eventually happened. The night of 18 April 1911 was misty with a light rain falling, and the Cape light was obscured by cloud. At ten minutes before midnight the Portuguese liner *Lusitania* of 5,557 tons, with 774 people on board, struck Bellows Rock immediately below the lighthouse. The crew had time to launch the lifeboats and all but four people were saved, but the authorities got the message. Another lighthouse was built 500 feet below the original one, which still stands as a monument to misplaced philanthropy.

The land here is as deceptive as the weather. The hike to the old lighthouse is fairly easy but, a few steps beyond, the peak falls away sharply to a knife-edged ridge, with sheer cliffs on either side besieged by surging seas. Black birds were wheeling across cruel rock faces, their cries barely audible above the din of the South Atlantic battering the shore below. From this height the Cape of Good Hope some distance away is unimpressive, a low headland jutting into the sea. An undulating path leading towards it skirts precipitous drops, meanders along a ridge and scrambles up a steep incline. Then you are there, sitting on a clump of grey rocks, with nothing between you and Antarctica but the icy waters of the Benguela current.

In fact Good Hope is not the end of Africa. The most southerly point of the continent is a spit of land called Cape Agulhas, about 100 miles to the east. But this is where Dias realised he had found a route around Africa, when he spotted it on his way home. A monument to a great navigator, a few years later it became his tombstone, when he died in a storm off the Cape he had christened.

For once the skies were clear and the sea was calm, and I enjoyed a moment of solitude contemplating the vastness of the ocean and the journey that lay before me.

5

I have as much right to be here as anybody else

It took Europeans two centuries from finding South Africa to show any interest in exploring it. This happened in 1679 with the arrival of a new governor of the Cape colony. Simon van der Stel carried with him orders from the Dutch East India Company to extend its settlement, and within two weeks he duly did so by riding into the interior and finding an agreeable spot to build a town that he modestly named Van der Stel's Bosch.

The Dutch word *bosch* means 'bush', of which there were plenty in the river valley where van der Stel pitched his camp. But the farmers who moved in were energetic types, and by the turn of the century they had transformed the place into a land of milk and honey. They also produced wine and deciduous fruit in abundance, in a patchwork of vineyards and orchards that sparkled in fertile valleys framed by dramatic mountains. They sprinkled the lower slopes with whitewashed farm buildings in the Cape Dutch style, grown-up dolls' houses with ornate gables and picture windows, but otherwise they wisely left the countryside as they had found it, which was absurdly beautiful. One suspects that people born here did something saintly in previous lives.

The town that grew up with the more manageable name of Stellenbosch is a sleepy service centre for the farming community and home of a university that has produced squads of politicians and international rugby players. The historic heart of the town is a genteel, unhurried place of oak-lined avenues and Cape Dutch and Georgian buildings that have changed little since their architects flounced around in corduroy knee breeches and high-heeled shoes with silver buckles. It is a living museum peopled by students and burghers who are uniformly polite, well dressed and white. I asked a friend why there were hardly any black or coloured people in the town centre, and he said there was no reason for them to go there because they couldn't afford the prices in the shops.

There seemed no reason for them to go to the university either, because there were few dark faces on the campus. This was a temple of Afrikaner academia from whose hallowed portals had emerged six of South Africa's eight prime ministers, but you would not know it from the entrance, which was a glass door in a plain building besieged by a car park. I strolled across a square of landscaped gardens surrounded by Georgian faculty buildings and headed for a neon sign that said 'student centre'. This was a shopping mall built around a multi-storey space known to students as 'the hole'. I could see why. Fast-food joints littered the ground floor, dreary rock music was blaring from loudspeakers and bored-looking teenagers were watching a bad science fiction film on a giant screen. Junk food, head-banging music and mindless movies – no wonder the students went loopy and came up with bright ideas like the Prohibition of Mixed Marriages Act.

There were exceptions, of course. One was a gentle bohemian character called Strydom, who had graduated from the university relatively sane and made a living from drawing circles in sand. He also planted rows of red flags in saltpans, and made designs from tall grasses in snowy landscapes. Then he took photographs of them which he enlarged and sold in limited edition prints that were starkly beautiful. He called himself a land artist, whose canvas was nature. Strydom and his wife Hermine lived in a small cottage in the grounds of a wine estate in the Jonkershoek valley, a lovely place of streams and mountains and meadows near Stellenbosch. Through a mutual friend they invited me to stay, and it was while sitting on their *stoep* one evening that I sensed again the magic of Africa. It is a union of huge skies, and hazy mountains, and mysterious rustlings in the bush, a sense of space and timelessness and ancient rhythms that quicken the pulse and calm the spirit.

Strydom told me a story about his father. The man was intelligent and well travelled, but every time his children spoke English at home he confiscated their pocket money. This was because his own father had been killed in the Anglo-Boer War and his mother had died in a British concentration camp, and when an aunt came to look after the children their farm was torched by British soldiers. 'To this day, if he cannot be served in Afrikaans in a shop, he will quietly walk out,' Strydom said. A century had passed since the Brits bludgeoned the Boers into submission, but in some Afrikaner homesteads it was remembered as if it was yesterday. Now Strydom was coming to terms with another transition. 'I think everybody's fear is what will happen when Mandela goes. But for now I feel relief that I don't have to feel guilty any more. Of course I feel sorry about what happened before, but it's over now.'

The scale of inequality in South Africa is so huge that most people shrug their shoulders. You can't solve everybody's problems, so the heck with it. There are others who extend a helping hand, because that's the way they are. Strydom's contribution to the redistribution of wealth was to fill his *bakkie* once a week with unsold produce donated by a supermarket and deliver it to a black township on the outskirts of Stellenbosch. One day I went with him.

The community of Kayamandi straggled in varying degrees

of dilapidation over a hillside by a road leading into town. A boundary wall was painted brightly with scenes of township life and inspirational messages like 'Every child needs a home' and 'Let's build our country without drugs'. The squatter camp of recent arrivals was the usual ghastly sprawl of cardboard and tin, but in a 'formal' district a few streets away were what the newcomers aspired to, a development of modern brick bungalows with neatly tended gardens. The grounds of the Kayamandi High School were teeming with pupils and they were all, as usual, kitted out in smart uniforms.

Our destination was Mandela Square, where a woman called Eunice lived at No. 149. The square was a cul-de-sac of shacks, a log cabin church, a foodstore made of cardboard and a derelict car without wheels resting on bricks. Eunice's home was a four-roomed affair enterprisingly cobbled together from bits of wood, chipboard and corrugated iron. The stone floors were covered with broken linoleum and worn carpets, and there was a shabby settee and a rough wooden table. Daylight showed through the roof and gaps in the walls, and you knew that the wind would find ways through and that when it rained the shack would leak like a sieve. But it was neat and tidy, and at the door a patch of sandy soil had been planted with flowers and herbs. Eunice had been promised a new house and had filled out the application forms, but she wasn't holding her breath. 'Maybe one day,' she said. In the meantime, she helped us lift the covers off the *bakkie* and soon a dozen women were carrying away piles of bread and fruit and vegetables. South Africa is a prosperous country in African terms, capable of feeding its people and spared so far the horrors of mass starvation. But this was a chance to save money on basic supplies, and within minutes everything was gone. 'Every little bit helps,' Strydom said as we drove past the squatter camp, back into the valley of whitewashed farmsteads glowing in the sun.

Another Stellenbosch University graduate lived nearby at the foot of the Helderberg, a distinctive mountain with green flanks sweeping to a sawtooth ridge. Pieter 'Hempies' du Toit was a quintessential rural Afrikaner, tough, independent and proud of ancestry that went back six generations to French Huguenot immigrants. When I first met him in the pre-Rainbow era, he had been a controversial figure. As a former Springbok rugby player and a winemaker who produced award-winning vintages, he had been a popular character. As a thoughtful man who expressed reservations about apartheid, he had raised conservative hackles. His doubts began on a rugby field, when he was invited to add his considerable stature and skill to a national squad of young coloured players. As a child, the farm labourers had called him *klein baas* (little boss), and as he grew older he became *meneer* (sir). 'When I played for that team, the others called me by my first name. That was the first step. When you're in a team, everybody is equal and I realised I had no right to be called sir. That was a turning point in my life.'

Hempies's vineyards had not changed, a rich, green carpet on the lower slopes of the Helderberg, simmering in the sun as I drove up a dirt road into a yard littered with tractors and dogs. He came out at my approach, a big middle-aged man in a rough woollen sweater with tree-trunk legs encased in shorts and leather boots. He was the kind of man, if he was in a hurry and missed the door, who would come through the wall. 'Things have changed a bit,' he said as we climbed into a Land Rover for a tour of the farm. 'My people have joined the union, and the vibes are different. In the past you felt they put their trust in you as their employer, now they look elsewhere and the relationship is not the same.' We were bumping along a muddy path beside a field in which scarecrows were playing rugby. Half of them were adorned with the blue and white jerseys of the local Western Province, and the others were in the Free State strip. Above them was a scoreboard, reminding passers-by that Western had recently beaten the Free Staters in the final of the country's top rugby competition. Most farmers in the area had scarecrows, but only Hempies had them positioned in loose scrums and line-outs.

He was describing how the paternalistic relationship between white farmers and coloured workers that had developed over generations was being undermined by new labour and land laws. In the old days a good farmer looked after his employees, providing food and accommodation, health care and education for their children. In return, the workers provided loyal service from father to grandson. The system was open to abuse, and on bad farms the conditions were little better than slavery. There was also the argument that if workers had been paid better wages they could have looked after themselves. But Hempies was regarded as a fair man who provided decent housing and wages, and he regretted the unravelling of personal bonds. 'For me it was sad when they joined the union. I have no trouble with the organisers because I treat my people well, but it's not the same. What it boils down to now is a man must work according to a contract and then go home. It's just a working relationship. There's nothing extra.' He used to lead his workers in prayers in a toolshed every morning, but no longer. 'I don't know why, but they weren't interested any more.'

But some attitudes die hard. As we passed a group of coloured women tending the vines, one of them thrust a sheaf of papers at Hempies. She called him *baas*, and they conversed in Afrikaans. Her son had been struck by a car, and she wanted to know how to apply for compensation. Hempies warned her to be careful of lawyers, and promised to help.

The view from the heights of the mountain was glorious. A valley hazy with morning mist stretched languorously towards the sweep of False Bay and Table Mountain. A white horse shook its mane in a green field, and a buzzard hovered above the vines. We stood for a while, our feet in the red earth. 'This is a magnificent valley,' Hempies said. But shadows were creeping over it. Virtually every week there were attacks on farmers, and a woman working in a local farm shop had been shot dead for the few rands in her till. The gunman was arrested, and when police brought him to the scene of the crime he was laughing. Hempies said: 'I love Africa. I feel I have as much right to be here as anybody else, but if my kids want to leave one day I'm not going to stand in their way. We were very hopeful and positive at the beginning. There was a lot of goodwill towards the black and coloured communities, and regret about wrong things done in the past. But now with all this crime . . .'

A restorative glass of wine was in order and we repaired to a cavernous shed musty with oak barrels and adorned with gold certificates from wine competitions. There were few visitors, partly because the estate was not on the wine route promoted by tourist offices. Hempies considered this too commercial. If people came to his farm it was because they knew their wines and they wanted to taste his, although one day he might get round to putting up a sign at the bottom of the road. I reflected that his estate was worth finding as I savoured a vintage described in a national wine guide as 'big forceful bouquet, ripe plums and liquorice, succulent but still chewy, long finish, great potential'. I didn't quite get the liquorice, but the rest of it seemed on the button and the world began to assume a rosy glow. 'Come,' my host said, 'I want to show you my dream place.'

When van der Stel camped by the first river he came across in 1679, he earmarked a portion of the land he had found for himself. Four years later he sold it, and it was part of this farm Hempies had just bought as a place to retire to one day, cultivate a few favourite vines, and contemplate the grandeur of the Helderberg. We drove off a country road, slewed down a path and scrunched to a halt by an old stone house and barn by the stream which van

der Stel had predictably named *Eerste* (first) *Rivier*. The previous
owner had run the place as a riding school, and a row of rose
bushes along a path by the water marked the burial places of
her horses. She had called it Memory Lane. 'There are good
vibes here,' Hempies announced as he wandered happily over
the rough ground, scrambling among fallen trees and picking
blackberries and guava. He had cleaned out a pond and was
planning to divert a water channel and stock it with trout. He
also thought he might lead tours of the winelands by horseback.
The barn would serve to store casks of his best wines, and the
house would have a veranda from which he could admire a
prospect of the mountain unblemished by any sign of habitation.
Just as van der Stel had first seen it, in fact. The historical
perspective was intriguing, as Hempies's ancestors arrived from
France not long after van der Stel came from Holland. In the
house we found references to his family in the mildewed pages of
a leather-bound book entitled *Travels in Southern Africa 1803–06*
by Henry Lichtenstein, doctor of medicine and philosophy at the
University of Berlin. The author wrote of meeting a Willem van
der Merwe and his wife (forebears of Hempies's mother) in a
nearby town, and reported that 'both parents and twelve children
were of almost colossal size and stature'. The erstwhile prop of
the Springbok rugby pack looming over me mentioned that his
physique came from his mother's side of the family. Meanwhile
his father's family was already in the wine-making business,
according to Dr Lichtenstein, who called the following day at
the home of the du Toit family and was served 'an excellent
deep-red wine'.

 Outside, Hempies pointed with pride at delicate whorls in
the old window panes that indicated they were made from
hand-blown glass. A breeze was stirring oak trees planted in
the time of van der Stel, and an ibis was pecking in the long
grass. 'This is true wealth,' Hempies said. 'Not in money, but

in land and culture. How can anyone say I have no right to be here? There is no way they can argue that.'

The beauty of the winelands and the relatively low cost of living had brought new settlers from overseas. This was apparent from the road that climbs out of Stellenbosch and sweeps over a high pass to reveal a majestic profile of the Great Drakenstein Mountains. It is among the finest views in the Cape, and an enormous German flag billowing above farm buildings on a hillside had not improved it. It was an arrogant blot on the landscape. I have never liked displays of nationalism; I did not care where these people came from, and I especially did not want to see their stupid flag planted there like a symbol of conquest.

At least the descendants of the Huguenots were more discreet. The town of Franschhoek in the next valley was founded after French Protestants, fleeing the Catholic thugs of Louis XIV, arrived in the Cape with Bibles, muskets and a talent for producing good wines. The French connection was preserved in red, white and blue signs erected by the *Vignerons de Franschhoek* and in establishments such as the Café Piaf and the Ballon Rouge guest house, but the biggest flag by far, flying above a pizza restaurant, was German.

Franschhoek is essentially a one-street town of prettified old buildings leading to a Huguenot monument of three arches symbolising the Holy Trinity. The central figure is a woman standing on a globe with her feet on France, who looks as if she is preparing to dive into a lily pond at her feet. A bus was disgorging a party of French tourists, and I found myself hoping the statue would jump into the pond and be declared a miracle. Protestants are short on miracles. In an adjacent museum I learned that about 200,000 of them had fled the realm of the Sun King in the late seventeenth century. Most remained in Europe, but about 270 sailed for the Cape and settled along the Franschhoek River. Looking for traces of Hempies's family, I discovered that

Guillaume du Toit and his brother Francois had arrived from Lille on the ship *Vrijheijt* on 23 June 1686. They established farms north of Stellenbosch, and soon both were married and producing wine and potential rugby players. A portrait of one Andries du Toit, born in 1762, shows an unmistakable development. From his high-collared frock coat protruded the neck of an ox.

My friend Paul was another burly character. A German journalist based in Africa for many years, he had given up a job in television, bought a wine farm at Villiersdorp on the less fashionable side of the Franschhoek mountains and settled with his wife and children to cultivate a decent pinotage. He was now sitting in a mountain restaurant, savouring a local wine with lunch, and discoursing on his adopted country's transition to majority rule. 'It's amazing how well it's worked, all things considering. I think part of the reason is there's so much space here. It's not like Europe, there's still room for everybody.' Below us the Drakenstein valley seemed to go on for ever, and beyond the mountains lay the arid plains of the Northern Cape, an area the size of France where hardly anybody lived.

Our discussion was interrupted by Paul's mobile phone. 'Got to go,' he said apologetically, 'there's a problem on the farm.' The problem was that his neighbour's cows had got loose among his vines. So off he went, a European in the process of becoming an Afrikaner. He had fallen in love with Africa, he spoke Afrikaans fluently, and he did not have a German flag at his farm.

The first time I heard Afrikaans, I assumed the speaker was clearing his throat. A correspondent of the *Cape Argus* in 1877 was equally unimpressed by the publication of a newspaper called *Die Afrikaanse Patriot*: 'An attempt is being made by a number of jokers near Cape Town to reduce the "plat Hollands" (common Dutch) of the street and kitchen to a written language and perpetuate it. They are carrying their joke well. They have a newspaper, have published a history of the Colony, an almanak, and to crown the joke – a grammar. It is impossible to read these productions without laughing . . . the promotors of the *Patriot* movement are laughed at and ridiculed by their sensible countrymen, but they stick to their joke.' Evidently it was a good joke, because at the last count it was estimated that more than 6 million people were still enjoying it. Their 'kitchen Dutch' has developed into a language that lends itself to dry humour, coarse insults and fine poetry. One of the most imaginative derogatory terms is reserved unsurprisingly for English-speakers. *Soutpiel*, which means salt penis, derives from the perception that the original British settlers had one foot in Africa, the other in their homeland and their member dangling in the ocean between. The language is also good for maxims, such as one coined by *voortrekkers* that says much about rural Afrikaners' approach to life. It is *Hou noord en fok voort*, which means 'Keep north and fuck on'. There is a monument to the language on a hilltop overlooking Paarl, a farming town near Stellenbosch where the *Genootskap van Regte Afrikaners* (Fellowship of True Afrikaners) was formed in 1875 to promote Afrikaans as an official language. From a distance the memorial looks like a rocket ship, a minimalist structure of granite and concrete dominated by a tower almost 200 feet high. I wandered around it, wondering why the gift shop in this cradle of Afrikaner culture was selling T-shirts depicting Bushman cave drawings. Then I looked back at the distant profile of Table Mountain for a glimpse of familiar territory. Behind lay places and faces I knew well; ahead lay mountains I had never crossed before.

6

So we came here to shallower waters

The road I chose to leave the winelands climbed steeply up the face of the Slanghoek Mountains into another world. These highlands were not green and pleasant like the valleys below. Even in summer sunshine they were barren and harsh, with rocks by the roadside separating the traveller from sheer drops. Ahead, the prospect was of similar mountains rising abruptly from plains shimmering in the heat.

This was my first reminder of the huge, open spaces of Africa. I was the only person on the road, and possibly the continent as far as I could see. When I stopped on a high pass it was easy to imagine European pioneers carving wagon trails through the wilderness and the dwindling race of Bushmen retreating before them. On the long, winding descent I played a tape of a Mozart sonata, and it seemed that classical music and mountains were the most perfect harmony that could be achieved between mankind and nature.

Apart from a well-placed pub, of course. The Calabash Bush Pub and Tea Garden beckoned at the foot of the mountain, a stone-walled outpost of civilisation that looked like a converted barn. Inside it was dark and cosy, offering respite from the heat and the prospect of decent food and cold beer. In a shady spot in the garden four men from Paarl, merry from a boozy lunch, invited me to join them. 'Listen here,' said Piet, a big man with dark glasses, 'you want to invest in the Western Cape. I'm in real estate, so I know what I'm talking about. There's nowhere else in South Africa, man. This is the only place where the kaffirs can't say this is their land. This is the California of Africa, man, I'm telling you.' Surprisingly this was the first time I had heard the K-word since arriving in South Africa almost a month before. It has an interesting derivation, having been first applied to Asians banished to the Cape in the seventeenth century for crimes in other Dutch colonies. They were recruited into an elementary police force known as 'kaffirs', whose duties included the flogging of black slaves. I considered recounting this historical anecdote to Piet, but decided on balance it was not a good idea. Mandela was a good bloke, my companions agreed, even if he was a kaffir; the problem was he couldn't last for ever and who knows what would happen then. In the meantime I was invited to go well, and come back and see Piet and his buddies any time I felt like acquiring a piece of the Rainbow Nation.

It was late afternoon by the time a switchback road deposited me in the town of Ceres, which claims without much conviction to be the Switzerland of South Africa. During the brief winter when there is snow on the surrounding mountains there might be a passing resemblance, but in high summer the valley of fruit farms in which it lies bears no resemblance to Switzerland whatsoever. Also, roads in the Alps do not have signs warning of baboons. Ceres was established in 1854 on the farm of Jan Frederik Munnik, and named after the Roman goddess of agriculture and fertility, which is much better than Munnikville. It is the most important deciduous fruit-producing area in the country, and packets of fruit juices bearing its name can be found in virtually every store and café. The town was a pleasant little place with a river running through it, so I booked into an old-fashioned hotel by the river and recovered from my first day's serious travelling with a jog in a park and a swim in the hotel pool, and had both to myself.

It is in such *dorps* that one can observe a curious fact of South African life – streets that change colour. At one end it is mainly white, with smart shops and cafés, somewhere along its length there is a grey area, then it is entirely black or coloured with cheaper stores catering for those races. There are no visible dividing lines or barriers; it just happens in the space of a few steps and people accept this as normal. It is a form of apartheid that has existed since van Riebeeck planted his almond hedge, and everybody seems to have grown used to it. Since the abolition of statutory racism, citizens of the 'new' South Africa are free to ignore such anachronisms, but few do. It is as if people of different races have established 'comfort zones' in which they move around happily among their own folk but feel ill at ease in other groups. The logical extension of this is that people who shop together live together. Thus while the cities have lots of grey areas, conservative *dorps* in the country remain rigorously segregated: white folks live in town or comfortable suburbs, and blacks and coloureds live in satellite townships and squatter camps. South Africans are not alone in such tribal behaviour, of course, it's just that here it is glaringly obvious.

The museum in Ceres is devoted to *Togryers*, which means transport riders. In the nineteenth century the town was on the main supply route from the Cape to the interior, which became a kind of freeway for wagon trains after the discovery of diamonds at Kimberley in 1870. Ceres cashed in on the bonanza by building wagons, some of which required teams of up to twenty oxen for big loads. The most dramatic exhibit in the museum was an ornate hearse draped in a black canopy that looked as if it had been designed for Count Dracula. I was more intrigued by accounts in the museum of an event that took place at three minutes past ten on the evening of 29 September 1969, when the earth moved beneath a railway station ten miles away, wrenching the needle off a seismograph on the coast and wrecking most of Ceres. Eleven people were killed, water and electricity supplies were cut off, and there were fires in the mountains. According to a local newspaper, seconds before the disaster a farmer saw something hurtling through the night sky. He was quoted as saying: 'As the bright object crashed into the mountains there was a shower of flames which shot up into the air and then we had the earthquake.' Similar sightings were reported by coloured labourers, and the wife of another farmer said she had been driving on a dirt road when her car was shaken violently by the shock of a flying object smashing into a mountain a few miles away. Sadly the newspaper led its story with an explanation of how the upheaval had been caused by a geological fault, and there were no further references to unidentified flying objects. This may be the only report of extraterrestials landing on Earth and being swallowed by an earthquake.

Before leaving Ceres, I sought advice on the best route north. There were three choices: a gravel road through high mountains, a tarred road through a valley, or a road that crossed a plateau between the two and was surfaced most of the way. The lady in the tourist information office said: 'We've had a lot of rain recently, so I can't say what condition the mountain road will be in. Even if it's okay, it will take you at least four hours. The main road in the valley is boring, so maybe you should take the middle one.' This seemed sensible. A long slog alone on a dodgy mountain road did not appeal, and my guide book spoke highly of scenic passes on the middle road. The only snag was that it was not surfaced through the second pass that led down to Citrusdal, where I planned to stop for lunch. I mentioned to the information lady that I was not at my happiest and most carefree when negotiating rough roads above long drops. 'It's not so bad,' she said encouragingly, 'just drive slowly and you should be fine.

And if you don't like it, just stop.' As far as it went, the logic of this advice was impeccable.

The first road sign I came to said: 'Heavy vehicles no through road to Citrusdal'. My car was as light as a feather, of course. We had no difficulty reaching the first pass, bounded on one side by rearing walls of rock and on the other by empty space falling to the valley I had come from. From the summit the road traversed a plain of wheatfields surrounded by iron-grey hills and dotted with lonely farmsteads. At one end of the plateau a mountain rose to a flat top in a distinctive mesa formation, and beneath it was a bungalow with a red roof among a plantation of small trees. I stopped for half an hour, hearing only the lowing of cattle and the occasional cry of a bird. In that time not a single vehicle passed.

The gravel section towards the end of the road was not bad, at first. At least it was on the level, snaking through a ravine between gnarled rock faces, and people were even living here. A wooden sign pointing up a dirt road said Riversong Farm, and another warned of children crossing by a small building I took to be a school, but the place seemed deserted. I had just passed the next sign, which said 'Danger: heavy vehicles proceed beyond this point at their own risk', when a dust cloud thundering towards me materialised as a large truck. Oh well, I reasoned, if he can make it, so can I. To be on the safe side, as the road began climbing towards a ridge, I played a tape of cheery music. I supposed nothing could go seriously wrong while I was listening to a rendition of 'Take me to where the daisies cover the country lanes'. Then the road momentarily disappeared. In its place was a heart-stopping void, with a vista of a valley ludicrously far below. At this point a sign suggested 8 kilometres per hour would be a reasonable speed limit. Personally I considered this excessive, and crawled around a succession of hairpin bends until the mountain grew tired of scaring me and levelled out. On reflection it probably wasn't so bad, although the steering wheel seemed to be sweating profusely.

The road led into the Olifants River valley, so-called because midshipman Jan Danckaert, the first white man to venture this far from Cape Town in 1660, claimed he saw hundreds of elephants in the area. Since then it had been taken over by fruit and vegetable farmers and wine producers whose fame had spread far beyond the area. When Napoleon was in exile on St Helena, he insisted on and was supplied with dessert wines from this valley. Citrusdal appeared as an agreeable little *dorp* of bungalows and shady lanes, with an information centre stuffed with kitsch gifts and kindly ladies in floral dresses who gave me a list of local eateries. The directions were fairly clear. One was described as the green building on Main Street, and another was the yellow building on Main Street. I chose the latter because it looked brighter, and was rewarded with home-made pancakes in a homely place that made a welcome change from the wild landscapes I had been passing through.

The information ladies suggested I visit mineral springs in the area. After a couple of days on the road, a bit of rest and recuperation was clearly called for, so I took their advice. The spa lay in a wooded ravine 10 miles south of Citrusdal, beneath mountains with incredibly twisted faces. One looked as if it had suffered first-degree burns, which I suppose it had in its youth. The existence of the springs was known to the Cape authorities in 1739, when it was proposed that a homestead and huts be built for visitors. They were bought at public auction in 1903 by James McGregor, a legendary figure who arrived from Scotland penniless and ended up owning 40,000 hectares of the valley. His family still owned the land on which the springs delivered a constant flow of hot water with a therapeutic cocktail of potassium, sodium, calcium and magnesium. All this good stuff was flowing into an open-air pool surrounded by lawns and ivy-covered walls. I eased myself in gratefully, and instantly began to relax. The water felt soft and soothing, and it was remarkably clear. I noticed with interest that fossils of dragonflies trapped in the cement bottom of the pool resembled little palm trees. Above, weaver birds were flitting in and out of nests that looked like twiggy igloos. Swimming was out of the question, being far too strenuous. I tried various lounging positions, and eventually found that by lying on my back with my heels resting gently on a submerged step, I could achieve a state approaching bliss.

Clanwilliam (pop. 4,172) lay at the foot of the Cedarberg mountains, and I liked it immediately. It was originally called Jan Disselsvlei, after a botanist who pottered around the area in the eighteenth century, until a governor of the Cape did everyone a favour by renaming it in honour of his father-in-law, the Earl of Clanwilliam. Its claim to fame was plantations of *rooibos* (red bush) tea, a herbal brew reputed to relieve everything from nervous tension and insomnia to heartburn and nappy rash. Not that the locals looked as if they needed any tranquillisers. There was a laid-back, frontier feel to the place. Time was not quite standing still, but it was in no hurry to go anywhere. As I stepped from the car, two old coloured men touched their hats and bade me good day in Afrikaans. Half of the buildings on Main Street seemed to be national monuments, including the old jail, which had become a museum. It stood on its own at the head of the street, a single-storey whitewashed building with a flat roof and barred windows dozing in the heat, a scene from a spaghetti western before the shoot-out with Mexican bandidos. It was High Noon in Clanwilliam, but the only stranger in town was myself and the locals seemed friendly.

There were no security fences or razor wire or slavering guard dogs here, but there was a wooden rail near the jail where you could sit and watch the world go by. There was some activity in *Die Tweedenhandse Winkel*, which is Afrikaans for The Second-Hand Shop, and incidentally explains how Rip van Winkle got his name (Rip of the shop). A man with a ponytail ambled towards the hotel, waving at passing motorists, a group of men in blue overalls was working not very hard at tending a lawn at the crossroads, and a fat woman rolled by holding the hand of a pretty little girl in an orange dress whose laughter tinkled in the still air. It required some effort to get off the rail and check into the hotel. I could have camped by a reservoir on the outskirts of the village, but this would have required a tent and a willingness to forgo the pleasures of a country inn, neither of which I had. A soak in a hot bath and a good dinner by candlelight were what were required. Even after dark, the air was warm. The sky was ablaze with stars, and the crickets were making more of a racket than the few cars. In the bar next to the hotel four coloured men and two grizzly old whites were nursing brandies and Coke while watching the news on television, and they all turned around as I entered. One of the whites patted a stool beside him and offered me a drink. He spoke at first in Afrikaans, then in laboured English. I gathered he had come to South Africa from Germany at the age of eight, and that he had formed the opinion the ANC was like the Nazi party. I looked over at the coloured guys, and they just rolled their eyes and grinned. I liked the place so much I decided to stay another day, and make a side-trip to the seaside.

It was less than an hour's drive to the coast at Lamberts Bay, which looked interesting on the map. In reality it was a dreary cluster of fish-processing plants backing on to a maze of stores and bungalows that stank of dead fish and bird droppings. I drove around aimlessly for a while looking for the town centre, until it dawned on me there wasn't one. I had given a couple of coloured boys a lift from Clanwilliam, and we kept bumping into each other. It was not a big place. Trying to find the harbour, I saw a notice outside the Lamberts Bay Canning Company Ltd. It was a safety scoreboard, declaring that the current total of days worked without a disabling injury was 196. The previous record was 307, and the company target was 350, so if they got through a year without somebody being crippled it would be a record. This cheery news was displayed above an enigmatic slogan: 'Living Beyond Care Costs'. Proclaiming Lamberts Bay a tourist resort required considerable vision, but a South African magazine had tried that month to make it look attractive, and was offering as first prize in a competition a weekend for two in the town's only half-decent hotel. The joke about the second prize being two weekends came to mind. It had a museum, of course, devoted largely to memories of a Springbok rugby player who had attended the local school. The exhibits included his school desk, a catapult, an inkstand and a homework book with essays on picnics and holidays by the sea. Unsurprisingly I was the only visitor.

The main attraction lay offshore, or at least it used to. Bird Island was no longer an island, having been connected to the coast by a breakwater, but it did have birds on it. Thousands of them in fact. There were two kinds, white ones and black ones, and they kept scrupulously apart. The whites had commandeered the prime real estate on the only flat ground, where they congregated in dense, fractious crowds, while the blacks were nesting more precariously and quietly on rocks around the edges. This is true. It was apartheid on the wing. The whites were Cape gannets, and this was one of only six sites in the world where they bred, in a screeching, foul-smelling community of snapping beaks and beating wings. I watched fascinated as those who failed to find their mates and landed in the wrong place were pecked mercilessly until they could drag themselves to the edge of the colony. The black Cape cormorants were smaller and their nests were spaced further apart, which seemed to make for a more peaceful neighbourhood. After more than a century of being pestered by guano collectors, the good news for the birds was that the site had been declared a nature reserve. The bad news was that the breakwater, built in 1959, served as a runway for hungry rats and cats. The only restaurant in town with a view of the harbour was a rambling wooden shed by the canning factory with a blue awning that provided shade and an agreeable ambience. Fortified by fish and chips and cold beer, I regarded Lamberts Bay more charitably. After the heat of the interior I enjoyed the sea breezes, but I shuddered to think what it was like when it was raining.

Clanwilliam had a golf course, a scrubby nine-hole affair a couple of miles out of town. The only birdies I am familiar with are the kind that fly, but I like golf courses because they provide grass to run on. It was just after sunset when I went for a jog around the Clanwilliam course, and the craggy faces of the Cedarberg mountains to the east were softened by a rosy glow. There was nobody around, but the sound of voices and laughter drifted from a black squatter camp on a nearby hill. I was about halfway round when I was joined by a couple of barefoot urchins from the township who wanted to sell a golf ball they had found. When I declined they seemed happy to run with me for a while. By now I was clipping along at a steady pace, but my companions in ragged shorts who could have been no more than ten years old were loping beside me with ease. As we approached my car I suggested a sprint. I fancied I still had a turn of speed, but the older boy flew away from me and when we finished he was laughing. His name was Joseph, and any coach in Europe would have given his best stopwatch to train a youth with such natural ability. As I got into the car, the smaller boy was still trying to sell the golf ball. Joseph shepherded him gently away and closed the door for me. We shook hands through the open window and I drove away, and in my mirror I saw them jogging through the twilight, up the hill to the shacks of wood and iron.

That night I dined in a restaurant owned by a man who had emigrated from England many years before. 'Spend a few nights in the bar and you'll learn all you want to know about life on the farms,' he said. So what was it like, I asked. Well, he said, the relationship between Afrikaner farmers and coloured workers was complex. When he came out at first, he believed the paternalistic approach was wrong. Instead of helping workers with housing and schooling, employers should pay them a decent wage and let them be their own men. Let them be independent and stand on their own feet, he thought. Then he became an employer, and he found his workers were always coming to him for help and advice, and when he raised their wages they spent the extra on drink. So he gave the money to their wives, or he gave them a chicken instead. And in the end he found himself being drawn into the system he had opposed. 'It's not perfect, and I still feel uneasy about it. But it's the way these people themselves seem to prefer.'

He returned to England every couple of years, and he was fond of the old country, but he could never live there again. 'I love the space in Africa. The open roads, the big skies. Every time I go to England now I feel hemmed in.' His daughter said they used to live near Cape Town. It had been a small place where people knew and cared for each other, then a squatter camp appeared on a hillside and the population soared and so did crime. So we came here to shallower waters, she said. Karma currents, she called it.

7

It's good for sheep

In the dining salon of the SA *Sederberg* that had brought me from
England hung an oil painting of the mountains after which the
ship had been named. It portrayed bizarre rock formations and
dramatic, rust-coloured peaks, and somewhere off Mauritania I
resolved to go and see them. My next destination lay in the heart
of these mountains. At the end of a dirt road that snaked for 40
miles along a high ridge lay a valley where German Lutherans
had founded a mission farm in 1830. There they taught their
coloured flock and freed slaves who joined them the word of
God and how to make shoes and gloves and build houses. The
population of Wuppertal had grown to almost 2,000 in a village
and outstations that were now owned entirely by the Moravian
Church, one of South Africa's 'non-white' denominations. To
live there, you had to be a practising member of the church, and
preferably coloured.

The tarred road ended a couple of miles out of Clanwilliam,
and thereafter my car became a mini dust cloud crawling up
a rust-red trail into a landscape that looked as if it had been
incinerated by a nuclear bomb. Great slabs of bronze-coloured
sandstone loomed over the track like petrified skyscrapers, worn
and pitted into fantastic shapes that produced weird sounds when
the wind blew. Martians would have felt right at home. To the

north, the mountains fell away to reveal arid plains and treeless, flat-topped hills receding in waves to the horizon. This was my first view of Bushmanland, a swathe of the Northern Cape about the size of the Benelux countries, with a population of barely 50,000. Among them were only a handful of the San people, descendants of the nomadic hunters and gatherers we called Bushmen who had virtually ceased to exist as a separate race. The Afrikaners, with their succinct imagery, called one of the valleys on the edge of this desolate region *Knersvlakte*, the Plain of Gnashing Teeth.

I was still in the foothills of the Cedarberg when I came to the grave of Graham Vinicombe Winchester Clowes, Lieutenant, 1st Battalion the Gordon Highlanders, killed in action at the age of twenty-one on 30 January 1901. Clowes and his batman Clark had set off from Clanwilliam to find a route for cavalry over the mountains towards Boer positions in the north. At the Wuppertal turn-off they came under fire from Boer scouts. Clowes was killed instantly and Clark died later of his wounds in Clanwilliam. Clowes was buried where he fell, and after the war his mother arranged for a memorial to mark the grave. Another was erected at Eton, where Clowes had sung in the school choir.

I found the spot screened by a big old tree by the side of the gravel road. Beyond a rusting iron railing was a marble cross with the inscription 'Brave and True' and a marble slab bearing Clowes's name. A pile of stones lay on the grave, and dead leaves and flowers were scattered among them. A sturdy branch of the tree had grown protectively over it, providing shade and a requiem of rustling leaves. I looked around, across the bushland and up to the mountain ridges, and thought of young Clowes and his companion riding to their death. A few miles back they would have forded a stream, and probably stopped to water their horses and rest. I thought of them resuming their journey, chatting as they went. The road rises slightly at this point towards a ridge. They would have been moving slowly, easy targets for marksmen. I wondered where the shots had come from. There were rocky outcrops nearby, perfect positions for snipers. So the Boers shot the young British soldier, and being Christians they buried him where he lay. They probably said a brief prayer for him before riding on. Standing by Clowes's lonely grave, I felt a profound sadness at the stupidity of war.

The road climbed on to a ridge and stayed there for a while, offering glimpses of the wilderness to the north, until it lost interest in the mountains and dropped into a valley and an oasis of greenery around a cluster of whitewashed cottages. I parked beneath a tree in an open space beside a store that seemed to be the hub of Wuppertal. A few youngsters sitting around smiled shyly but said nothing. Rows of cottages with thatched roofs stood on a slight rise overlooking tilled fields, but it was Friday and the village had downed tools early for the weekend. In an old house with a sign that said tearoom, I asked a woman if lunch was a possibility. 'We are closed and there is nothing to eat,' she said. So I wandered off to look for the local tourist officer, and found him in a *bakkie* about to drive to an outstation. He was a middle-aged man in a T-shirt with religious mottos on it, and he was not particularly pleased to see me. I should have called in advance, he said. I had tried but there had been no answer, I said. Well, he would see if he could arrange a room for the night, but he had to go somewhere just now. He was too busy to show me round, and anyway the shoe and glove factories were closed for the weekend. Come back later, he said. So I found a café with a couple of tables where I was able to buy a soft drink and eat sandwiches I had brought with me. Three youths came in and sat at the other table eating fruit and ignored me.

The information office next door had photographs of the village and a brass band in blue tracksuits, and scraps of faded newspaper cuttings, and religious texts. Otherwise it was empty. But a few people were still in the glove factory, stitching heavy denim gloves for gold miners. They glanced up as I entered, but paid me no particular heed. I was beginning to wonder if I existed. Maybe I had wandered into a parallel world where I was invisible. The only 'Welcome to Wuppertal' sign I had seen was on the wall of a dilapidated shed that purported to be a petrol station, although there was no sign of a pump. The church at the head of the main street was a handsome white building with a bell suspended from an arch in the grounds. Inside it was decorated in Lutheran minimalist style, familiar from my Scottish childhood: bare whitewashed walls and wooden ceilings, plain mottled glass windows and a naked light bulb. The only cross was a silk one on a black cloth hanging from the pulpit. None of your fancy High Church nonsense here, not so much as a vase of flowers to detract from pious devotions. At least the minister was friendly. I came across him in his garden near the church, and he bid me welcome and invited me to come by later for tea.

In the meantime the tourist officer, *aka* local grocer and lay preacher, had returned in a more communicative mood. He said Wuppertal was a largely self-sufficient community raising cattle, goats and sheep and cultivating fruit and vegetables. Everybody had to belong to the Moravian church for the simple reason that the church owned the mission. 'People know everybody here,' he said. 'It is a safe place. When I go away on business I leave my house open and the keys in my *bakkie*. When there is a funeral, everybody will attend.' On that cheery note he handed me the keys to a guest cottage behind the church and bade me good night.

Life seemed fairly relaxed in this parallel world, but there were tensions and Reverend Willem Valentyn was a troubled man. 'I was attacked in church the other day,' he said. 'Some people said the church should only concern itself with spiritual matters, and not control social life. I said the church is not only our spiritual father, it must guide us in our daily lives as well, but some people do not agree. It is worrying.' Already the mission was succumbing to social evils, like smoking *dagga* in the fields. Revd Valentyn was also worried about his parish shrinking, as young people left to seek higher education and work. 'I was born here, and it was a privilege for me to come back after sixteen years away, but the best and brightest leave. The ones who stay are what I would call the labouring class.' As I left his house, two boys passed by in an ancient cart drawn by donkeys and smiled at me. At least I was visible again.

The minister had shown me a path to the 'swimming place', so I took a pair of trunks and walked over a hill to a gorge where a river flowed into dark pools beneath overhanging rocks. It was early evening, the sun had gone and the blackness of the water was not appealing, so I retraced my steps. The village was quiet, old men were sitting around chatting and a couple of children were riding bicycles, and I felt again like an unseen visitor from another dimension. I returned to the empty guest house feeling tired and lonely, and microwaved a slice of pizza saved from dinner the night before. This was a mistake. Within minutes I felt unwell, and then I was violently sick. I tried reading by candlelight, but the words kept dancing around the pages. Eventually I fell into a fitful sleep, in which I dreamed I was running through Wuppertal with no clothes on and nobody noticed.

The impression that the Moravian mission lay on the edge of nowhere was confirmed next day when I returned on the gravel road to a pass that led out of the mountains and deposited me on the moonscape of the Northern Cape. I was heading for the Orange River, some 350 miles to the north through arguably the bleakest and harshest region of Africa outside the Sahara. Most of the itinerant tribes and white men who passed this way had wisely left it to the Bushmen, establishing a pattern of settlement in eastern regions that has not changed. We are talking seriously dry country here. In a good year it gets about the same rainfall as Scotland on a summer day, and good years are one in ten. The rivers are euphemistically called 'episodic', which means there is usually somebody who remembers his father talking about a flash flood in one of them. The result is a vast plateau with brown, flat-topped hills and perennial shrubs and thin lines of thorn trees and not much else. But it has stark beauty, and it is a strong antidote to delusions of grandeur. Anyone with an inflated ego has merely to stand here for a while to regain a perspective on his place in the great scheme of things.

After a couple of hours on a deserted dirt road, I was beginning to wonder about my own place on the planet. I didn't seem to be getting anywhere, and for some technical reason (like a stuck needle) the petrol gauge kept showing a full tank. It seemed as if I was doomed to travel for eternity through this wasteland, a terrestrial *Flying Dutchman*. Then I came to a little brick house with a tin roof by the side of the road. There was a row of similar dwellings on a hillside, and a sheep farmer's *kraal* on the other side of the road, and they were the only signs of life as far as the eye could see. When I stopped for a drink, two young coloured girls emerged from a mud and straw hut and looked at me shyly. I could hear a man's voice indoors, but he did not appear. A flock of geese was squatting in the shade of a rusting tanker truck, and a donkey was standing motionless in a dusty pen. The liveliest thing in the place was a line of washing, flapping in a hot wind blustering across the plain. On through hills that looked like monstrous slag heaps, and over parched river beds, and then there was a lone house on a farm the size of a European principality and you wondered what they did for company.

*   *   *

The answer was that they headed for Calvinia. This was a town, named after a dour Swiss Protestant reformer, that was famous in the nineteenth century for its religious services, which on one memorable occasion drew 6,000 people on 500 carts and wagons. Now it survived on merino wool and mutton, and boasted the biggest pillar-box in the world, a bizarre red giant with a blue top standing near the neo-Gothic church. It was about 20 feet high and a sign said it had a volume of 43,000 cubic metres, which I supposed would hold all the mail from the town for a century. There was no explanation why it was there. One was left to assume that people who spent a lot of time with sheep in blazing heat tended to develop a peculiar sense of humour. The other curious thing was that the street on which it stood was deserted, and so were other streets around it. I passed a petrol station, a row of houses and a coffee shop and there were no signs of life. So it was true. The hot wind in the desert had been the dying breath of a thermonuclear catastrophe, and I was the last person on earth. Then I turned a corner and was caught up in a street market. It was lunchtime on Saturday, and people were stocking up on beer and groceries for the weekend. I cruised around, checked out the available accommodation in about three minutes, and settled for a plain hotel where a friendly girl gave me a room that was cool and clean.

In the afternoon a crowd gathered in the bar to watch a rugby match between South Africa and England on television. The coloured guys were fired up for the game on brandy and Coke, but the burly whites in khaki shorts watched impassively as the South Africans ritually stuffed England. I tried to strike up a conversation, but after a couple of monosyllabic responses I gave up. So I went for a stroll before dinner, and the town was virtually deserted again. I stopped a policeman patrolling in a van and asked him if there was anything to see. 'I can't tell you that,' he said with a laugh. His English was awkward but I got the point. In the distance a ridge of the Hantamsberg range began to glow rust-red in the sunset, and this was the best show in town. That night I met some farmers in the bar of another hotel, and I asked them about life on the moon they called home. 'It's good for sheep,' one of them said. 'But it's hard. At night sometimes it's so hot you sweat in bed.' His son said they were plagued by mosquitoes and scorpions and snakes, but the barman said they loved the wilderness. They came to town to visit friends and pick up supplies, and after a couple of days they were itching to get back on the farm. 'Born and bred,' one of the farmers said. 'That's the answer. Born and bred to the life.'

Next morning I spent a few hours sitting on the *stoep* of the hotel with the owner and his wife, watching the world go by. This consisted mainly of giant trucks towing trailers between Cape Town and the interior. As one of the leviathans thundered past, the woman raised her arm in a pulling motion and the driver pulled on his klaxon which gave a deeply satisfying blare. It was Sunday and there wasn't much else to do. The museum had a stuffed four-legged ostrich chick, but it was closed. So I went for a jog around a rugby field until I got bored. Earlier I had noticed a couple driving through town slowly in a *bakkie* with three children. They didn't seem to be going anywhere, and I came across them again while jogging back to the hotel. They stopped and waved me across the street with a smile. I supposed this was the highlight of their day, and I imagined a conversation: 'I want to see the supermarket.' 'No, we did that last week. Let's look at the garage and the post office.' I suppose when you live on a farm on the moon you get your kicks where you can. That evening the only other people in the hotel dining room were a Chinese couple. When I entered they were eating quietly, oblivious to a horrible screeching from a tape player that had gone wonky. The room was filled with a cacophony from hell, but they gave no indication of being aware of it. It was like a scene from *The Outer Limits*.

Route 27 running north out of Calvinia was also spooky. It was a black ribbon on a treeless plain that stretched endlessly like a dirty brown sea, and in the distance it shimmered in the heat as if it had turned to water. This was a land of mirages, in which trucks swam through the haze and floated past and then disappeared, and you wondered if they were real. Unlike the trucks, the heat had nowhere to go. So it lay there, trapped in the still air, burning the land. I stopped at a thatched shelter by the road and sat listening to the tick-tick of the car engine cooling. Passing vehicles sounded like low-flying aircraft, a grumble that became a roar as they swept by, then there was only the sigh of the wind and the droning of insects. This was lonely country. I thought of Africa's first people, the Bushmen who had roamed this plateau for thousands of years, small people with high cheekbones and honey-coloured skin who fought with lions to survive until they lost their hunting grounds and eventually their identity to black and white incomers. I had visited one of the last San settlements in Namibia, and I knew that they trod lightly on the ground, leaving few traces of their passage. A tribe could have passed this way the day before, and I would never have known.

Now and again there was a copse of trees near the road, and in its shade would be a bungalow with an iron roof and outbuildings squatting close to the earth, as if cowering from the sun. Among them there was always a metal windmill, clanking as it drew water from an artesian well that was the lifeline of the farm. I passed a homestead that had a graveyard inside a black iron railing a few yards away, which set me to musing on the brief journey between life and death on a farm in the middle of nowhere. This is one of the attractions of travelling alone in solitary places. As the miles roll by, you gaze at far horizons and your mind drifts around the edges of everything and nothing. You understand the nomadic instincts of the San, and you sense the lure of the desert that makes Aborigines go walkabout. Such places leave indelible images and vague longings. Occasionally, months later, I felt a yearning to return to the space and silence of the empty lands.

After a hundred miles I came to a mirage that refused to go away. The town of Brandvlei materialised as a few dusty streets of iron-roofed bungalows by the side of the road. Its name means 'burning marsh', after a *trekboer* who stopped to rest his oxen and accidently set the *veld* on fire. The local marshes are periodic, and most of the time are salt pans that finance the town's continued existence. It took less than a minute to cruise the main street, which had a bank, a post office, a municipal office, a hotel and a couple of stores and ended at a salt factory. The only place for lunch was the hotel bar, where I was joined by a big sheep farmer in rugby shorts who sat on the next stool and ordered a brandy and Coke. It was the middle of the day, and the heat outside was like an animal trying to claw its way in. I wondered how they could drink that stuff in this climate without pickling their brains. I said: 'It's hot.' It's only the start, the farmer said, wait till January. Off-hand I could think of nothing worse. He conceded it was a hard life, with the heat, the dust, the wind and the mosquitoes. But it's a living, he said. You had to be born to it.

He was an amiable, soft-spoken man accustomed to physical hardships, but he didn't like the way things were going in what he called the Mandela era. Three weeks before a local butcher had been shot dead while delivering meat to a township near Cape Town. The farmer shook his head. 'We are suffering now. People overseas don't understand. We are different people, the whites and the coloureds. We will never be one.' He said I should stay the night and enjoy the local attractions: nice farmers, nice swimming pool out back, nice girls, nice steakhouse at the end of the street. I had a vision of staying a night, then a week, then being trapped for ever in this slow-motion time warp. As I drove away, I felt as if I was escaping from something.

The next 100 miles ran as straight as an arrow through the stony heart of Bushmanland, skirting salt pans glaring hard and bright in the sun. On one of the largest, called Verneukpan, Malcolm Campbell attempted to break the world land speed record in 1921, and failed by 13 m.p.h. Somebody should have told him the name of the place means pan of deception. There were few signs of life. A brown, stoat-like creature scurried across the road in front of me, and a big bird with black wings blundered up from a carcass as I approached and returned to its meal when I had passed. Occasionally there were signs to unseen farms along gravel roads that disappeared in the distance, and I thought they were among the most forlorn signs I had ever seen.

The town of Kenhardt had a camelthorn tree more than 500 years old, a monument to two Boers executed by the British in 1901 and a comfortable old hotel with animal skins on the walls and a crazy German in the bar. I stopped at the hotel for a drink, liked the look of the place and decided to stay for the night. I had driven far enough for one day, I was beginning to see mirages with my eyes shut. The German was an intense young man with a drawn face who babbled interminably about Bushmanland. He had been there for months, wandering alone through its furthest reaches, taking notes and photographs for reasons that were unclear, even to him. During one of his monologues my eyes strayed to the pelt of a lynx splattered on a wall beside the bar. 'They prey on sheep,' a farmer sitting beside me said by way of explanation.

I dutifully inspected the camelthorn tree, where a special magistrate and fifty mounted police set up camp on 27 December 1868 to protect stock farmers against rustlers and hostile tribes and thereby founded the settlement of Kenhardt. Half of it seemed to be dead, but the other half was still producing foliage, which I thought was remarkable for a tree that had been around before Dias turned up at the Cape. I touched one of its withered arms with respect. The monument to H.L. Jacobs and A.C. Jooste, martyrs to the Boer cause, was a granite obelisk on a hill overlooking the town. Hundreds of death sentences were passed on Afrikaners during the Anglo-Boer War, but only thirty-three were carried out, including these two. As I was trying to decipher the Afrikaans inscription a hot wind came from nowhere, blustering across the dusty earth and whistling among the telegraph wires; as I turned to leave it died away.

That night in the hotel two huge farmers were drinking at the bar. On the counter was a wooden carving of a hippopotamus, and the men bore a striking resemblance to it. The German *naturkind* was wittering on about west-flowing rivers being free of bilharzia, so I stepped outside to look at the stars. The air was warm and still, and I caught my breath as I looked up at a cosmic extravaganza I had never seen with such exhilarating clarity.

The Orange River signalled its presence with a band of vegetation cutting a green swathe across the plains. At this point it had flowed for hundreds of miles from its source in the mountains of Lesotho, irrigating vast tracts of land on its journey westwards to the Atlantic. I stopped by a concrete bridge and watched this river of life tumbling in brown torrents over rocks and around grassy islets between banks of tall reeds. The air smelled sweet, and the sounds of running water and birdsong were joyous after the stony silences of Bushmanland.

Shortly afterwards Route 27 came to an end, leaving me on a highway that followed the river to Upington, the commercial capital of the Northern Cape. It had supermarkets, and sports fields, and guest houses in pretty gardens by the river, and the longest airport runway in the southern hemisphere that was the only place outside the United States that the Challenger spacecraft could make emergency landings. So they said, anyway. The reason for such a ludicrously long runway outside a small town where nobody flew further than Johannesburg had something to do with the military, which figured.

There were a lot of foreigners in town, which the owner said was because Upington was the gateway to the Kalahari. It was one of the world's last great destinations, he said. 'It's a place for travellers, not for tourists. It's for people who have been all over the world and are still looking for magic. This is where they find it. The magic is here.'

8

The black people don't want to stay here

It is more than a hundred miles from Upington to the Botswana border, and in all that way I saw one thing of interest. It was a *warrelwind*, a sand devil that appeared from nowhere. It began as a whirl of dust that grew and spiralled into a crooked white column about 10 feet high, spinning near the road. After lurching around like a drunk for a while it seemed to break in the middle, then it faded away. It was impressive for its size, and I decided I was in no hurry to see a full-blown tornado.

Ahead lay the largest expanse of sand on earth, the Kalahari Sand Beds. It is not a real desert like the Sahara or the Gobi, because occasionally it has rain, which produces brief profusions of grass and flowers. But for most of the time it is blisteringly dry savannah, flat and featureless apart from eye-searing salt pans and sparse scrub. So I ignored signs pointing ahead to the Kalahari Gemsbok National Park, and turned right. The main reason I took the gravel road along the southern edge of the Kalahari was because it led to specks on a map called Hotazel and Lower Dikgatlhong that had intrigued me for years.

The first place off the main road was Askham, which comprised a church, a primary school, a petrol station, a shop and a few houses. It served the local stock farming community and had a population of about ten. When I was there it also had four big Afrikaner farmers in khaki shirts and rugby shorts leaning on a petrol pump discussing hunting rifles. I wondered the pump didn't collapse under the weight of them. 'It will bring down an elephant,' one of them said of the gun under discussion. 'Only if you stick it up his arse and give him both barrels,' another opined. I have this literal translation thanks to Connie, my friend from Cape Town, who had flown to Upington to join me for a few days. She was a cheerful companion who could tell me all I needed to know about Afrikaner culture and also liked to hitch up her skirt and extend her bare legs out of the window on country roads, which somehow helped the miles to roll by.

The Kalahari farmer with the pet cheetah, recommended to me before I left England, was called Llewellyn Stadler and he raised sheep and cattle on 30 square miles of savannah that a Scottish surveyor had marked out in 1921 and called Loch Broom. His family name came from Swiss ancestors and his Christian name came from a Welsh cookery book. 'That's South Africa for you, the rainbow nation,' he said. His farm lay east of Askham on the banks of a river as dry as the local humour. The Kuruman River is marked on maps with a broken blue line, which means that it flows sometimes but mostly it doesn't. It had appeared in 1921, then four times in the 1970s, and once in the 1980s. Its course was usually marked by a shallow depression between dry banks of reddish sand, but it was still a lifeline for farmers, yielding water from boreholes 300 feet deep.

We were welcomed to Loch Broom by a peacock prancing on a wooden fence. Llewellyn's wife had transformed her portion of the desert into an oasis of sweet-thorn trees, and washingtonia palms, and sprays of delicate white flowers called Butterflies in the Mist. The peacock seemed at home, along with the cheetah, called Maggie, who liked watching rugby on television. Llewellyn had adopted her as a cub after her mother had been shot in Namibia, and she had become part of the family. 'When the rugby's on she can't take her eyes off the screen. My wife thinks it's the figures running around that bring out her hunting instincts.' I admired her from a distance as she prowled around a large fenced enclosure, a fully grown specimen with all the lithe grace and beauty of her breed. She strolled over to inspect me, discouraged any intimacy with a snarl, and loped off to gnaw on the carcass of an antelope. Any rugby player that sparked her interest as potential prey would not stand a chance. In theory she was the fastest natural killer on earth, but as an orphan and a television addict her prospects of survival in the wild would have been remote. Which is where Hennie the panel-beater from Upington came in. We were introduced to *Groot* (Big) Hennie and his son *Klein* (Little) Hennie over a barbecue dinner with the Stadlers and their son, who farmed nearby. Afterwards I saw the men loading guns and spotlights on a *bakkie*, and Big Hennie said: 'We're going to shoot some steenbok for the cheetah, do you want to come?' And so I went on my first hunting trip.

Riding on the back of a pick-up truck on undulating dirt roads is like balancing on a small boat in a choppy sea. You sway a lot, and sometimes you feel queasy. Little Hennie, who was manning the spotlights, was having fun. 'This is the life,' he said. 'I love being back in the bush. You really feel alive here.' I thought: Which is better than some steenbok will feel soon. Steenbok are small, delicate antelopes with big eyes and a surprising range of enemies. Predators partial to their flesh include leopards, eagles, pythons, monitor lizards, jackals, hyenas and panel-beaters. For this reason they tend to hide in long grass much of the time.

It was a cloudless night and the heavens were full of stars. I was reflecting that the Kalahari by moonlight was a haunting stage for the ultimate drama of life and death when a pair of green eyes glowed in the dark, transfixed by the lights, and we stopped. In the silence there was a rustle of movement as the black barrel of a rifle emerged from the *bakkie*. A soft intake of breath as Big Hennie steadied his aim, then the shot sounded like a dry cough, echoing across the *veld*. It missed. We saw a puff of dust where the round had impacted beside the animal about 100 yards away. Still the eyes sparkled like emeralds, mesmerised by the embrace of death. *Run*, I wanted to shout. *Get away*. The rifle coughed again and this time in the distance there was a sound like sheep bleating; the green eyes danced briefly, then disappeared. It had not been a clean shot. When we approached, the steenbok was squirming in the dust, its little head twisting and turning in shock and fear. It looked like Bambi. Any minute its forest friends would come running to the rescue and chase away the bad men with guns, and Bambi would recover and bound away. Then Big Hennie took something from behind his back and knelt down. There was a ripping sound, and a whimper that was almost human. 'What did he do?' I asked his son as the carcass was loaded into the back of the truck. 'He put a knife into the skull through the back of the neck.' Just then the animal began kicking, its hooves slamming on the side of the vehicle. 'He didn't do a good job,' Little Hennie said.

The killing went on, some of it swift and painless and some of it messy, until half a dozen creatures were lying in eddies of blood beside me. I regarded them with immense sadness, confronted for the first time with the reality of dying animals I was accustomed to buying in sanitised supermarket packaging. Then the life went out of them, and they became bundles of fur and bone, and the beauty of the night restored my spirits. Back at the farm I walked away from the truck as Hennie began to butcher his kills. It was natural, no different from a European farmer preparing rabbits for the pot, but I didn't want to see it. In the house I said to Llewellyn's wife Mariana that my first hunt had been an interesting experience. 'That isn't hunting,' she said. 'That is killing at night.' In this wild place, surrounded by big game trophies, she was a kind woman with a fondness for the animals she lived among.

The next morning I noticed with interest that her bosoms appeared to be moving of their own accord. She reached into her blouse, and extricated a bedraggled dove chick that had fallen from its nest and been drenched by a garden hose. 'This is the best way to keep it alive, with body heat,' she said. Behind her, I noticed that the cheetah had reduced one of the steenbok to bloody scraps. You win some, you lose some.

This was the youngest farming area in South Africa, having been settled in the 1920s, and Llewellyn said it was the best: 'No ticks, no parasites.' Apart from his main stock of sheep and cattle, he bred ostriches for their low-fat meat and skin that produced fine leather. His other sideline was grazing peacefully among thorn trees in an enclosed area of the *veld*, a small herd of rare Arabian oryx. Hunted almost to extinction in their native land, they were thriving in the Kalahari. 'I started with them partly to make money, by selling them to the Saudis, but mostly because they are beautiful to look at,' Llewellyn said. They were the most graceful antelope I had seen, with light-coloured coats and long, curved horns like scimitars. By contrast the ostriches looked ungainly, like feather dusters on stilts.

The tidal wave of political change that had swept the rest of the country in 1994 had caused barely a ripple here, which was fine with the farming community. 'In this area the new government has made no difference,' Llewellyn said. 'The ANC and the black people don't want to stay here, it's too hard for them to earn a living. They want it easy. They want more land, but they're not farmers. They cut down the trees and kill everything.' So the paternal relationship between white farmers and their coloured labourers continued, with Llewellyn's workers calling him *baas* and relying on him to take them to hospital when they were sick as well as their children to school. He said there were mutual benefits to the system: 'If you have good relations with your workers you don't have to worry about security. We trust each other. I take care of my people and they look out for me and my family. When I go on holiday I know they will protect my house.' That night we drove to a neighbour's farm for a barbecue, and over drinks in the garden the woman recounted her adventures on a visit to Johannesburg: 'As we were coming to the city, the bus driver said we must hold tightly to our handbags, and take off our jewellery because they will steal it from your neck.' Her tone implied her shock. 'Everything is locked, and covered with bars and barbed wire. How can they live like that?' In the darkened bush, a male ostrich intent on mating made a sound startlingly like a lion's growl. I looked at low hills ghostly in the moonlight and listened to myriad rustlings in the bush, and understood why these people shuddered at the thought of Johannesburg. Raised on farms, they were born free.

Mariana said the best thing was camping trips to Botswana and deserted stretches of the Namibian coast. You should come back in winter and sit around the fire and listen to the stories, she said. 'It's too tame on the farm, you have to get into the *veld* and be afraid a lion will get you. That's the great thing about Botswana; the whole time you're there you're aware of danger. It's the last wilderness.' Life on a Kalahari farm can be sufficiently perilous for the unwary visitor, however. I spent the next morning wandering barefoot around Mariana's garden, and on leaving I paused to admire the peacocks. 'Yes, they're good for the scorpions,' Mariana said.

'Sorry?'

'Scorpions. We've got lots of them in the garden and the peacocks eat them.'

Stop at Van Zyl's Drift, my friend in England had said. Wonderful, dusty little frontier town, he said. He was right about the ambience and close with the name. It lay at the end of a turn-off from the gravel road to Hotazel, beyond a metal sign that said: 'Relax this is Van Zylsrus'. The name meant Van Zyl's Rest, but who this character was and why he chose to get off his horse in this dead-end spot nobody knew. I liked it immediately. This is the way frontier settlements ought to be: no paved roads, no sidewalks, just a broad sandy street leading to a T-junction where trails branched off and petered out in the desert after 100 yards or so. There were no signs to the Botswana border 10 miles away, because there were no roads to it.

At the corner a coloured attendant was dozing by a petrol pump, summing up the pace of life in an outpost that comprised little more than a hotel, a post office, a store and a handful of bungalows. We wandered into the bar of the Gemsbok Hotel and savoured the cool interior after the heat and dust of the gravel road. The walls were festooned with a collection of battered old felt hats, some of them hanging from gemsbok horns, and cartoons of animals copulating. One of them featured an elephant with an arrow flying from its trunk while a man hammered its balls. The caption read: 'The army's new secret weapon'.

By way of greeting, the barman said: 'This place, if they give the world an enema, this is where they put in the pipe.' But he was smiling when he said it. He was a former civil engineer who had worked in the area, decided he liked it, and bought the hotel. During the winter it was popular with game hunters, but now it was quiet.

The only other customer, a crony of the owner with a face as creased as his bush shirt, informed us we would never be able to hit a gemsbok on the head with a stone. I couldn't think off-hand why I would want to, but he explained that if you threw stones at one of these big antelopes, it would hit every one with its horns. 'If it signed for a baseball team it would be the best batsman ever,' he said. I noticed a pair of gemsbok horns on the wall behind him. They were impressively long and straight, but they appeared unmarked. Evidently their owner had been hit by something other than stones.

There was also a blue, white and orange flag of the pre-Rainbow South Africa on the wall, which had been 'borrowed' from the local police station. 'This is still an ultra-conservative part of the world,' the owner said. 'If you want me to go bankrupt in a week I'll put up the new flag.' The rest of the country might be disappearing into the black hole of majority rule, but for the clientele of the Gemsbok Bar in the far north time was standing reassuringly still.

Go and see old Dudley before you leave, the owner said, he knows all about the history of the place. We stepped outside and the heat hit us like an oven blast. It was 42 degrees in the shade, which the locals said was a nice day. Last week it was 46, which meant it was 55 in the sun. This was a place for strong sunglasses and wide-brimmed hats, or staying indoors. We strolled along the main street, all 200 yards of it, to a hideous modern church as out of character with the dusty brick and iron buildings around it as a flying saucer. I found myself wishing it would take off. On the way back, a *bakkie* stopped and a farmer leaned out and said we should take a look at the museum. It was really interesting, he said, lots of old photos and things, and we could get the key from the woman who lived next to the hotel. Then the hotelier's crony spotted us and beckoned us to the store where he introduced us to Dudley. We had been in town for half an hour and it seemed everybody knew us.

Dudley was an old timer with sparkly eyes and an impressive white beard, whose great-grandfather had been a British general in Crimea. He remembered his grandmother talking about meeting Queen Victoria. His own story was similar to the engineer-hotelier's. He had come to Van Zylsrus as a travelling liquor salesman, liked the look of the place, and bought the hotel. After a while he sold it and bought the garage and store. Not much had changed over the years, except the primary school, he said. When it went multi-racial the coloured kids moved in and the whites moved out to the nearest schools, more than 100 miles away. It was felt standards in the local school had dropped, he said. I asked him about the museum, and he said he had been living in the town for twenty-three years and he had never been in it. So we filled up on water and petrol and headed out of town on the dirt road for Hotazel.

Be careful, people warned us, it's a bad road. And so it was. The surface was rutted, and alternately hard as iron and soft as mud; I discovered with interest that drifting sand has much the same effect as black ice, causing wheelspin and a slewing rear end in clouds of dust; vehicles travelling in the other direction were followed by mini sandstorms that blotted out the sun and everything else; and behind tinted windows and sunglasses my eyes were bloodshot from the glare. But it was good fun. We felt free and alone in a wilderness that made no concessions to mankind. It was bleak and hostile, a flat ocean of scrubby sand beneath a metallic blue sky. Barrelling along between the two with one hand on the steering wheel and two shapely legs dangling from the passenger window, we felt like Bonnie and Clyde. Hotazel, here we come.

Hotazel was a dump. It materialised as a garage, a beer shack and a railway goods yard at the end of the gravel road. Then there was nothing. Mystified, we turned round and saw a sign by a side road bearing the name of a mining company. So we followed it, and passed a black township and came to a small shopping centre. There were a few white people in cars, and a lot of black people just hanging around. I asked a woman where the town was, and she looked mystified.

'The centre of Hotazel?'

'This is it.'

'Where do people live?'

'Over there,' she said, pointing to a cluster of bungalows at the far end of the street.

'Is there anywhere to eat?'

'No, the social club sometimes does *braais* in the evening, but not just now.'

I wanted to take a photograph of a road sign saying Hotazel, but there wasn't one. The place was christened in 1917 by a man called Dirk Roos, who had been surveying farms in the area. Back at his camp after a blistering day in the *veld*, Roos checked his maps and named the farm he had just surveyed 'Hot as Hell'. A few years later a geologist passed his magnetometer over the area and it flew off the scale, indicating the richest deposit of manganese ore in the world. So now it was a mining town, with nothing going for it but a black mineral that made a lot of money for people elsewhere.

We drove to the residential district, which had a rugby field, an open-air swimming pool and a social club with an inspiring motto inscribed on the wall: *Gryp die dag* (Seize the day). Unfortunately it was closed. A poster on the gate was advertising a country dance that night and my friend said it might be interesting, but we agreed we would probably die of boredom before then. Anyway, the only guest accommodation seemed to be in barrack-like 'single quarters', which didn't appeal. So we went to the post office, where a nice woman sold me two postcards, which she franked with a Hotazel stamp. For good measure I went to the car and got my passport and she stamped that as well. She had been there for eight years, since her husband came to work in the mine. So how was it living in Hotazel, I asked. 'Hell,' she said with a laugh. 'If you like peace and quiet this is the place, but if you don't . . .' Her voice trailed off. But it wasn't so bad, she said; people made their own amusements, dances and *braais* and so on.

In accordance with this ethos, we bought meat pasties and

bottles of water from the grocery store and sat on an old bench outside and observed life in Hotazel. This consisted mainly of a truck standing with its engine running while the driver passed the time of day with friends in the store. We struck up a conversation with an elderly black man sitting beside us, who said he was a Tswana who had been working in the mines for fifteen years. Hotazel was a good place for work, he said; the money was good and the white bosses were good to work for, but his own people were a lazy, shifty lot. 'The management offered to build us houses and provide buses, but my people just talk and talk and can't agree so we don't get the houses.' Nothing had changed since majority rule, he said. 'Too many black people don't want to help themselves. They expect the whites to do everything for them.' He was a dignified man who held conservative views that were scorned in his own community, and we sensed the sorrow in him.

Given the uninspiring character of Hotazel, we gave its neighbour Lower Dikgatlhong a miss and headed south to the bright lights of Kuruman. Nature gave this town a good start by endowing it with a spring flowing from dolomitic rock and delivering more than 20 million litres of clear, fresh water a day, even during the worst droughts. Thus it became known as the 'Oasis of the Kalahari'. The London Missionary Society then provided it with Robert Moffat, a Scotsman who founded a mission station in 1824, and it was blessed as 'the fount of Christianity in Africa'. From then on it was all downhill. Kuruman was an ugly little town, inundated by crowds and litter swirling around noisy streets and seedy shopping malls. We drove around looking at crummy hotels and guest houses, and eventually headed out of town to a country lodge among rust-coloured hills where we were deeply grateful to find peace and quiet, a swimming pool open to the evening sky and friendly staff serving *al fresco* dinners by candlelight.

One of the waitresses had grown up on a farm and she was not impressed by Kuruman. 'There are a lot of lesbians there,' she informed us. My friend said that from the look of the men she was not surprised.

We ventured back next day to see the Eye of Kuruman, a pool fed by the spring. It was a real oasis, but it lay in a desert of tarmac and concrete in the middle of town, and it had to be fenced in because the locals kept trashing it. Still it was worth a nominal entrance fee to stroll around the haven of translucent water and palms and willows, teeming with dark fish and bright yellow birds. I tasted the water flowing from a rock fissure; it was fresh and sweet. It must have been an idyllic spot before the infernal combustion engine shattered its tranquillity.

Among the few white folks to have enjoyed it *au naturel* were Moffat and his wife Mary, who established their mission a couple of miles away. Another was a compatriot, a Lanarkshire cotton factory worker turned missionary and explorer by the name of David Livingstone who turned up in a bad way after a lion attack, was nursed by their eldest daughter Mary, and in due course became their son-in-law. The almond tree under which Livingstone proposed was subsequently reduced to a blackened stump by a bolt of lightning, but the garden in which it stood was preserved along with the mission as a national monument. We sat on a bench in the garden for a while, musing on the intrepid character who charted great swathes of the 'dark continent' while enjoying the view. It was a peaceful place, with wild flowers and pear and syringa trees dappling a meadow beyond an old wooden fence. A plaque on a wall said: 'Here David Livingstone said he learned the truth of Jesus' words: There is no one who has left house or brothers or sisters or mother or father or children or lands for my sake and for the gospel, who will not receive a hundredfold.'

In the stone and thatch mission there was a photograph of

Livingstone with his youngest daughter, Anna Mary. He was an avuncular figure with wavy hair and long sideburns, and she was a remarkably pretty eight-year-old girl who looked like Alice in Wonderland. In a bookcase beside them was a handsome volume bound in dark red leather with gold lettering, entitled *How I Found Livingstone in Central Africa*, by Henry M. Stanley.

The mission church in which Livingstone was married no longer had a congregation and was used mainly for weddings. It was a simple stone building with a high roof that was still supported by rafters donated by a Matabele chief in the 1830s, and its only adornment was a black marble plaque listing those who had served at the mission. Livingstone was the eighth name, in the period 1841–43. As we entered a white minister was conducting a marriage ceremony for two Tswana couples who were accompanied by relatives in their best dark suits and white dresses. They were nice people and I didn't think much of the minister, who treated them like children. At one point, when he was asking whether they wanted the service in English or Afrikaans, he rounded on one of them rudely and said: 'I don't care what you would like, I want to know what the bride and groom want.' I like to think that Moffat, who translated the Bible into Tswana, would have booted him out of the church.

On leaving the mission we were surrounded by a gaggle of black children carrying pots and pans and bits of woods for a *braai*. They were laughing and singing, and having a great time. Moffat and Livingstone would have loved it.

We returned to Upington along the great western highway to Namibia. This was the Wild West, badlands of dry plains and low brown hills and road signs riddled with bullet-holes by passing sharpshooters. Upington even had a saloon, actually an Irish theme pub, packed with Afrikaners watching a rugby match between Scotland and South Africa on big screens. It became apparent to even the most inebriated of them that I was the only person in the place not cheering the succession of Springbok tries, and eventually one of them leaned heavily on my shoulder. His brow was furrowed in concentration as he worked out what he wanted to say in English: 'Scotland is going to lose.' It seemed a reasonable assumption, since the score was Scotland 10, South Africa 60-something and rising. I consoled myself by sitting on the banks of the Orange River and watching the setting sun casting a rosy hue on a scene that was more attractive than a rain-lashed rugby stadium in Edinburgh.

Connie flew back to Cape Town, and I spent the night in a guest house whose owner was not a happy man. He had just returned from a visit to London, where he had been reminded of what it was like to live in a First World country without constant fear of violent crime. 'The problem here is the blacks feel they are owed something. Look, apartheid was a hell of a mistake for sure, but if we'd just handed over the country to the blacks in the sixties we'd have been like Mozambique now.' His family had deep roots around Upington, farms and so on, but he told his dad that if he had been a young professional guy who had gone overseas he doubted if he would come back. He thought I was crazy to travel alone through tribal homelands. 'Go well,' he said.

9

Interlopers in these outer zones of waste

The road south from Upington followed the Orange River, clinging to its banks as if afraid to venture across the parched plains. On one side were farms by the river, where white people lived, and on the other were clusters of matchbox houses on stony ground, where their coloured workers lived. In between, along the edge of the road, were the Walkers.

You see them all over South Africa, black and coloured people walking and trotting and carrying bundles, sometimes alone, sometimes in pairs or groups, often in the middle of nowhere. You wonder where they have come from and where they are going. They walk because there is no transport, or because they can't afford it. I have seen them in deserts and mountain passes, splashing through storms and striding out beneath umbrellas in temperatures over 40 degrees. Some glance hopefully at passing vehicles, but most seem content to walk because that is what they have always done. The cavalcade south of Upington included women crossing the road with bundles of firewood on their heads, a boy in tattered jeans wearing a T-shirt around his head like an Arab headdress and kicking a deflated football, and a lean youth loping at a brisk pace while carrying a heavy black cooking-pot. There were no houses to be seen, and the heat had begun to melt the tarmac.

I took a minor road that swung east across a plateau of red dust and bush and low hills for almost 200 miles to Kimberley. Drive carefully, a woman in a filling station said, there are a lot of accidents out there. Stop if you get tired, she said. Her advice was good, but there was nowhere to stop without being broiled by the sun. The land was already on fire, red flames and a huge cloud of dense smoke billowing from a bush blaze advancing across the *veld*. It looked like a strike by a B-52 bomber. I was becoming drowsy, and the road had begun to shimmer and dance in an odd manner when Kimberley appeared on the horizon. Its multi-storey buildings rose from the flat, desolate country like a colony on another world, and I felt like calling planet Earth to announce my discovery.

The big discovery that conceived this improbable city in the desert was made on 16 July 1871 by an African cook called Damon. He showed his employer, a diamond digger by the name of Fleetwood Rawstone, three stones he had found on a hill. To Mr Rawstone's delight, they sparkled. This precipitated the greatest diamond rush in history, during which the hill disappeared and became the biggest man-made hole in the world. The farm on which the find was made, named with uncanny premonition *Vooruitzicht* (Prospect), belonged to two brothers called Diederik and Nicolaas de Beer, who had paid fifty pounds for it eleven years before. Three months later they sold it for 6,000 guineas, packed their ox-wagons and trekked into obscurity, leaving their land and their name to the most powerful diamond cartel on earth.

The city that mushroomed around the diggings has the most haphazard layout in the country, as a result of buildings being erected along meandering paths between rows of miners' tents that in due course became streets. It is still a confusing place, but the Big Hole is easy to find. Given its size, it would be hard to miss. The crater is the main attraction of an excellent open-air museum featuring original buildings from the diamond rush, when the corrugated iron houses, tents and shacks echoed to the carousing of prospectors and the women and barflies who lived off them. It is approached through an elongated wire-mesh cage with a handrail in the middle. A few steps from the end you begin to glimpse the far wall of the hole, like a rusty cliff. With your last steps the earth falls away to reveal an awesome nothingness, and you have an idea what a meteor strike might look like. Sheer rock faces plunge to a milky green lake, silent save for the wheeling and crying of birds. Everything is dwarfed by it. The scale is such that the buildings perched beyond the distant rim, including skyscrapers, look like a toytown. A signboard gives the statistics: it is more than 600 feet deep, 1 mile around, and it produced 14,504,566 carats of diamonds, which is about 2.5 tons. For this, 22.5 million tons of earth were excavated. The feverish burrowing into the pipe of diamondiferous lava stopped in 1914, when war in Europe brought a slump in the diamond market. On my way back along the gangplank, I noticed three small mine trolleys filled with fragments of glass. A sign said that if all the diamonds from the Big Hole could be gathered together, this is what they would look like. For more than forty years of intensive labour, fierce competition and slick marketing, it didn't look like much.

Not all the miners struck it rich. One of those who toiled in vain on the nearby Vaal River diggings left this philosophical epitaph:

> Of course I thought that once on the field,
> Every load a stone would yield;
> But, I owned, after many a weary day,
> That gravel is gravel, and clay is clay.

The labours of another produced a cry of despair:

> Beneath the brazen sky and flaming sun;
> That lashes still the river and the man,
> As interlopers in these outer zones of waste.

Unfortunately there were no prizes being awarded for poetry in Kimberley in those days.

Judging by the museum, the Kimberley of old, with *The Diggers' Rest* saloon next door to Barney Barnato's Boxing Academy and diamond buyers' offices clustered around the Victorian bandstand, was more appealing than the concrete jungle that replaced it. A display of 'then and now' photographs taken at the turn of the century and in 1981 gave a classic illustration of how an array of splendid buildings had been decimated by the Neanderthal architects who ravaged the world in the 1960s. The colonnades and ornate wrought-iron verandas were almost all gone, replaced by ugly grey slabs in the neo-Gulag style. This is pretty standard for South African cities, whose commercial centres are called CBDs, or central business districts. Concrete box districts would be more accurate.

An elegant survivor of the early days was the Kimberley Club, a bastion of wealth and power founded in 1881 by the arch-imperialist and capitalist Cecil Rhodes. This was the character who outlined his ambitions by declaring: 'Why should we not form a secret society with but one object, the furtherance of the British Empire and the bringing of the whole uncivilised world under British rule, for the recovery of the United States, for making the Anglo-Saxon race but one Empire?' He was twenty-three when he penned this modest proposal. By the time Rhodes and his cronies founded the Kimberley Club five years later, he was a millionaire, joint owner of the De Beers Mining Company and a member of the Cape parliament. It was from the verandah of the club that he prepared his strategy for colonising the land north of the Zambezi, which in due course came to be called Rhodesia. The club was no longer the exclusive domain of millionaires and empire builders, which is how I managed to secure a room on the upper floor with antique furniture, sash windows and an enormous bath, redolent with the faded grandeur of yesteryear and musty carpets.

Visitors to the Kimberley Club passed through the field of fire of a machine gun in the doorway, presented by Captain B. Carden Stewart, MC, RFA, in appreciation of the hospitality shown to officers during the 1914–18 war. They were also subjected to critical inspection by a larger than life bronze bust of Rhodes, looming over a memorial plaque to club members who died in the same war. Given changes in the club over the years, it was no wonder Rhodes looked stern. Its ramparts of male dominion had been breached by women 'associate' members who were admitted in the 1960s, although *not* through the front door and only to the dining room and a separate ladies' lounge. They subsequently stormed the main entrance, but were still barred from the inner sanctum of the Gentlemen's Lounge Bar and card room. Here ceiling fans span lazily above a splendid curved wooden bar, and portraits of past chairmen and old soldiers gazed benignly upon leather armchairs, oriental carpets and an RAF plaque over the fireplace. Pride of place went to a portrait of Rhodes, and former club president Henry Oppenheimer was accorded a prominent position above the fireplace. Royalty in the person of Prince Phillip was relegated to a side wall beneath a Grecian-style urn, which seemed appropriate. The people who decorated this room knew who the important players were, and Phil the Greek was not among them.

Before being admitted to this gentlemanly refuge I was required to dress in an approved manner. In this I was aided by a printed card helpfully placed on my bedside table. It quoted regulation 17.2.4 as saying: 'Denim clothing of any description, T-shirts, golfing shirts, polo or turtleneck shirts, sweat shirts, windbreakers, sheepskin-type jackets (whether zippered or not), zippered jackets (other than tailored leather or suede leather jackets), hunting jackets, bush jackets, anoraks, tracksuits (or components of tracksuits), short pants, slip-slops, strops, running shoes and canvas or other types of athletic or gym shoes may not be worn by ladies or gentlemen.' Dressed accordingly in my smartest shirt and trousers, and regulation tailored suede leather jacket (unzippered), I presented myself for dinner to be informed politely but firmly that my khaki-coloured trousers were unacceptable. So I changed into a cheaper pair of navy trousers, which matched the jacket like brown chalk and blue cheese, and was ushered in.

There were few other diners, and most of them were noisy women exchanging gossip, so I retreated from a mediocre meal to the calm of the Gentlemen's Lounge. This was more like it: a couple of old buffers discoursing on guns and horses, and attentive waiters in black waistcoats standing by to proffer the Havanas and top up the tinkling whisky glasses. I settled back in a deep armchair, conjuring images from the past. Rhodes paced the room, and came out with another of his immortal lines: 'Africa is still lying ready for us. It is our duty to take it.' He was interrupted by a clatter of hooves, and an exhausted dispatch rider burst in with news of the relief of Mafeking. This was *Boy's Own Adventure* country.

I also mused on the club dress code, and what kind of mind could have dreamed it up. I believe I found it in the head of a podgy, pasty-faced man at the reception desk who identified himself stiffly as the manager. I had asked whether someone could spare a few moments to tell me about the history of the club, and he said: 'You are not permitted to write about the club without prior authority.'

'Sorry?'

'We do not allow people to write about the club unless we

know who they are, and what they are writing. You must put in a written application, and then submit anything you write for approval.'

I searched for a hint of humour, but the man was serious. I couldn't make up my mind whether he was an idiot or a pompous ass, and concluded he was both. When he left, one of the waiters happily told me all I wished to know.

The rip-roaring days of the diamond rush were gone, but Kimberley was still a wild place, judging by all the metal bars on store windows and armed guards lounging in doorways. I also noticed the locals had got into the car-protection wheeze, a scheme whereby self-appointed security guards patrol parking areas; if your car is in one piece when you return you are expected to reward the guard accordingly. It is a blend of protection racket and moral blackmail (the guards are poor), and by and large it seems to work. In Cape Town the guards had been black or coloured, but here they were white. On returning to my car one evening, I was approached by an elderly man carrying a baton who said: 'You owe me for looking after your car all day.' I was getting fed up with people with their hands out looking for money, and his blunt approach didn't help. 'But I didn't ask you to look after it.' We then had a pointless argument about how 'some black guy' might have smashed my car windows, and how I didn't intend to pay for a service I hadn't asked for. In exasperation I gave him a handful of coppers that was more of an insult than a gratuity. We both remained polite and I drove off, feeling bad.

The next evening I drove to a park for a jog and a swim in a municipal pool. This time I was glad there was a guard who could keep my keys while I was running, and when I returned we had a chat. He was an Afrikaner called Herman, and on a good day he earned the equivalent of six pounds. I asked him why he did it, and he said: 'You have to live.' He used to work as a panel-beater and spray-painter, but he lost his job when it was given to a black man who was prepared to do it for half the pay. 'Now you've got old white women in the streets with cardboard signs saying please help me. That's getting dangerous,' Herman said.

Back at the club, I asked one of the waiters about the mood in local black communities. He was a thoughtful, articulate man and his view was so far, so good. The premier of the Northern Cape had delivered most of what he had promised: 250,000 houses built with substantial grants. 'I want to thank him for that, there is hope for people now.' But there were problems for blacks who moved into white neighbourhoods. 'Some whites accept us, but there are still some racists. It will take more than one generation.'

Meanwhile Kimberley was losing its sparkle. The city founded on greed and nurtured on vanity was running out of its most precious commodity. Soon there would be no more diamonds. Only three mines were still operating, producing barely enough gems between them daily to fill a dinner plate. I learned this from Corrie, an ex-miner who led tours of one of the last working mines called Bultfontein. We were standing at the pit head with a group of local schoolteachers, waiting to descend to a network of tunnels four times deeper than the Big Hole. In fact we were about to drop more than 2,500 feet into an extinct volcano that had spewed up chunks of crystallised carbon from the bowels of the earth 3 billion years ago. This was the stuff, worthless apart from its beauty, that slick marketing had transformed into the ultimate symbol of wealth and romance.

The first thing you see on entering the lift shaft at Bultfontein is a chart of noise levels from a falling leaf (10 decibels) to a jet engine (140). Most mining operations, such as drill-sharpening, crushing and the use of a device with the wondrous name of the twin boom rockdrill, fall into a danger zone between 'high noise level' and 'threshold of pain'. This explains the ear plugs dangling from your hard hat. You then step into an aluminium box with a block and tackle device suspended from the ceiling on a heavy chain, reminiscent of Poe's 'The Pit and the Pendulum', and metal gates clang shut behind you. There is a shudder, and with much shaking and rattling the cage plummets about half a mile in three minutes. This is an emotional time for the inexperienced, ranging from anxiety to panic. I noticed the colour draining from the faces of the schoolteachers as if by magic.

At the bottom we emerged into a surprisingly large, light, and well-ventilated chamber with broad tunnels branching from it in several directions. We followed one of them for about half a mile to a steep staircase that went down, and down, and down, to another warren of smaller tunnels leading into the heart of the mine. This is where we encountered monsters. They came rearing out of the darkness, mechanical gorgons devouring the earth in a cacophony of hisses and roars and shrieks and screams, the full repertoire of scary noises. The tunnels and caverns seemed to tremble under the mad assault as the machines ripped away huge slabs of granitic rock in search of the last diamonds. It was the Temple of Doom, and we were being led to the altar where the high priests Rhodes and Oppenheimer worshipped the gem god Solitaire.

Happily the miners seemed to be in control of the monsters. Mostly they were sitting behind protective screens of wire mesh, sending mechanical diggers careering down side tunnels like wild animals. When a scoop returned with rubble drooling from its jaws it was switched off, and a miner would walk alone to inspect the far end of the shaft, his headlamp becoming a pinprick of light in the heart of darkness. Then we were taken to the Crusher. It was as if we had stumbled into a giant's workshop. It filled a cavern, a dusty machine about the size of a three-storey house that reduced boulders to pebbles. Everything about it was immense, including 4-foot spanners hanging on the walls. For the moment the machine was silent, so we climbed an iron ladder and peered into it. We were dutifully inspecting its massive jaws when a sudden loud, harsh noise caused all of us except our guide to briefly leave the ground. It was a telephone ringing. Back near the lift, we passed conveyer belts of rocks heading for the surface, rivers of diamonds in disguise. I asked Corrie what would happen when they dried up, and he shrugged and said maybe somebody would come up with new technology that would prolong the life of the mines. But as things stood, they had barely ten years left and that meant 30,000 jobs on the line. At the Kimberley Club next day I overheard more promising news. Three businessmen, a South African and two Europeans, were discussing acquiring a farm in the area for prospecting. Surveys indicated they could expect 13 carats per 100 tons, which they considered a reasonable haul. It was like an echo from the old days, and from above a portrait of Rhodes looked on approvingly.

At the time I was reading an interesting article on the front page of the *Diamond Fields Advertiser* (founded 23 March 1878): 'At the very moment you are reading this newspaper, 98 years ago exactly, the Scottish soldiers of the Highland Brigade were lying pinned down two hundred yards in front of the Boer trenches at Magersfontein, many of them dead, wounded, or dying.' I read on to an account by a survivor, Lieutenant Freddie Tait: 'The men on each side of me were hit straight away, and in a few minutes very few were left unhit. It was quite impossible for any ambulance or doctor to advance, so all our wounded lay within two hundred yards or so of the Boer trenches all day in a broiling sun, being shot at whenever they moved until seven o'clock at night, most of them without a drop of water . . . Our brigade was simply thrown away; hundreds of splendid fellows were killed and wounded, and nothing gained in the end.' I consulted my map and found Magersfontein was only a slight detour from my

intended route, so I went to see the place where more than seven
hundred of my countrymen had been shot for nothing.

The men who shot them were a tough lot. Courageous, fiercely
independent and expert marksmen, the Boer commandos proved
a match for the most powerful army in the world. For a sketch
of their character, I defer to the opening lines of Arthur Conan
Doyle's *The Great Boer War*, written in 1900: 'Take a community
of Dutchmen of the type who defended themselves for fifty years
against all the power of Spain at a time when Spain was the
greatest power in the world. Intermix with them a strain of those
inflexible French Huguenots who gave up home and fortune and
left their country for ever at the time of the revocation of the
Edict of Nantes. The product must obviously be one of the most
rugged, virile, unconquerable races ever seen upon earth. Take
this formidable people and train them for seven generations in
constant warfare against savage men and ferocious beasts, in
circumstances under which no weakling could survive, place
them so that they acquire exceptional skill with weapons and in
horsemanship, give them a country which is eminently suited to
the tactics of the huntsman, the marksman, and the rider. Then,
finally, put a finer temper upon their military qualities by a dour
fatalistic Old Testament religion and an ardent and consuming
patriotism. Combine all these qualities and all these impulses
in one individual, and you have the modern Boer – the most
formidable antagonist who ever crossed the path of Imperial
Britain.'

The battlefield where their paths crossed at Magersfontein
lay at the end of a dirt road below two low hills, on a plain
of ochre earth and thornbushes. It was here, on the night of
10 December 1899, that General Lord Methuen ordered 3,400
men of the Highland Brigade to launch a frontal attack on Boer
positions, which he assumed were on top of the hills. Nobody
had actually checked where the Boers were, so it came as a bit

of a shock when they popped out of trenches at dawn and began firing into the massed ranks of Scots, who had begun deploying from a dense column 40 yards across. Nor had anybody told the Highlanders about the barbed-wire entanglements. Those who tried to charge were cut down within a few steps, and the rest were pinned down and shot repeatedly during a day in which the temperature rose to 44 degrees in the shade. Later I came across an old cutting from the *Natal Witness* newspaper, which quoted a Boer volunteer telling a British officer: 'We admit that the British soldiers are the best in the world, and your regimental officers are the bravest, but we rely on your generals.'

The killing ground at Magersfontein was now strewn with memorials. There were at least nine of them, to Brits, Boers and Scandinavian volunteers who had fought with the Afrikaners. The most imposing was a Celtic cross more than 20 feet high, carved at the Aberdeen Granite Works in 1902 and paid for by public subscription after an appeal organised by the *Glasgow Herald*. Its inscription read: 'Scotland is poorer in men but richer in heroes.' It was a depressingly familiar refrain. I found a photograph of one of the heroes in a small museum nearby. Captain E.B.B. Towse of the Gordon Highlanders had been a handsome fellow with an impressive handlebar moustache, and he cut a dashing figure in full dress uniform. He was awarded the Victoria Cross after holding a position with twelve men against 150 Boers. The caption said: 'When called on to surrender, he opened fire and continued firing until severely wounded (both eyes shattered).'

I strolled around the hill to an observation point that had a relief map of the battle. After a century the positions of the Boer trenches were still faintly visible as scars in the earth among the encroaching thornbushes. In the distance a bush fire created an illusion of artillery. Looking across the huge open *veld*, it was easy to imagine rifle bolts being slid back, the terrible fusillade, the skirl of bagpipes, the cries of wounded men. Torn bodies

and bloody kilts. I had with me a copy of a poem written by
a soldier of the Black Watch who survived the carnage. One of
the verses read:

> All day long in the same position,
> Watching our own shells burst,
> Lying with dead men and wounded,
> Lips swollen blue-black with thirst.

For a while I was alone with my thoughts, then I was joined at
the observation post by two South African soldiers in uniform.
They were Afrikaners, but on learning I was Scots one of them
said to me in English: 'There's nowhere to hide down there. It's
all open ground. It wasn't a fight, it was a slaughter.' He then
spoke at length to his companion in Afrikaans, and the younger
man looked gravely at the trenches, and said: 'Bloody hell.'

Inevitably there were ghost stories. The curator was a grey-
haired lady who had lived in a cottage by the museum in the hills
for thirteen years. She had never seen anything strange, but others
had. Her sister had seen a lone bagpiper by the Celtic cross, and a
local soldier swore he had met a Highlander who had put his hand
to his head, complained of pain, then disappeared. The curator
said: 'My sister says they are not bad ghosts, but she couldn't
live here, it's too heavy.' Her maid came out and said yes, she
had seen foreign soldiers in skirts and Boers in big hats, and she
had heard horses' hooves drumming on the plain. 'I used to see
them often, but now they are quiet.'

A couple of years before, the ghost stories had attracted a
crowd from Kimberley on the anniversary of the battle. They
brought *braais* and crates of beer, and after dark they gathered
near the Scots Memorial with their cameras and videos. Then
two local soldiers crept up a *koppie* behind them, and on the
stroke of midnight started playing bagpipes. It was wonderful,

the curator said, there was total panic. Everybody ran for their cars and took off; you couldn't see them for dust.

There was a lot of dust on the way to Modderrivier. And ant hills. Tens of thousands of them, rising like monstrous boils from the dark red earth, a vast construction site of worker ants. I imagined crashing into one and being devoured in seconds. Modderrivier was a fly-blown truck stop and railway siding that was as appealing as its name, which meant muddy river. But it was lunchtime, I was hungry, and there was nowhere else. Round the back of the petrol station was a dilapidated tin-roofed building grandly called the Crown and Royal Hotel. It had another sign, above a doorway, that said: '*Blanke Kroeg* – European Bar'. (The Afrikaans is actually more direct, meaning 'white bar'.) I wondered whether it might be a joke, but evidently not. The *blanke kroeg* was empty and coloured patrons of the establishment were kept firmly in their place, which was a bare room next door. A big, craggy-faced old Afrikaner in shorts appeared and I asked for food. 'It's a bit late,' he said grumpily. It was twenty past one. So I left, possibly the only European to have been in the European Bar of the Crown and Royal for years, and went to the garage where a nice woman sold me a steak pie and a milk shake. Then I drove south to a Never-Never Land on the banks of the Orange River.

10

White tribe dreaming

The first time I came to Orania, the loudest sound was the banging of doors in the wind. The cluster of prefabricated bungalows by a minor road had been built as a camp for canal construction workers who had moved on, and it was virtually a ghost town. It was still quiet, but now people were living in the houses and not all of the gardens were choked by weeds. In the space of six years the vision of an Afrikaner *volkstaat* free of blacks, coloureds, Indians and English pinko-liberals had drawn 500 souls to this lonely settlement of barely a dozen streets on the edge of the Great Karoo desert. Led by a relative of Hendrik Verwoerd, the architect of apartheid, they had trekked here to make the wilderness bloom into a new Afrikaner Fatherland that would stretch from the Free State to the Atlantic. That was the theory, anyway.

In essence it was a fairly simple idea. Apartheid had not worked mainly because there were so many blacks, and admittedly people kept complaining about it, and the whole thing had become unwieldy. The obvious way to safeguard Afrikaner culture and values from the threats of black nationalism and communism was to create an autonomous mini-state as far away from the rest of the so-called Rainbow Nation as possible. Thus Verwoerd's son-in-law Carel Boshoff and his followers bought Orania lock, stock and water barrel as the nucleus of a white community they dreamed would eventually reach across the plains of the Northern Cape to the sea. They would boldly go where no white South African had gone before by dispensing with black and coloured servants and fending for themselves. While most of the country was moving in one direction, they turned around and headed defiantly in the other.

The town was still surrounded by a wire fence, a legacy of the days when it belonged to the Department of Water Affairs, and its new residents seemed unsure whether to welcome visitors. At the main entrance a sign said Welcome to Orania in Afrikaans and English, but another nearby said: 'Strictly Private'. By a lucky coincidence I arrived on the eve of the Day of the Vow, the most sacred day in the Afrikaner calendar, commemorating the rout of a Zulu army in 1838. The good news was that I would witness rituals at the heart of this misfit society; the bad news was that the only guest house in town was full. A roadside café had rooms and I was given one with a view of two petrol pumps manned by a lean, weather-beaten character in shorts, bush shirt and a battered old leather hat, who spent most of the time sitting on the *stoep* chatting with his cronies.

In the café a woman was giving me directions to a park where some sort of ceremony was going on, when I looked out the window and saw a black man getting out of a truck that drove off. He crossed the road, came into the café, and asked for something in Afrikaans. The woman spoke to him sharply and he turned away, hesitated, and left. The next customer was a white man in khaki with a pistol at his hip and a doberman in his *bakkie*. This time the woman smiled and served him. Evidently the town didn't welcome dark strangers.

To those of a lighter hue, Orania seemed a neat, friendly little place in which people greeted one another by name. It had a modern community hall, an open-air swimming pool,

tennis courts and inspirational signs with a cartoon bird saying
things in Afrikaans like 'I speak Afrikaans' and 'We work for
ourselves'. It was even quieter than usual because most of the
Oranians were down by the river, dedicating a new park to
Boshoff's wife Anna. When I arrived a small brass band was
playing 'Rock of Ages' as a prelude to speeches and the guest
of honour unveiling a plaque. Picnic tables had been laid out on
the grass, and students from the University of the Free State had
created a fountain and pond with rocks, ferns and plastic ducks.
There was even a motor launch called *Volkstaat* for excursions
on the river. Interestingly it had no neutral gear, and could move
only forwards or backwards. Its captain was a roofing contractor
from Pretoria who had been living in Orania for two years, and he
was happy to explain why he was there: 'Look, I'm not a racist,
that's for sure. I just don't want to live and work with blacks any
more.' He seemed to be quite clear on this.

Wilna, a retired computer training officer, was equally succinct: 'If you want to have a country of your own, your own
people must be in the majority.' Apparently it was a question of
numbers: there were coloureds and Bushmen living in the area,
but they were a small minority and didn't pose a problem; in the
same way, Orania was no threat to the government because it was
so small. There was also safety in numbers. Wilna was happy
giving pottery lessons, playing the recorder in a wind ensemble
and caring for an old woman in a community that didn't have a
police station because it didn't need one. A few loonies had turned
up in the early days, thinking they could stage mini-Nuremberg
rallies and shoot blacks on sight, but they had not stayed long.
Nor had the dreamers who could not face toiling for a meagre
living in a hard land. Those who remained were inspired by the
pioneering spirit of the *trekboers*, and on special occasions they
wore traditional short *dopper* frock-coats and lace *kappies*.

And already they had a museum, in one of the prefabricated

offices. Most of the exhibits were guns dating from the Anglo-Boer War, but one room had been made into a shrine to the Dutch-born icon of apartheid, Hendrik Frensch Verwoerd. A bad oil painting depicted him being acclaimed by a crowd, his pasty face creased in a smile and his right arm raised in what looked like a Nazi salute. Beside it, an election poster proclaimed him *Man van die Volk* (Man of the People). There were photographs of him looking proud, sincere, determined and porky, a larger than life wooden bust and bric-a-brac such as spectacles and a tennis racket. One item was given pride of place in a display case. It was the dark suit that Verwoerd was wearing in parliament in Cape Town at 2.14 p.m. on 6 September 1966, when he was attacked by Dimitri Tsafendas, the deranged son of a Greek immigrant and a Mozambican woman, and stabbed to death. Four red arrows, each bearing a number, indicated the position and sequence of the knife thrusts that killed the man that gave the world 'separate development'. The ragged holes in the suit had been roughly stitched.

The curator was a retired aircraft engineer from Transvaal, a white-haired man with watery eyes and an abiding bitterness towards the British. His opening line was: 'If the British hadn't been on our necks from day one, things would have been different today.' He shared the views of the river boat captain: he got on well enough with black people, but he didn't want to live among them and he found it incredible that a land built by whites had become Mandela's country. I found it equally surprising that Mandela had visited this fly-blown *volkstaat* a couple of years before, but there was his signature in the guest book beneath a diplomatic comment: 'We had an interesting visit to this museum which contains an important aspect of the country's history.'

At dinner in the guest house that night I was joined by a building contractor and his wife from Pretoria who had bought a plot in Orania. If things got any worse they would move, he said. 'Where we live everybody has their own prison, you lock yourself in at night.' There wasn't much work in Orania, but the soil was good and they could grow most of what they needed. 'For the whites the good times are gone,' he said. But they still had their moments. At the community hall later a group of children livened things up with a concert of country music on guitars, accordions and keyboards. Flanked by flags of the old Boer Republics, they played jaunty tunes with titles like 'Kliprivier Polka', and the audience loved it. They smiled, they clapped, they tapped their feet, and they cheered at the opening bars of old favourites. The mayor was there, stamping his feet and wearing a ceremonial claret neckerchief, boy scout style, with *Groot Trek 150, 1838–1988* written on the back.

Surveying this happy band of *voortrekkers*, it struck me it was fear that had brought them here: fear of losing their language and culture, fear of being overwhelmed by what they perceived as an alien race, fear of violence in a society of which they had lost control. Here on the banks of the Orange River the descendants of the 'bitter-enders' – the Boers who fought to the last against the Brits at the turn of the century – had drawn their wagons into a *laager*, the flags of the Transvaal and the Orange Free State were flying again, and dreams of freedom were being reborn. History was being repeated. Only this time the rest of the country had moved on, and it had no room for pioneers with guns and Bibles any more.

In the meantime they were putting their trust in God and building an airport. A model of development plans in the community centre had a little aeroplane on a gravel runway, beside a field of tomatoes and pecan nut trees. I was inspecting it next day, during a break in the Day of the Vow ceremonies, when the mayor gave me an update on progress. They were reclaiming arable land from the desert with piped water from the river, developing intensive farming techniques and planning a herd of a thousand dairy cows.

'I feel that our countrymen, although they laughed at us in the beginning, are slowly coming to realise there may be something in this concept,' he said. 'In the outside world they call us racists, and some call me fascist, but all we want is the freedom to live according to our own culture. We don't wish to deprive black people of the same rights.' So the ethos of Orania was live and let live – let us live here and let all other races live somewhere else. The mayor admitted there were problems. There was an extreme faction that wanted Orania to be a white enclave totally isolated from the rest of the country, which he thought was impractical. So I asked about non-whites currently living in the prospective *volkstaat*, and he said it was hoped they would move of their own free will. He said: 'Our vision changes from day to day, depending on what happens outside.' It seemed to me their vision changed every five minutes, depending on whom you spoke to.

The highlight of the Day of the Vow was a dramatic stage presentation by three women and a man of the history of the Afrikaner nation in three acts. The basic plot was how they had lost their freedom, won it back and were now in deep trouble again. The tone was gloomy, and there seemed to be a lot of wailing and gnashing of teeth. The star was a big blonde woman in a floral dress, whose voice quivered and bosoms heaved with indignation as she recounted injustices heaped upon her *volk*. There were repeated cries of *vaderland*, to the satisfaction of two boys sitting beside me in khaki uniforms. They had neat blond hair and blue eyes and earnest expressions, and looked as if they were ready to invade Poland. A youth leader sitting behind me leaned over to explain the action on stage: 'They are saying that people are not defeated if they lose their land, they are defeated only when they lose their will for freedom.' Flashback: Nuremberg, 1938.

Having rescued his people from the perils of black majority rule, Carel Boshoff had mellowed over the years into an avuncular figure with white hair and a neatly trimmed beard, and he had refined his views on race relations. After the performance, he explained that apartheid had been misconceived: 'We had become strangers in our land and it was our own fault. We tried to occupy too much. We integrated the whole black population in a minority-ruled country and that couldn't be done.' Now the idea was for Afrikaners to determine their own future without imposing themselves on anyone else: 'We don't wish to perpetuate apartheid, it's unthinkable. But South Africa is like a big river that will flow over us if we try to stop it. We have to accept that, and get out of it.'

So they had formed a little white stream that was meandering along the edge of the wilderness, in the hope that the rest of the world would leave it in peace. And by and large it had, apart from the time President Mandela came to visit. The reason he had come was to pay a courtesy call on Betsie Verwoerd, the widow of Hendrik, who was still alive and amazingly well in her late nineties. Wilna the potter, who looked after her, arranged an audience for me. The erstwhile First Lady of apartheid lived in a bungalow that was a time capsule of memories filled with dark, heavy furniture and dominated by a portrait of her husband sitting on a farmyard wall. Just a simple country lad at heart, obviously. Betsie came into the drawing room shrunken and stooped with age, but walking steadily with the aid of a cane and as bright as a button. She was wearing a smart floral dress, her grey hair was tied neatly in a bun, and her eyes were clear. Speaking in fluent English, she said she had been in an old folks' home in Pretoria when Carel had told her of his plans for Orania and she had insisted on coming. 'They said the weather was too harsh, so hot in the day and cold at night, but I grew up in the Karoo. I know what the climate is like here. I knew I was coming to the end of my time, and I wanted to be here.'

I asked about Mandela's visit. 'It was really quite pleasant. He is a gentleman. Some of my people thought it was wrong for him to come, but we just took each other as we were.' Better late than never, I supposed. Wilna said they had planned to have tea in the house, but they had to meet in the community hall because there were so many officials with Mandela and they were afraid the journalists would trample the roses. When I asked what she thought of the 'new' South Africa, Wilna interjected that Mrs Verwoerd did not take an interest in politics any more. Betsie had a gold lapel badge bearing Hendrik's image pinned to her dress like a Mao Tse-Tung badge, and I felt I ought to press her on what she thought now about her husband's big idea. But what the heck, she was nearly a hundred years old and it was a long time ago. Outside in the garden, Wilna explained that Verwoerd had been misunderstood by history. Apartheid had become a dirty word, but really all he had wanted was to give each race a bit of South Africa to live in as they wished. That was his grand vision, she said.

In the guest house I sat at dinner with two thin-faced men with goatee beards who had invested in Orania. They were intrigued by political devolution in Scotland, drawing parallels with Afrikaner aspirations, and they were surprised by my lack of enthusiasm for it. My opinion that another bunch of bickering politicians in Edinburgh would not materially improve the lot of their constituents disappointed them. Searching for another model, they said the Palestinian homeland was the kind of thing they were aiming for. The landlord, a young man from Natal, added a historical perspective. 'The English,' he said with feeling, 'we still have an account to settle with them.' When I pointed out that most of the casualties at Magersfontein had been men of Highland regiments, he said: 'Ach, shame man, we had to kill so many Scottish.' That night a bush fire glowed on a distant hill beneath a full moon, and it looked like a volcano. Next day the town was seared by a hot, dry wind blowing clouds of dust.

Before leaving this white tribe dreaming in the desert, I went
for a jog on dirt roads around the town in the cool of the evening.
As I was returning I saw a statue on a hill that I hadn't noticed
before, and trotted up a path to find the *Man van die Volk*.
This time Verwoerd was a bronze pygmy, barely three feet tall,
standing on a marble plinth. His profile was etched against a
dazzling sunset of gold and violet, his eyes scanning the plains
where his followers envisioned a Boer homeland. As I looked at
the statue it seemed to move. I thought at first it was a trick of
the light, then I touched it and realised it was trembling in the
wind. It had come loose at the base, and a strong gust would
probably have sent it tumbling down the hill. It was almost 500
miles from the embryo republic of Orania to the Northern Cape
coast, so its burghers had a long way to go to create a white
corridor to the sea. Most of their own people thought they were
loopy, and so far the government had ignored them as a bunch
of harmless eccentrics. Personally I tend to take people as I find
them, and without exception the Oranians were courteous. But
then I was the right colour.

Crossing the Orange River again, I left the lunar terrain of the
Northern Cape and returned to earth on the *platteland* of the
Free State. The barren plains gave way to cultivated fields in
a panorama of blue, gold and red – blue of a huge sky, gold
of cornfields and red of newly ploughed earth. It was flat and
empty, apart from files of electricity pylons marching across the
veld to nowhere, like an army of giants with outstretched arms
carrying the power cables. I thought of a headline: Giant Aliens
Invade Earth But Get Lost in Free State.

Then I spotted a weird character on the road ahead. It was
black and white and walking on two long, thin legs in a stiff,
precise manner like an arthritic waiter in a Parisian café. On
closer inspection it seemed to be a cross between a stork and an

eagle, with the spindly legs of the first and the raptor's profile of the other. As I approached it spread huge silver and black wings and glided over a fence into a field where it walked about as before. Apparently it was too hot to fly. I learned later this mixed-up creature was called a secretary bird, and the guide book I consulted admitted its features were confusing. One of the rewards of travelling off the beaten track is meeting other denizens of the planet. Thus on country roads in the Free State I encountered troops of monkeys, eagles perched proudly on telegraph poles, a tortoise crossing the road agonizingly slowly (I stopped and lifted it to the other side), and troops of furry animals like stoats that stood on their hind legs and gazed at me with interest as I passed by. Yet the most extraordinary sight was man-made: a range of wrinkled hills around the old diamond mining town of Jagersfontein that glowed a luminescent lime green. It looked like something nasty that had landed from space, and was lurking around till nightfall to creep into the town. This was stuff the mining companies had kindly left to beautify the landscape after they had removed all the diamonds.

About fifty miles from Bloemfontein I stopped at a place called Petrusburg, drawn by a road sign promising refreshments. In a café beside a petrol station I asked a woman if I could have coffee. 'Nie,' she said. How about tea? 'Nie.' Was there anywhere in town I could get a cup of tea or coffee? 'Nie.' She was beginning to sound like a donkey so I drove away, past the sign that said Welcome to Petrusburg.

One of the reasons I went to Bloemfontein, the most centrally located city in South Africa, was because it was the birthplace of the magician who conjured a heroic hobbit called Frodo Baggins and sent him on an epic crusade against evil in the Land of Mordor. John Ronald Reuel Tolkien was born on 3 January 1892 above a bank where his father, who came from Birmingham, was the manager. Three years later his mother took him and his younger brother to England for a holiday, during which his father died of rheumatic fever. J.R.R. never returned to South Africa, although it has been suggested his memory of it as 'hot, dry and barren' influenced the landscapes of Mordor. His fantasy world of Hobbiton in the Shire was preserved in a guest house in a leafy district of Bloemfontein. Created by a Tolkien admirer, it was a high kitsch warren of antique furniture, patchwork quilts, old rugs and low ceilings. I was allocated Frodo's Room, which had 'Keeper of the Ring' in counterpoint by the door, an Edwardian closet bath and a teddy bear with a red ribbon around its neck on the bed. Old-fashioned windows overlooked a hobbit-sized garden where a pepper tree rustled in the wind. I would not have been surprised if Gandalf had materialised in the loo.

Tolkien's birthplace was a disappointment. The bank had been demolished after a flood in the 1920s and replaced by a furniture store in the dreary concrete box style. A brass plaque commemorating the author had been fixed to a street pillar, but somebody had stolen it. I wondered whether any of the store's customers knew about Tolkien, but I doubted it. When I returned to the guest house, I found the teddy tucked up in bed, and beside it a Book of Psalms lying open with a tartan ribbon beneath the verse beginning: 'I to the hills will lift mine eyes . . .' I was suffocating in schmaltz, and the next day I went to stay with friends who had never heard of hobbits.

Another writer who visited Bloemfontein in the 1870s found a haven of tranquillity: 'The town is so quiet and seems to be so happy and contented, removed so far away from strife and want and disorder, that the beholder . . . is tempted to think that the peace of such an abode is better than the excitement of Paris, London or New York.' Anthony Trollope's vision of a serene backwater evaporated on 13 March 1900 when Field-Marshal Lord Roberts of Kandahar led the British army into the Boer republican city to claim it on behalf of Queen and country. Six months later its citizens were introduced to a new British invention, called concentration camps.

At first they were not so bad. They began as 'refugee camps' for families of Boers who had surrendered voluntarily. Then British troops began burning farms in reprisal attacks and to deprive Boer commandos of support, and the homeless women and children were concentrated at points close to railway lines and water sources. Hence the name. The British army was hopelessly unprepared to deal with so many refugees and soon they began to die of pneumonia, measles, and dysentry – not in their tens or hundreds, but in their tens of thousands. By the end of the war two years later, more than 26,000 Afrikaner women and children had died in the camps. I mention this because Bloemfontein is where a remarkable monument was erected to them in 1913.

The National Women's War Memorial is an obelisk over a hundred feet high surrounded by a circular 'whispering wall' designed to convey around its circumference any sound made near it on the inside. A paved path leading to it is lined with twenty small marble tablets, each bearing the name of a concentration camp and its death toll: Balmoral 427, Belfast 247, Bloemfontein 1,695, and so on, until Winburg 487. By far the greatest number of victims were children. When I walked along this avenue of sorrow and recrimination I felt angry and ashamed. In an adjacent museum I saw a photograph of a victim of the Bloemfontein camp named Lizzie van Zyl. She was eight years old and looked vaguely familiar. I stared at her for a while before remembering where I had seen the skeletal limbs and death-head look before. It was in photographs of Auschwitz. The British in South Africa were guilty of incompetence on a monumental scale, rather than a deliberate policy of extermination, but the effect had been much the same.

I went to the site of the Bloemfontein camp on the outskirts of town. There was nothing to indicate where it had been, and I had to ask directions before I found a field of coarse grass by a main road. A dirt track led to a copse of trees, where there was a well, a flagpole and a sculpture of a woman and two children walking up a slope on a trail of crosses. The death toll here was 459 women and 1,236 children. I wandered around the field where the rows of tents had stood, but it was a forlorn and empty place that had forgotten the horrors of a century before. Britain's scorched-earth policy also left thousands of black tenant farmers and labourers destitute. They and their families were herded into separate camps, principally to provide a labour force for the British army. The known death toll in these camps was 14,000, more than 11,000 of them children, but nobody kept a complete tally and no memorials were erected to them.

The next day friends took me to the front line of another conflict. It was an old farmhouse with book-lined studies and antique furniture, and climbing roses around the windows, and a well-armed defence force ready to respond to calls for help with guns blazing. The militia had been formed by farmers in response to attacks on isolated farmhouses by lunatics apparently intent on killing as much as stealing. Every morning and evening a roll-call of two dozen farms in the network was made by short-wave radio and at night patrols inspected all of them. In the event of an incident a 'reaction force' would be on the scene in minutes. I learned this from a farmer who had been a judge in the highest court in the land, and evidently had no problem with taking the law into his own hands. The police did not have the manpower to protect farmers, so they were doing it themselves and the police were glad of it, he said. They hadn't caught anyone yet, but word of their activities was getting round and the farms were safer.

That day it was hot: 40 degrees Celsius (104 degrees Fahrenheit) in the shade to be precise, according to a newspaper that said it was the hottest day since records began. 'West wind,' a man told me, 'straight from hell.' Actually it came from the Namib desert, which was much the same thing. It was time to head for the hills and green pastures of the eastern Free State, and meet the peaceful Warriors of the Rainbow.

11

The most important thing is to reach out

After weeks of plains and prairies, it was a relief to find a road winding into hills dotted with woodland and meadows. Of a sudden the air was cooler and the grass was greener, and there were streams and orchards. When I stopped by a farm track to stretch my legs, I was surrounded by butterflies and wild flowers and birdsong. Cresting a rise, I beheld to the east the awesome ramparts and pinnacles of the mountain kingdom of Lesotho tumbling along the horizon like a monstrous tidal wave. I was heading for Rustler's Valley, a remote canyon in the foothills of the Maluti Mountains that used to be a good place for hiding stolen cattle and was now a good place for getting spaced out on nature and drugs and weird music. The dirt road to this alternative Elysium ran past fields filled with bales of honey-coloured wheat and cattle that were fat and sleek, in a land dozing contentedly in the afternoon sunshine.

The first indication that Rustler's Valley was at the other end of the social and political spectrum from Orania was a camp of white tepees on a hillside. The tribe inhabiting them was a motley band of ageing hippies, disillusioned yuppies and easy riders in search of eternal verities and good dope. I was allocated a room for the night in a stone and thatch cottage which was more conventional, apart from mysterious symbols by the door and a larger than life head of an American Indian chief painted on the bedroom wall. In the bar and buffet restaurant the ambience was hippier than thou, with beads, dreadlocks, and strange pendants on bare chests competing for attention. The music blaring from speakers sounded like a dinosaur dying of a hernia. On the wall was a notice for a 'Sweat Lodge' to celebrate the winter solstice, which explained this was a purification ceremony and no alcohol or drugs should be taken beforehand. Beside it somebody had painted a maxim attributed to Einstein: 'The most beautiful and profound emotion we can experience is the sensation of the mystical.' In my room an information leaflet helpfully outlined the genesis of 'neopagan eco-warriors'. It seemed there was an American Indian prophecy about a tribe called the Warriors of the Rainbow, who would be born at a time of widespread environmental destruction to save Mother Earth. Meantime Rustler's Valley was laying the groundwork for them. Sort of holding the fort till the cavalry arrived, I supposed.

The chief of the valley was a middle-aged Afrikaner with a crinkly face and a ponytail streaked with grey called Frik. 'We don't see ourselves as warriors, just as people aware of our responsibilities to the environment,' he explained to the sound of dying dinosaurs. After years of travelling he had settled in the valley and bought a half-share in a farm. Unhappily this coincided with the beginning of a drought that lasted for eight years. With nothing much to do he missed having a social life, so he created one by inviting up to 5,000 people at a time for open-air raves. He said the idea was to create a model, through music, dance, and gardening, to teach environmental awareness. And also to have a good time, of course. On the drugs thing, Frik said: 'We are totally against drug abuse. The only way to deal with drugs is to use them sensibly.' In the beginning his eco-tribe was hassled by security police and narcotics squads, but eventually they gave up. 'We don't produce or sell drugs here, in fact we advise moderate consumption.' In a commendable pursuit of knowledge, he had invited an expert from Brazil to give lectures on the origin and use of *ayhuasca*, a shamanic substance of the Amazonian rainforest. It was a mixture of eight plants, and it had healing properties. But was it hallucinogenic? 'Well, yes, of course.'

At least the horses were real. They were tethered at the entrance to the camp, and next morning I went for a ride with a band of apprentice Rainbow Warriors. It was a glorious day and the horses were frisky, apparently enjoying the trail through tall grasses and beneath soaring bluffs as much as we were. At one point I lingered behind the others, and struck off alone into a canyon. A herd of buck looked up as I approached, but scenting only the horse they continued grazing and we passed within a few feet of them. On the way out we disturbed an eagle. I heard it first, a beating and rushing of wings, then it burst from a copse of trees, circled once, and soared up and away to the crags. It was a wondrous sight that left drug-induced fantasies for dead.

There was no room at the eco-tribe inn that night because of a two-day open-air concert/rave/happening, so I moved down the valley to stay with a farmer who had a string of polo ponies. It had been a popular sport in the days of British colonial administrators and soldiers, but there were hardly any teams left. 'Playing polo costs money and the farmers round here don't have that much to spare any more,' he said. Working the land was hard because of frequent droughts and frosts, and many families had given up and moved on. In my bathroom there was a sad oil painting of a scene from English urban life, an unkempt little garden crowded in by red brick houses. I was pondering it, being drawn into the world it portrayed, when there was a clatter of hooves and I turned to see a herd of thoroughbred ponies cantering up a dirt track towards a highland meadow, their manes and tails flying in the dust. Maybe the owner, who was of English stock, kept the painting to remind him that no matter how tough farming was in the eastern Free State he was better off beneath its big skies.

Back at the Rainbow Ranch, the eco-warriors were limbering up for their marathon rave being staged by electronic whizz-kids who called themselves Return to the Source and Flying Rhino. One of them had explained to me earlier that they played 'trance music', aimed at inducing a state of heightened awareness. What they produced was a moronic cacophony that induced a headache. They also projected computer-generated patterns on to a big screen, which became tedious after a couple of minutes. My problem of course was that I was not on drugs, unlike most everybody else who seemed to be wandering about with daggas drawn, so to speak. This did not encourage interesting or even barely intelligible conversation, but what the heck – they might have achieved nirvana and they weren't harming anybody but themselves.

At least I could appreciate the beauty of the night. A full moon had risen above a sharp outline of black mountains, washing the valley with silvery light. A group of Africans had gathered around a wood fire in a stone circle, forming a timeless image as they stared at the flames. Nocturnal raptors were active, and their dark shapes fluttered beyond the light of the fire. The Rainbow Warriors appeared oblivious to all of this, having gone to metaphysical happy hunting grounds. Strobe lighting had created a fluorescent effect, and in a corner I noticed a man with glowing red, green and yellow symbols on his face carefully painting the face of a girl in a similar manner. This seemed to be a meaningful experience for both parties. A couple of hours of the head-banging music was all I could stand, and it was a relief to head back down the valley and fall asleep to the sound of wind in the trees. Next morning I left the space cadets playing at being Red Indians, and went to a land of real tribes that rejoiced in the name of QwaQwa.

*   *   *

I was uneasy. I had been in similar situations in other parts of the world, but this was South Africa and much had changed since I was here last. Be careful, friends had told me. When you're in unfamiliar territory keep your wits about you, they said. So here I was in territory about as unfamiliar as it could get, I was travelling alone, and as far as I could tell I was the only white person in a black town with an unpronounceable name that nobody had heard of. It was called Phuthaditjhaba. There was no obvious cause for concern, but I felt on edge.

The restaurant had few customers, and none of them paid me any heed as I sat reading a book at a corner table. Then a big man rose from a group at another table and walked towards me. He paused, towering over me, and said: 'Excuse me, they say you are a writer.'

'Yes.'

'I like to read good books. I was reading one last night by George Orwell, called *Animal Farm*. It reminded me of the recent ANC conference at Mafikeng.'

'Sit down,' I said.

Fusi Mokubung was a genial giant of a man with a youthful face who looked like an overgrown schoolboy. In fact he was a local government officer who owned an office supplies business and had a keen grasp of Orwell's vision of totalitarianism. He asked about my travels, and if I had drawn any conclusions. I said that superficially little seemed to have changed, with various races living apart and remaining largely ignorant of each other's cultures. 'Yes, that would be a good title for your book,' Fusi said. 'South Africans that have never met.' I ordered a couple of beers, and began to relax and enjoy QwaQwa.

It was an improbable name for one of the absurdities of apartheid, a black tribal homeland called 'whiter than white'. The term was said to have been bestowed by Bushmen on a flat-topped mountain that dominated the capital, probably because of its snow cover in winter. And if it was good enough for a hill, the apartheidniks reasoned it was good enough for an obscure fragment of their bantustan jigsaw. I found it at the end of a highway sweeping down a hillside to a sprawling patchwork of shacks and matchbox houses, with a scattering of bungalows and offices bequeathed by the defunct homeland administration. The first thing I saw when I stopped at a crossroads was a man getting out of a car, walking to another car, pulling out the driver, and beating the daylights out of him. For good measure he had a go at a passenger who unwisely intervened. *Be careful*, my friends had said. I took off before the lights changed.

The glitziest building on the main street of Phuthaditjhaba was the QwaQwa Funeral Parlour, a brash glass-fronted structure adorned with red and blue arches. A few doors along, Thando Funeral Services was committed to 'dignified and affordable services' that included tents, toilets, and flowers. The burial business was clearly booming, along with taxi services that filled the streets with dilapidated minibuses that made up their own highway code as they went along. Taxi driving and undertaking must be among the most lucrative employments in black communities, one providing a steady stream of customers for the other.

I checked into the QwaQwa Hotel, a drab concrete adjunct to a shopping precinct, and found a guide in Simphiwe Mhlati, a cool dude in a gaudy shirt, shades and dreadlocks who worked at a cultural village out of town. He was packing his bags for a trip to Belgium on a cultural exchange visit, but he happily took time to show me around. 'Economically, we were better off under apartheid,' he said. We were standing in a dusty road of little brick houses, attracting shy smiles from barefoot ragamuffins playing with tin cans and punctured footballs. 'When tax incentives to exploit cheap labour went, so did most of the companies. And when the government services moved away, our economy collapsed. We still have good schools so we have a high literacy rate, but there are hardly any jobs. It's a bit of a mess.' It was a familiar problem in the erstwhile 'self-governing' homelands. When the system was abolished, state-subsidised industries on their borders packed up, and then the administrators moved out and there was no manufacturing and no money any more. In the case of QwaQwa, a population of around 300,000 *Sotho ba Borwa* (southern Sotho) people had swelled to 1.5 million with the return of contract workers laid off elsewhere in the country. Across the road was a bar called If Tomorrow Comes, which said a lot about the general outlook.

We walked over to three old women sitting outside a house of plywood and corrugated zinc, and one of them immediately stood to offer me her seat, which was an inverted paint tin. They were a lively, friendly bunch and we were received with interest. Mandela was a good man and he was doing his best, they said, but it seemed he hadn't got around to them yet. One day things would get better. In the meantime, would I like tea or home-made beer? I wondered again about the fatalism of Africans, and the absence of rancour after a generation of apartheid. Simphiwe said: 'South Sotho are warm, receptive people. It's a God-given thing. When I go into a white nightclub, I can sense tension. When you come into our restaurants and clubs you are welcomed. When we talk about nation-building, we mean what we say.'

Our conference assembly on paint tins was growing, and one of the new arrivals invited us into the house next door. His name was Petrus and he scratched a living as a handyman. His wife and three children lived with relatives and he stayed with friends because they couldn't afford a home of their own. This house belonged to his mother, an old woman wearing a red knitted hat who smiled as we entered. It was a one-room shack with a single bed, a few sticks of furniture and a gaudy portrait of Jesus on the cross; tiny, but neat and spotlessly clean. The woman was dusting a big old kitchen cabinet of enamel and chrome, and she continued polishing it all the time we were there. 'We like the new South Africa but there is no improvement,' Petrus said. 'It is the same as the old order, there is no progress for us.' Dealing with officials was a nightmare. He and his mother had been told to go to a local office and wait for new birth certificates, and so far they had gone every day for five days and they were still waiting. 'If there is no white person controlling the department there is always problems,' he said. I looked questioningly at Simphiwe. 'It's part of our culture. We have to be directed. It's a very silly thing.' As we left, he added: 'We don't build a castle in one day.'

The shebeen across the road had been built in bits and pieces over several generations by the look of it. In the old days it had been an illicit drinking den that required only four walls, preferably a roof, and a plentiful supply of beer. Now it was legal it had gone upmarket, complete with red velvet sofas with broken springs, unsteady metal tables and chipped plastic chairs. When we went in there were only a couple of customers who looked as wrecked as the furniture. African jazz was blaring from loudspeakers, and we stood by a metal cage that passed for a bar and Simphiwe talked politics. 'In 1994 we didn't vote for policies, or even a vision. We voted for a man. There is a lot of frustration now. I think in the next elections we will be looking at policies. If somebody gives us a good promise, we will go for it.'

I drove alone to the top of a hill where a modern glass and concrete building once housed the Mickey Mouse 'parliament' of QwaQwa. The offices had been taken over by the local education department and judiciary, but it was a Saturday and there was nobody around apart from a security guard and a bunch of kids kicking a ball around one of the world's great playing fields. It was a patch of grass high in the sky, with panoramic views of the miniature Table Mountain above the town and a sea of low hills and grasslands sweeping towards the mountains of Lesotho. It was an irresistible field of dreams and I duly trotted onto it and became Roy of the Rovers, dazzling my diminutive team mates with a spectacular goal.

It was after dinner that night that I met Fusi, the admirer of Orwell. Having observed the installation of democracy in his country, he had concluded that people on both sides of the ethnic divide had to change attitudes. 'There is a need for all of us who have benefited from the new dispensation to roll up our sleeves. Nobody wants to work on the farms any more, they all want big offices in Johannesburg. And on the other side of the bridge there are a lot of people who are complaining. The most important thing in South Africa is to reach out.' After we had set the world to rights with the help of Orwell and a few more beers, I began to feel at home in QwaQwa. I no longer felt uneasy, and the racism I had encountered, with its prejudices and fears, seemed senseless. For a while I forgot about the killer-muggers and rapists wrecking things for everybody, whom friends confidently expected to blow my brains out in places such as this. It was another eventful day on the Rainbow Roller-Coaster.

Next morning I was almost thrown off it. Cruising a quiet highway to the Basotho cultural village in the hills, I was surrounded by a cavalcade of drivers who appeared to be insane. They formed a motorised samba, careering over the road in a blur of balloons and streamers, oblivious to the possibility of being horrifically crunched at the next blind summit or corner. It remains a mystery to me how they left the highway alive. But they did, in a cheerful swarm of red dresses and green suits that formed a double file behind a brass band and went rocking and rolling up the hill to the cultural village. It was a wedding party, coming from dingy little brick and tin houses to have their photographs taken outside brightly painted clay homes of their nineteenth-century ancestors that were much more practical and attractive. It was here that I saw whites for the first time for a couple of days, and they came as a shock. They were ordinary, nice tourists festooned with cameras and sun hats, but somehow they seemed strange and I felt uncomfortable at being associated with them. The sentiment was unfair to the tourists, and probably precious of me, but it said much about the community that had accepted me and made me feel welcome. The cultural village was an interesting display of Sotho life through the centuries, but it bore no relation to the modern realities of Phuthaditjhaba. I felt like saying to the tourists: take a step further, go to town and meet people, and watch the barriers coming down. Like Fusi said, the most important thing was to reach out.

Then I drove north, reaching out with a sinking heart to the menacing sprawl of Johannesburg. The conurbation it lay in had been renamed Gauteng, which was Sotho for 'place of gold'. Somebody had worked out it was also an anagram of 'get a gun'.

12

Don't get out the car.
Unless it's burning.

It could have been anyone, but it was an Australian stonemason and prospector called George Harrison who found it. He was building a house extension for a widow on a Transvaal farm when he saw traces of shiny stuff he correctly identified as gold. George appears not to have been a man of great vision, because a few months later he sold his claim for ten pounds. This is all he walked away with in exchange for discovering the richest goldfield on the planet.

This was in 1886. In came the ox-wagons, up went the tents, and within three years the new municipality of Johannesburg was the biggest town in southern Africa. It was a rowdy, rootin'-tootin' boom town in which men were men and women were cheap. By the turn of the century it had ninety-seven brothels employing more than 1,000 prostitutes, which was one prostitute for every fifty white inhabitants. When a journalist from Harrison's old country turned up in 1910, he wrote: 'Ancient Nineveh and Babylon have been revived. Johannesburg is their twentieth-century prototype. It is a city of unbridled squander and unfathomable squalor.'

Not much has changed. The only reason anyone chooses to live in Johannesburg is to make money. That is the sole *raison d'être* of this ugly, violent city squatting among mine dumps on a featureless plateau more than 5,000 feet above sea-level. It is devoted lock, stock and gun-barrel to the single-minded pursuit of the rand; you either make it, or take it. Over the years it has made a lot of people rich, and attracted many more who have remained poor, thus precipitating an unofficial redistribution of wealth by violent men. The result is that Johannesburg is in a permanent state of siege. Much of its population lives in mini-fortresses guarded by high walls and razor wire, slavering dogs, electronic alarm systems and the hired guns of 'instant armed response' security companies. When they leave these compounds they drive with their doors locked, keeping a wary eye out for car hijackers, to offices and shopping malls guarded by other security companies. At night, they go to restaurants and clubs that provide enough firepower to protect them and their vehicles. This is what they call 'jolling', or having a jolly time in Joburg. To amuse themselves, they tell each other horror stories. No dinner party is complete without anecdotes about people being shot/robbed/raped/blown to bits. My favourite was a non-violent tale about a couple whose car was stolen. Next day it was returned with a written apology on the windscreen for having 'borrowed' the vehicle in an emergency, along with two cinema tickets. When the couple returned from the movies, they found their home ransacked. Some people reckoned this was an urban myth; if it had happened in Joburg, the thieves would have come back for the car and raped the maid.

When I lived here as a journalist, I acquired by chance a security device that came with floppy ears, a quizzical grin and a ferocious growl. This stray mutt bounded up to me one day when I was jogging in a local park, playfully knocked me off my feet and followed me home. He quickly established his territory in the way that dogs do, and thereafter protected my hearth and home with commendable vigour. For a medium-sized mongrel of amiable disposition, Flophead I, Laird of Dumbreck (Floppy to his chums) was a fearsome sight when he reared on his hind legs and bayed like a wolf at any stranger with the temerity to approach my house. In this he was not alone. When we jogged through residential suburbs at night, our passage provoked a mad cacophony of barking and growling and howling and slavering, and sounds of chains and leashes being strained to their utmost. It was like a scene from *Night of the Werewolves*. Transvaal by day, Transylvania by night. I recall a sign outside a house that depicted a ferocious dog with blood dripping from its fangs. It said: 'Trespassers will be eaten.'

I called a friend in Joburg as I drove north from QwaQwa.

'How are things?' I asked.

'Worse,' he said.

According to the Ministry of Safety and Security, a splendid example of Orwellian irony if ever there was one, this was not strictly true. Serious crime was falling, and it had the figures to prove it. In the year in which I toured the country, a mere 18,000 people were murdered. There were also 36,400 rapes and 170,000 domestic burglaries. This worked out at one murder, two rapes, and ten housebreakings every half hour, Sundays and public holidays included. And these were only the ones the police knew about. A significant proportion of this mayhem, by general agreement, was taking place in and around the city I was heading for.

Approaching the profile of grey concrete towers etched on the highveld skyline, I felt my spirits dropping as I passed through a wasteland of mines and factories, then monotonous suburbs of red brick bungalows, on to a freeway that skirted the city centre and dropped me in the northern suburbs where the well-off white folks lived. On a whim I went to have a look at the tree-lined street where Floppy and I were wont to stroll of a balmy evening. It looked as if it had been requisitioned by paratroops. I found my old house with difficulty, because the gate that once opened on to a pretty garden path lined with flowers had been bricked into a 10-foot wall topped with razor wire. Another innovation was *sentry boxes* at each end of the street, with hard-looking men in uniform watching me as I drove past. It would be only a matter of time before they started laying mines, I thought glumly. In the meantime a buzzing, sparky sound alerted me to another new feature, electrified fencing, and I wondered why nobody had thought of it before.

When you live in Johannesburg you gradually become accustomed to the paraphernalia of urban survival, and security precautions become an instinctive part of daily routine. Even after a long absence, you soon get the hang of it again. By the time I returned to my friend's house at the end of my first day back I was pretty relaxed, an old hand on familiar territory. As I entered the driveway, I pressed a gizmo in the car to open the electronic gate and nothing happened. I tried again, and it still didn't budge. Then I noticed the gate was slightly open, which in Joburg conjures up the words 'suspicious' and 'danger'. My engine was still running, so I backed off and looked around. It was dark, and rain was drizzling across dim street lamps. It was the classic scenario for an ambush, the kind you hear about at every dinner table where the good guy ends up with a hole in his head. I was not a happy traveller, but there was nothing else for it, so I got out of the car and walked warily to the gate. When I pushed, it slid open easily. The motor that operated the gate was gone, apart from four discarded bolts and two neatly snipped wires. My friend said later it would be worth a lot of money to its new owner. I assumed the gate had been too heavy to take away.

Car hijacking was the big new entrepreneurial activity in Get-a-Gun-Gauteng. Because of electronic alarms and disabling systems, car thieves were targeting vehicles when their owners were in them. The idea was to pounce when a likely victim was stopped at a red light or waiting for a home security gate to open. They then took the car, any valuables *in situ*, and if the owner was a woman they might also take her. I asked a taxi driver for his advice on what to do in such a situation. 'Smile and give them the car,' he said. 'You only got one life.' Happily, an impressive deterrent to hijacking had just been invented by a man called Fourie. It was a flame-thrower. I kid you not, it was a device activated by the driver with a push of a concealed button that emitted balls of flame from both sides of the vehicle. The gas-fired contraption had been approved by the South African Bureau of Standards, and it was legal providing it was used in self-defence. An attorney was quoted in a newspaper as saying it should make no difference if an attacker was shot or burned. Mr Fourie called his invention the Blaster, and it was proving so popular he was adapting it for use in shops and homes. The newspaper report on the invention featured photographs of it roasting a dummy villain, above the caption: 'Flambéed hijacker, anyone?'

Being Blasterless, I felt vulnerable when I disregarded warnings in my guide book to avoid downtown Joburg at all costs and went to see a chum about fixing my laptop computer, which seemed to be having panic attacks. The concrete box district came as a shock. It used to be a lively, unlovely dynamo of a place swirling with multi-racial crowds of office workers and shop assistants and even tourists. Now it looked rough and dangerous. Most of the offices were abandoned or half empty, the smart stores and hotels had closed and all that remained were seedy shops that looked as run-down as their customers. The reason was simple – the white business community had fled *en masse* to the northern suburbs, and itinerant street traders and shady characters had moved in. The result was a city in its death throes, a bad dream on the verge of becoming a nightmare. I took a wrong turn and lost my way, and stopped to ask for directions. An old black man approached the car and asked if he could help. He showed me the way, and said: 'Close your windows and lock your doors, *baas*, and go now. Go quickly.'

The area around the Market Theatre where my pal Steve the computer wizard worked had always been seedy in an interesting kind of a way, but now it was just forlorn. A popular pub and restaurant opposite the theatre had changed hands and lost most of its customers. Guards and car park attendants provided a measure of security in the immediate vicinity, but a couple of blocks away lay the spooky streets of an abandoned commercial district. When Steve began wrestling with the innards of my laptop I mentioned that I was going for a stroll to the Carlton Tower, one of the tallest buildings in the city, to have a look at the view from the top. 'Drive, don't walk,' he said. Then he brought out a book I had written and asked me to sign it. 'Just in case you don't get back,' he said. He had a weird sense of humour. I think.

In the five years I lived in Johannesburg, I had never been in the Carlton Tower. It's always the same. I lived in Paris for longer and only went up the Eiffel Tower once when my parents came to visit. I was always doing more important stuff, like going for walks in the country or playing football, so this was an interesting new experience. On the ground floor I paid for a ticket to ride an express lift to a viewing platform on the fiftieth floor, called the Top of Africa. A sign by the lift said: 'Africans do it 50 floors up.' What they do is gaze at a panorama of urban disaster. To the north and west tower blocks jostle like entries in a competition for the world's ugliest building. To the south and east, low-rise offices and workshops sprawl towards mine dumps and a haze of pollution over Soweto. The prospect in every direction has no redeeming feature whatever. Bring on Godzilla, I say.

It was not always thus. The viewing platform offered another perspective on the city, in a display of photographs taken a century before. Joburg was never a pretty place, but once it had broad streets of imposing buildings adorned with the intricate wrought-iron lacework favoured by Victorian architects. In its heyday the City of Gold was brash and boisterous, but it had a raffish charm in its crowds of fortune seekers in trilbies and straw boaters swirling among horse-drawn trams and carriages. Beneath them lay a gold-bearing reef extending for more than 300 miles, and it showed in the opulence and self-confidence of the metropolis they built to exploit it.

One of the most spectacular modern buildings was a soaring obelisk of blue-tinted glass, a hotel that thoughtfully provided armed guards for guests who wished to go shopping. Unsurprisingly it was virtually empty, and a few weeks later it closed. Nearby was a shopping arcade where I used to browse at lunchtimes, but it had since become a notorious muggers' alley. It had become so infamous that Mandela had walked through it, with a hefty security entourage, to demonstrate that law and order would be restored. Shortly afterwards the police station in the arcade closed, and the official reason given was that it had made no contribution to crime prevention and was harming the image of the force. A police spokesman was quoted as saying: 'The station looks bad inside, it is very run-down. Certain media have also criticised the effectiveness of the station.' So they closed it.

The only cops crazy enough to venture into the frightened city after dark are the men of the Johannesburg Flying Squad, who are marginally less homicidal than the bad guys. The essential difference between the opposing sides in this urban combat zone is that the policemen are supposed to shout a warning before they shoot, although whether they do or not tends to become a minor detail when the bullets start flying. When I mentioned to a friend that I had arranged to go on a night patrol, he offered this advice: 'Don't get out the car. Unless it's burning.' At the squad headquarters, an enthusiastic public relations officer briefed me on the successes of the *Johannesburg Blitspatrolle* over the previous year – more than 1,000 stolen vehicles and 300 firearms recovered, and hundreds of suspects arrested, including sixty for murder. He then issued me with a vest designed to stop the high-velocity bullets of Kalashnikov rifles. It was surprisingly light, but a manufacturer's leaflet cheerfully assured me all I would feel would be hammer blows that would cause bruising. As long as the bullets hit the vest, of course. Outside I was introduced to my guides for the evening, Johan and Eugene, short, stocky men with close-cropped hair, lounging against a high-speed German saloon bristling with aerials.

Johan was the quiet one. A former soldier who had fought in a particularly nasty war in Angola, he had joined the police because he liked discipline, wearing a uniform and guns. At the moment he had a 9mm Beretta pistol and a 7.62 R1 infantry assault rifle. He would have preferred a Kalashnikov, but they were not standard police issue. I asked if he was ever afraid, and he said when you were under fire there was no time for fear. 'You have an adrenalin rush, and sometimes afterwards you might feel a bit shaky.' Eugene was the lively one. His reason for joining the force was simple: 'I'm a total adrenalin junkie. I'm not happy unless I'm shooting or driving fast. It's better than sex.' He had a strange light in his eyes when he said this. After two weeks' leave he was suffering withdrawal symptoms, and he couldn't wait to get into action. To up the stress factor we were accompanied by a radio reporter who turned out to be a hackette from hell. Beneath layers of make-up she had a motormouth that was jammed on full throttle. She had opinions on everything, and expressed them in a shrill babble that threatened the sanity of anyone within earshot. I learned to walk away when she was in full flow, but this was impossible in a car being driven in a manner that would have been familiar to *kamikaze* pilots.

We took off like a bat out of hell. The alleged reason was that
another unit had called for help to deal with car hijackers, but
I suspected it was because Eugene badly needed an adrenalin
fix. With the exception of a couple of excursions in Beirut
and Belfast, it was the scariest drive of my life. Eugene was
apparently trying to set a world land speed record, irrespective of
minor obstructions like traffic, pedestrians, and red lights. As we
screeched through the darkened streets I fumbled desperately for
a seat belt, discovered there was no buckle, and hung on grimly
to the strap like a bomber pilot being thrown around by ack-ack
fire. I could not bear to watch the near collisions and closed my
eyes. The smell of burning rubber was in my nostrils, and I had
a vivid image of the car rolling and bursting into flames. *Don't
get out the car. Unless it's burning.* We were brought up short
by an elderly man driving slowly in a narrow street, oblivious to
the flashing lights behind him. When eventually we roared past
him, Eugene grabbed a microphone and growled something in
Afrikaans. The hackette from hell translated: 'He said why don't
you go home and die.' I think Eugene would have been mystified
by Dixon of Dock Green.

The suspect vehicle turned out not to have been stolen, so
we resumed our patrol at a less frantic speed, which permitted
conversation. Johan said violent crime had increased significantly
since the government had abolished the death penalty. 'The
politicians say it's getting better, but it's not. It's getting worse
all the time. We are on the streets, we see it every day.' Eugene
said bribery and corruption was rife among the police, and he
couldn't blame them. It was a dangerous job; you said goodbye
to your wife in the morning and you didn't know if you'd ever see
her again. And for what, a wage that hardly paid the mortgage.
Johan agreed; morale in the force was as low as the pay.

At the time we were cruising the Hillbrow district, a clutter of decaying apartment buildings that had been among the

first multi-racial communities in the country. My guide book described it as South Africa's answer to Soho and Greenwich Village, but said it was on the verge of becoming outlaw territory. This had now happened. A few days before, newspaper billboards had proclaimed 'Mayhem in Hillbrow'. This was a reference to New Year festivities that included shootings, stabbings and hurling bricks and bottles from balconies of tower blocks for the hell of it. A front-page photograph in *The Star* showed a pedestrian sensibly carrying a sheet of corrugated iron above his head to protect himself from missiles. The police had patrolled in armoured cars, but one of them had been injured when a bottle came through a hatch and struck his head. A vehicle set alight by high-spirited revellers burned merrily out of control because firemen who tried to extinguish it were beaten up. By all accounts it was like Belfast in the marching season.

By night it was seriously spooky. Most of the street lamps were out, and crowds of men prowled around cheap food and drink stalls on the pavements, their dark features illuminated by the flickering light of cooking fires. Hard, bright eyes followed the patrol car. There was a palpable sense of menace. 'These are Nigerians,' Eugene said. 'Illegal immigrants dealing in coke and heroin and they don't give a shit for the police. They'll even come up to cop cars and try to sell stuff.' The next street was a hang-out for pimps, prostitutes and junkies. Among them were pre-teen glue sniffers, already little tough guys with criminal records. A week before, Johan had stopped a stolen car and the thief was an eleven-year-old who could barely see over the steering wheel. You wondered what prospects of decent lives kids had in this neighbourhood, and the answer was not much.

A radio call from headquarters, armed robbery in progress, set us off on another scary slalom through the city centre to an indus-trial suburb, where we squealed to a halt outside a warehouse. Eugene and Johan were instantly out of the car, aiming guns at a dozen men around a truck and barking orders at them to lie down. Another squad car arrived and more guns appeared. *Don't get out the car*. Through the windscreen I saw three white men raise their arms, but one of their black companions panicked and ran. Johan raised his rifle. It seemed to be happening in slow motion, with horrible inevitability. I waited for the crack of the rifle, but instead the man stumbled and fell, and Eugene was on him with a pistol to his head. Later Johan said: 'I almost shot that guy. I had him in my sights. He shouldn't have run.' There followed a farcical exchange involving suspicious cops, a fat frightened white man in baggy floral shorts and a mysterious employer on the other end of a mobile telephone. The truck crew claimed it had been sent to pick up a load of sugar, but nobody had told the warehouse staff. While they were trying to persuade sceptical detectives of their innocence, I asked Johan how this work compared with military service on the Angolan border. 'It's about the same situation,' he said. 'There you hunt the enemy in the bush, here you hunt the enemy between buildings. The only difference is that here we don't have artillery and land mines.' You could tell by the way he said it he wished they did. Eugene had been in the force for six years but he was still a constable, partly because he kept shooting people. Every time this happened an internal inquiry was held, and he could not be considered for promotion until it was concluded. I asked him how many times this had happened, and he scratched his head and thought. 'Eighteen,' he said.

The truck crew had been given permission to leave when the radio crackled again, and Eugene whooped with delight. This was the big one, he said, a raid on a hide-out of armed kidnappers, special forces called in, and a good chance of a shoot-out. 'There's a shitload of guns involved,' he announced happily. But he had been told to return his passengers to headquarters first, for which I was quietly grateful. The man was beside himself as we raced back to the station, bouncing around in his seat with excitement and humming surprisingly the triumphal march from *Aida*. It occurred to me that *Ride of the Valkyries* might have been more appropriate, but I let it pass. 'This is a dream job for a policeman,' he said as we narrowly avoided a high-speed collision with a furniture van.

'You're crazy,' I said.

'*Ja*, of course. You've got to be nuts to do this job.'

There was no time for farewells. As soon as we had stepped from the car it sped away on screeching tyres, Eugene aglow with the prospect of a nineteenth notch on his gun. Back in the control room, I asked a policewoman how I could keep track of developments in the impending shoot-out, and she directed me to 'section three', which comprised a policeman in an alcove with a communications headset and a computer screen. As I approached, he put his head in his hands. When I said excuse me, he looked up, snarled, pulled out his pistol, and slammed it on a metal filing cabinet. Then in English, apparently for my benefit, he said: 'I'm going to put down my gun before I fucking shoot myself.' When he began yelling in Afrikaans into his headset I retreated to the policewoman behind a desk. 'He's busy,' I said.

An hour went by, then two, and there was still no word from pals Joey and Gene. I watched a TV murder mystery in a rest room, but I was tired and hungry and bored. So eventually I handed in my bullet-proof vest, left Radio Motor Mouth babbling into a mobile phone and headed back to the northern suburbs for a beer and a curry. It was two days before the news reached the papers. Police units and a special task force had arrested a dozen armed kidnappers in a nightclub and freed three hostages, one of them an eight-year-old girl. The bad guys were notorious drugs smugglers, but they had given up without a shot being fired. Eugene must have been disappointed.

13

The only rainbow country in the world is New York

It seemed like a good idea at the time. Put the black people of Johannesburg in a place outside the city where they could be controlled and recruited as cheap labour for the mines and ancillary industries that fuelled the country's economic powerhouse. The geographical location of this experiment in the early 1950s gave it the collective name of South-Western Townships, or Soweto for short. Then the townships began to grow. And grow. And grow. So that when they erupted in a mass uprising against apartheid in 1976, it was like a declaration of civil war. It was a spark that lit the fuse that blew away statutory racism little over a decade later.

At the last reckoning the conglomeration of dingy brick bungalows, tin shacks and urban wasteland ranged over 25 square miles of undulating terrain south of the main gold-bearing reef, and had a population of more than 3 million, which was about the same as Ireland. One of them was a middle-aged woman called Ivy, who lived with seven children and grandchildren in a two-roomed shack of corrugated iron, number 1233, which was painted light blue. I met her when I joined a group of tourists on a township tour. Her opening line was: 'My name is Ivy. I have three children. Only God helps me, the government gives me nothing. Before, apartheid was oppressing us terribly but at least we could get jobs. Now it is very difficult to get work.' There it was again. Freedom was fine but it was a mixed blessing.

A sign of better times was that she no longer hid beneath her bed at night. It had been set high against a wall to provide shelter during a murderous conflict between supporters of rival political parties that ravaged black communities before the 1994 elections. There had been no serious outbreaks of violence for a couple of years, so now she stored belongings beneath her bed. 'People like me who don't know about politics, we just say thank you for the changes,' Ivy said. She had come from her village in Transkei more than twenty years before in search of work, and now she would like to go home although there was little prospect of earning money there. She would live like generations of her people before her, by sharing the labour and fruits of subsistence farming. The only problem was she had no money for the bus fare to her village.

Ivy was an amiable, articulate woman who seemed to enjoy the attention of foreigners poking around her home. 'Before, we had no chance to talk to people like you. We welcome you. Be happy and enjoy our country, it is a good country,' she said. There was no electricity in her home, because the shacks around it were packed so densely together that it would have been a fire hazard. Our guide Max, who came from Soweto, said houses were being built, but it was not easy to see the improvements because as soon as somebody moved from a shack into a new house somebody else moved into the shack. There seemed to be a never-ending flood of humanity from the rural areas, and most of it was washing up in the flotsam and jetsam of squatter camps. But amid all the debris there were signs of people striving to rise above the squalor: simple workshops and food stores, scrap metal yards, and here and there modern houses with verandas and lace curtains that signalled the emergence of a middle class.

Our group included a gay couple from the United States, and

one of them was interested to know why the government had recently legalised homosexuality. Max said he didn't know, because in his culture they didn't have that sort of thing. 'Well,' the gay man replied indignantly, 'I've got news for you, you most certainly do.' The exchange was in danger of becoming heated, when Max changed the subject by taking us to the only street in the world that had been home to two Nobel laureates.

Vilakazi Street in the Orlando West district of Soweto was an unremarkable place that had played a role in the lives of two extraordinary men. A house on the corner had belonged to Desmond Tutu, and halfway up the street was a brown brick bungalow where Nelson Mandela lived until his behaviour attracted the attention of the security police. His estranged wife Winnie had moved to a grander house nearby, and turned their old home into a museum. At least that's what it said above the turnstile where you paid three rands to visit the property where Mandela plotted revolution in the early 1960s. The garage was filled with tourist junk and framed tributes, most of them to Winnie, who had achieved a certain fame independent of her former husband. This was because of her own aberrant behaviour, and the activities of an entourage of thugs who had terrorised the neighbourhood. Before Mandela was released from prison, I saw a slogan painted on a wall in Soweto that said: 'Free Nelson, Hang Winnie'. Her fall from grace was not recorded in the Mandela Museum, which was selling T-shirts proclaiming her to be 'Mother of the Nation' and commemorative plates and posters portraying her in heroic poses. Her assistants were also peddling bottles of earth with vouchers saying it had come from the Mandela backyard. I looked around the garden with interest to see where these samples of holy ground had come from, but was left to surmise that somebody had discovered the secret of self-replenishing soil. The house was an untidy clutter of odds and ends of little interest, other than a gown said to have been worn by Mandela during his treason trial. It was sad and tacky, unworthy of one of the greatest public figures of the twentieth century. Happily one of the gay men cheered us up with a hushed aside: 'I'd like to ask if I can use the toilet, but it's probably a shrine.'

For the few whites who venture into Soweto, the place is full of surprises. The first is that they are more likely to be greeted with smiles than be mugged on every street corner. Then they begin to notice unexpected things like an SPCA office with a queue of people carrying sick dogs and cats and horses grazing in the grounds. We passed a bowling green with manicured lawns, which mystified the American tourists, and a funeral procession led by a fancy stretch limousine, which made them feel at home. Black communities do not have the resources to build big shopping centres, so local entrepreneurs make do with what is available. Among the most common business premises are freight containers with doors and windows cut into the metal walls and smart logos painted on the sides. They have the advantages of being cheap, portable, windproof and watertight, and they are ideal for trading in fast food, car spares and telephone services. They are also good places for hanging out with friends.

The last stop on the tour was a huge graveyard, where at least three funerals were taking place. The only whites buried in Soweto lay in a corner plot called Heroes' Acre, reserved for those who had fought against apartheid. Joe Slovo, the doyen of the South African Communist Party, and fellow campaigner Helen Joseph lay among unmarked graves of black freedom fighters in muddy ground that was trampled and neglected. It had been raining heavily, and ribbons in the black, gold and green colours of the ANC lay in forlorn twists among the puddles. Only Slovo had a memorial worthy of his struggle, a tombstone of marble bearing the hammer and sickle emblem. He died of cancer shortly after apartheid had been defeated, and I remember him in the end as an avuncular, elderly man with a ready smile. I suspect he would have chuckled at the fancy monument raised to him in the mire of a township he knew well enough.

If you want to know about what's happening in Soweto, go see Godfrey Moloi, my friends said. He's the man.

I found him sitting at the bar of the Blue Fountain, his nightclub and restaurant in the Mapetla district, wearing a trademark straw boater. A bit of a showman, was Godfrey. In his day he had been a gangster, bootlegger, movie star and jazz saxophonist. Then he had become a born-again Christian, philanthropist and self-styled 'Godfather of Soweto'. He had been around, had Godfrey. It was early morning and he was sitting alone at the bar, a heavily built man of medium height, past middle age but still physically strong. Despite the boater at a jaunty angle, he looked what he had been for most of his life, which was a hard man. Press cuttings said he had a reputation for being fast and deadly with fists, knives and guns. Now he organised an annual amateur soccer tournament that attracted crowds of 20,000, and chartered military helicopters to bring handicapped children to the games.

But he had no time for the Rainbow Nation. 'Europe should be the first to do that, all you buggers look alike,' he announced after ordering me breakfast. 'In our country it might happen after a thousand years, when everybody is mixed race. If the Rainbow Nation is possible, let twin brothers from the same womb live all their days in the same house. We can meet in the street, we can work and play together, but at the end of the day we must go home and do our own rituals. No country needs federalism like South Africa. It's the only way we can have peace. Let the Sotho eat his horse, the Shangaan his worms, and the Dutch his *boerewors*.' It was safe to say Godfrey had conservative views. So how were things in Soweto? 'I see no good things. Young people nowadays have no respect for their elders, because they have no fathers. Why is White City (a notorious Soweto gangland) a nest of crime? Because 99 per cent of the creatures there have no families. Women give birth to children, then children give birth to children. It's a madhouse. How can we have a nation like that?'

It was the same everywhere he looked. The police were useless, jail was no punishment any more, and now the Nigerians had turned up with all their drugs nonsense. White investors were building shopping malls in the townships, which meant the end of small local businesses and a return to white master and black servant economics. Somebody would start a row, and in ten years Soweto would be up in smoke again. 'We are moving away from our culture and Christianity. My heart bleeds when I think what's going to happen to our beautiful country when there is no longer Xhosa or Zulu.' Ever a man with an eye for a business opportunity, however, Godfrey had just opened the first officially registered guest house in Soweto. It was his family mansion and he was proud of it, but he hadn't had any guests so far. I asked if I could be the first, and he said: 'I would be very happy.' In the meantime, he summoned a man to show me around Soweto.

My guide was called Difference Khaba, who was known as Defy to his friends. He had been named after an uncle who had been a professional footballer, but how his relative had got the name was anybody's guess. 'What's the difference?' he said with a smile, although it was an old joke. We walked across the street to the sports ground where Godfrey staged his annual 'Goodwill Games'. It was an uneven patch of red earth without a blade of grass, but for two weeks every December it was a field of dreams for youngsters hoping to impress scouts from professional soccer teams. It was presently the venue of a match between Mapetla Youth and Chiawelo Champs, teams of ten-year-olds who made up in enthusiasm what they lacked in stature. They were evenly equipped, with Mapetla wearing smart black strips but barefoot, and Chiawelo with boots and ragged T-shirts. As a graduate of similar football pitches in Glasgow in the 1950s, I appreciated the skills on display with the eye of an aficionado. Then we got into my car and skirted three districts that Defy said were known collectively as the Wild West. 'The people there do crazy things. They like fighting. When you drive through, you always see people fighting.'

We gave the badlands a miss and headed for the oddest place in Soweto. The Sir Ernest Oppenheimer Tower is a small stone column set in landscaped gardens on a slight rise that is the highest point in the township. Its iron gates were locked, but a lady in a nearby office gave us the keys and we climbed an interior staircase to a platform that afforded panoramic views of one of the most densely packed communities in the world. The peaceful haven of the gardens was a surprise, but the remnants of a traditional healer's *kraal* near the tower was astonishing. It was like stepping into the pages of an early anthropological work on tribal Africa. Out of woodland reared giant statues of Shaka and Ngungunyan, the Zulu and Shangaan chiefs, guarding a complex of mud huts and ceremonial arenas populated by bizarre effigies. There was a man with three faces, a giant green woman bearing three children and a spear, and a creature that was half eagle and half man. Beyond them a man-cockerel was scowling at a humanoid with an enormous, misshapen head. A few yards away grey and yellow commuter trains were trundling to Johannesburg, and here were thatched huts protected by stone leopards; two cultures a world apart, one fading before the demands of the other. 'It is beautiful artwork, but it is wasted now,' Defy said. 'In a year or two it's just going to be rocks.' The mystic who created it had upset the locals a few years before and had been forced to leave Soweto. His extraordinary powers were apparently unaffected, however, because he had risen again as a television star.

On leaving, I passed a hand-painted sign on a wooden board

that I had not noticed before. It identified the place as *Kwa-Khayalendaba* (Home of the Story), and said it was a holy place where African cultures, religions, and indigenous sciences were recorded and preserved. The notice politely requested visitors to respect the site, and concluded with a spectacular warning: 'All liars, fools, skeptics (sic) and atheists must please keep out! A curse lasting seven years shall fall on all who destroy any part of this place, they will be unlucky in all they do, be hunted like beasts and finally die in lonely places and the vultures of the sky shall eat their flesh. Beware!' I carefully replaced a shard of carved stone I had absent-mindedly picked up, and stepped gingerly back into twentieth century Soweto.

The good, the bad and the ugly exist in South African townships like anywhere else. A school term was beginning and we passed a crowd of girls in smart uniforms, escorted by proud mums with parasols, milling around outside the gates of a high school. Education was a high priority, and every child attending school was as well turned out as the family could afford. It was a bright, hopeful little scene that made you feel good. Around the corner I swerved to avoid a dead dog in the middle of the road, and almost hit two men urinating into a pile of rubbish. Driving around with Defy I felt relaxed, but that day two television journalists working in Soweto were robbed at gunpoint in the driveway of a house. One of the victims said later what struck her most was the unconcern of the locals. She recalled that a girl came out of the house and said calmly: 'You can get up now, they've gone.'

Defy seemed to be enjoying showing me around. It made a change from his daily routine of looking for odd jobs. He used to work as a government clerk in Pretoria, but it meant rising at 4 a.m. to catch the train and spending most of his wages on transport, so he packed it in. He was thirty-six, he had three children, and he did not have a clue how he was going to feed them next week. Something would come up, it always did. Today it was me. And today I had decided we were going to eat at Wandie's Place, an upmarket restaurant by Soweto standards, popular with local yuppies. When we arrived a smartly dressed party was enjoying a leisurely lunch on a terrace beneath sun umbrellas, and all of them were speaking English. The decor was Greek taverna, with flowers and bottles of wine on checked table cloths. Defy had never been in such a posh place and he was uneasy, but deferential service and good food perked him up. I had a brief chat with the owner, Wandile Ndaba, during which he complained that the economy was still in white hands. 'We don't have the resources, and neither does the government. We just have to help ourselves.' We were interrupted by the arrival of a party of tourists, confirming that Wandile's self-help philosophy was a success.

Another Sowetan who had made a name for himself was 'Baby' Jake Matlala. Standing 4 feet 10 inches high and weighing little over 8 stone, the biggest thing about him was his smile. He also had a lightning right hand that had felled a string of opponents and made him flyweight boxing champion of the world. Jake's training headquarters was a small brown building with a red iron roof in a patch of wasteground. It looked like a Scouts' drill hall, except that inside the brick walls were bare, the floor was hardboard panels on concrete and there were no changing rooms, showers or toilets. The training equipment comprised two punchbags and a few skipping ropes, and the 'ring' was imaginary, being roughly the area covered by four of the floor panels. This was the Soweto Boxing Academy that had produced nine South African champions, including Baby Jake.

When Defy and I walked in, the hall was echoing to the drumming of feet and ropes and the gasping of muscled youths doing endless press-ups. Jake was in a corner on his own, ducking and diving in a shadow boxing routine, his right jab a blur of movement. Above him yellowed newspaper cuttings peeling from the wall listed highlights of his career, with photographs portraying triumphs in Glasgow and Las Vegas. His manager Theo was a kindly, grey-haired man who earned his living as a sports journalist and spent the rest of his time helping township youths to realise their dreams of becoming great fighters. With Jake it had taken time: 'As a kid he showed great promise, then in mid-career he had a string of losses. People asked me why I continued with him. The reason was I could see the dedication in him, and the hunger. That's why this place has produced nine national champions. The boys here are hungry.'

Theo's voice was lost in a thunder-roll of feet as the boxers went into a high-stepping routine, then the trainer shouted 'Shadow box' and they split into pairs, dodging and jabbing, grunting with the effort, sweat streaming down strained faces. Jake was wearing a track suit to keep his weight down in preparation for a title defence, but he was still faster on his feet than any of his sparring partners. He was barely breathing heavily when he finished his training session and strolled over. I asked what made a little guy like him so special, and he laughed and said hardship. 'Things were tough in the townships in the seventies. You had to fight hard for what you wanted. It was only in the eighties that things began to change. It was only then black boxers could get into a ring with white boxers.' The world had opened up for the new generation, but the key was still having a set of goals and the dedication to achieve them. He told the kids they had to work hard at school and in the gym, focusing on what they wanted, and behaving as sportsmen in and out of the ring.

Jake was a good role model for the youngsters who idolised him. Success had brought an expensive home in Johannesburg, a smart car and a fast food franchise. He endorsed products on television, and he had taken his family to Disney World. But he still trained six days a week in the place where he learned how to fight. People were saying he should go into politics when he hung up his gloves, but he had other plans. 'I think by the time I give up fighting this place will be equipped like a real gym, and I will be able to come back and teach the kids.' I thought of a health club that I had visited in the northern suburbs of Johannesburg the day before. It had all the high-tech paraphernalia of the modern fitness culture but it would never produce champions like this dilapidated little hall of fame in Soweto. The people who went there didn't have the hunger.

Late afternoon is the best time of day in Soweto. The harsh light softens, the rhythms of life slow, and people stroll in the twilight chatting and laughing. I sat on a step outside Godfrey's club watching the cavalcade of life and feeling mellow. Boys were playing football across the street, and the thump of the ball long after darkness had fallen was an echo of my own childhood.

I was waiting for Godfrey to take me to his house, which turned out to be worthy of his Godfather status. Soweto's first official guest house was a neo-baronial concrete castle with lofty ceilings, marble floors and palm trees soaring above a fish pond in the central living area. On the roof was a sunken swimming pool, with sauna and steam bath en suite, overlooking manicured lawns. It was by far the most extravagant building in a cul-de-sac called Red Pear Street, and it stood at the end of the road like a sentinel surveying the Sowetan masses across an expanse of tall grasses. Godfrey had clearly done well in the bad old days before discovering the path of righteousness. A brochure pointed out that his guest house was near a police station and a hospital, which were presumably important considerations for visitors. It didn't mention the surreal pleasure of swimming by moonlight on a rooftop in Soweto, and then standing barefoot in the warm night listening to the voices of the township. They carried across the *veld* and seemed to hang in the air, reassuring sound waves of humanity punctuated by laughter, children crying and dogs barking. You knew there was squalor and violence out there, but there was a sense that decency prevailed.

Morality was a subject on which Godfrey held firm views, which he expressed over dinner in the hall of his concrete Camelot. Standards were falling because the police were failing to do their job, and foreigners were flooding in from all over Africa with their drugs and guns, making babies and polluting the South African races. And as for this Rainbow Nation nonsense – look at Europe, after 2,000 years it was going the other way, with countries fragmenting into ethnic homelands. 'The only rainbow country in the world is New York,' he said. He was a character, was Godfrey. A man who did bad things and then tried to atone for them, a conservative Zulu who thought apartheid had its good points, an ex-con who went back to prison to play his saxophone and tell inmates it wasn't the end of the road, they could rebuild their lives as he had done. Writing of my visit to his home I feel grateful and sad, because six months later Godfrey died.

Before leaving Soweto, I arranged to join Jake for a training run. He took heroic status literally in his stride, acknowledging the greetings of admirers with a smile and a wave. 'Hey, Baby Jake,' they would cry, and throw an imaginary punch. 'Hey man, how you doin',' he would reply and jab with his right. All of this while he was effortlessly running the legs off me. We met at a garage. It was mid-morning and serious heat had built up, but he kept on his tracksuit and to make things tougher he carried small metal weights. We set off at a leisurely pace along a busy road, Jake waving and laughing and chatting, me trying to maintain a rhythm as the thin air of the high *veld* began to take its toll. We turned on to a dirt track, past a cemetery, and on to a quiet road rising through open fields towards mine dumps on the crest of a hill. As the incline increased I began to struggle, and after a few minutes I told Jake to go on. We shook hands, I wished him well in his next fight, and I turned back to Defy, who had been loyally following in my car. My last view of Jake was his slight figure trotting past the mine dumps. He had picked up speed, his feet seemed to be barely touching the ground, and his right fist was jabbing the air. A few weeks later he successfully defended his title, which surprised nobody but his opponent.

While I was in Johannesburg, newspapers were giving a lot of publicity to a book that was billed as a survival guide to the urban jungle. Among life-saving tips for pedestrians, it suggested they walk tall and look confident, remove jewellery, and tuck away loose ends of scarves, belts and long hair that could provide a grip for an assailant. Instead of walking closely around a potentially dangerous corner, they should either stop briefly beforehand, which would throw a waiting attacker off balance, or take the corner several paces away from it. For anyone obliged to wait in a street, the book advised: 'Keep your back to a wall and hold your parcels firmly, without looking as if you are clutching them nervously; women should hold their handbags tightly to the side of their body like they would a rugby ball.' Motorists should ensure their windows were open no more than 4 centimetres, unless they were on a long stretch of open road, and a handy hint for home owners was to install a tape recording of a savage dog barking triggered by the doorbell.

I imagined a city full of people who had read this book, skulking around corners, their backs to walls, clutching their belongings fiercely like rugby balls. And driving cars fitted with flame-throwers. It was a scary thought, but it was already happening.

14

Of pioneers and Sun Kings

It was a relief to get out of Joburg. I felt my spirits rise as I drove away from the city that had lost its heart and headed north on the N1 freeway towards Pretoria.

This road reminded me of the highway between Glasgow and Edinburgh. They were roughly the same distance, about 40 miles, passing through similar rolling green countryside, and linking disparate cities – one historically a grimy hive of industry, the other a sedate administrative capital. The difference here was that the green belt between them was vanishing as developers acquired pastures new for foreign investors and businessmen fleeing downtown Joburg. It seemed inevitable that in a few years the urban sprawl would fuse the cities into a megalopolis.

A distinctive landmark still dominated the approach to South Africa's capital from the south. The Voortrekker Monument stood on the top of a hill, a huge granite cube commemorating the epic expedition of thousands of Afrikaners who quit the British Cape colony in the 1830s in search of land and freedom. Over the years the Great Trek has been romantically portrayed as an exodus of biblical proportions, although only a fraction of Dutch-speaking settlers in the Cape joined the wagon trains heading north. Yet it was a momentous migration, similar to the settlement of the American West which took place about the same time, and for many Afrikaners it is a cornerstone of their culture.

Die Groot Trek was the stuff that legends are made of. In the space of six years about 15,000 Afrikaners struggled over mountains and deserts, braving drought, flash floods, malarial mosquitos and hostile natives who were understandably reluctant to hand over their lands to the newcomers. Killing and looting was the order of the day, with the spoils of land and cheap labour going to the men with guns and Bibles. The indomitable spirit of the *voortrekkers* is depicted above the entrance to the monument in the sculpted head of a buffalo, which is reputed to be the most unpredictable and dangerous animal in Africa, particularly when wounded. I saw this metaphor come to life, in a manner of speaking, the first time I visited the memorial in 1988. It was the Day of the Vow and President P.W. Botha, apartheid's last enforcer, was warning his *volk* of the black-commie-liberal 'total onslaught' against them and of hard times ahead. Traditional short *dopper* coats as worn by the *voortrekkers* mingled with khaki uniforms and neo-Nazi symbols of neanderthal militiamen in a display of defiance and resolution, and the cry was no surrender. But the sun was shining, and the National Party was still in power, so the big men with beards and the women in long dresses and lace bonnets enjoyed themselves with beer and *boerewors* and bellicose speeches. Eat, drink and be merry, for tomorrow Mandela gets out of prison.

This time it was quieter. Only a few tourists were wandering around the sombre interior of the monument. It is a stark mausoleum with a high domed roof, and in the middle a granite tomb commemorating those who died in the trek is illuminated by natural light softened by yellow mosaic windows. Around the walls is a bas-relief depicting scenes of life on the trail: ox-wagons departing from the Cape, battles with natives, making peace with natives, more battles with natives, crossing mountains, more battles with natives, and so on. The most dramatic frieze depicts the Battle of Blood River in 1838, when a punitive expedition of 470 Boers under the command of Andries Pretorius defeated an army of more than 10,000 Zulus. This was taken as proof that God was not only on the Boers' side, but that He had given them a mandate to conquer and civilise southern Africa. Hence the Day of the Vow, to honour God and carry out His work.

From the roof of the monument there is a fine view of the city named after the victor of Blood River, nestling in a green valley framed by low hills. A prominent feature is the red roofs and sand-coloured façade of the Union Buildings, the seat of power from which ancestors of the *trekboers* administered the country for generations. The reason the government complex is still visible from the monument is that there are laws restricting the height of buildings to ensure that the view between the two is not obscured. Presumably the idea was to inspire the bureaucrats with the spirit of their forefathers, and to remind them that God was keeping an eye on them. Whether Mandela appreciated such forethought on his inauguration as president at the Union Buildings is not known.

The other thing I noticed at the monument was a hopeful little poster near the entrance, issued by the department of education, which spelled out the acronym LEARN: L is for love, E is for everyone, A is for achieving, R is for rainbow, N is for nation. The big news in South African newspapers that day was that half of the country's school leavers had failed their final exams.

On closer inspection, the Union Buildings are splendid. This is the way bastions of power ought to be. Designed by Herbert Baker in 1910 in the form of an acropolis, it is a Renaissance-style compendium of graceful arches and terraces adorned with Greek columns, Italianate roofs, magnificent studded brass doors and windows with attractive wooden shutters. The central feature is an amphitheatre with a lily pond, fountains, potted palms and domed towers crowned with figures of Atlas and Mercury. Spread upon the crest of a hill above the city, it is a palace fit for a Medici and altogether pleasing to the eye and the spirit. For Baker it was an opportunity to hone his skills for his masterpiece, the legislative buildings in New Delhi, for which he received a knighthood.

After the tumult of recent years, peace had returned to the palace on the hill. The security goons of the apartheid era were gone, and there was not even a policeman in sight as families strolled in the sunshine, taking snaps of each other in the *piazza* where the man from Robben Island had completed his long walk to freedom. The most energetic thing in the place was a green baseball cap worn by an Asian tourist, which was equipped with a small solar panel that powered a fan that blew air on to the man's forehead through a hole in the front. It was the kind of contraption that past presidents of South Africa would not have been seen dead in, and which Mandela would probably wear for fun, which was a sign the country was heading in the right direction. I sat in the shade of a terrace, observing part of the amphitheatre framed by an archway beneath a brilliant blue sky, and imagined I was in Florence. Then from a balcony I looked across the city to where the Voortrekker Monument brooded in the distance. Interestingly, the perspective meant that it was dwarfed by a 'Rainbow Nation' flag flying from the Union Buildings.

I had never liked Pretoria much. It was a city that had been founded by farmers and taken over by bureaucrats, who had produced a community whose idea of a good time was getting drunk at weekends. But the retreat of the grey men in dark suits from the corridors of power and an influx of foreign embassies and agencies had transformed it into a lively, cosmopolitan capital. The streets were full of agreeable, smiling people, and open-air markets that were well managed, and little old ladies in floral dresses carrying handbags who wouldn't have lasted five minutes in downtown Joburg. You could almost see a rainbow.

In a central square I observed an interesting contrast. In a corner glowered a gigantic bust of Johannes Gerhardus Strijdom, a hard-line prime minister of apartheid for four years in the 1950s. It was Orwellian in scale and design, a massive effigy of Big Brother staring sternly across the square. Well might he have been displeased, because nearby a cheerier figure was mocking his gravitas – a life-sized cardboard cut-out of a smiling Mandela, which an enterprising photographer had brought along to attract clients. While Mandela posed for pictures with admirers, Strijdom got peppered with bird droppings.

The next day I drove to a Make-Believe Land and met a confused peacock. It was standing on the fourth step of an escalator, considering whether to continue to the first floor cocktail lounge or return to the poolside bar. It is not every day one sees a peacock facing such tough decisions in a five-star hotel. But then it is not every day the son of Russian immigrants emerges from a tough Johannesburg suburb to build the most extravagant leisure complex in Africa. The resident peacock in the Cascades Hotel is a minor detail in the contrived splendour of Sun City, a fantasy world created in the Pilansberg Mountains of the erstwhile black homeland of Bophutatswana by an energetic little man who began his career by selling chips and chewing gum in his parents' café. At the last count the Sun International corporation of Mr Sol Kerzner owned more than thirty casino resorts in southern Africa, the Indian Ocean islands and the Bahamas.

Sun City remains the jewel in the crown of Sol the Sun King, a glittering monument to the enterprise of a very shrewd cookie. In the dark days of apartheid in the 1970s, Sol came up with a simple idea for bringing some pizazz to a country governed by Calvinist pedants. Stepping through the looking-glass of the bantustan system, he set up shop in the 'independent' republic of Bophutatswana, and offered South Africans lots of stuff they could not get anywhere else – gambling, topless showgirls, soft-core porn movies and the ultimate thrill of sex across the colour bar. This was at a time when fashion pictures in South African newspapers had black stars on the nipples of models wearing transparent garments. Thus a palace of illicit pleasures was founded on hypocrisy and thrived on greed, and the Court of the Sun King became a wondrous place renowned throughout the land.

The first time I visited it, with chums, I expected to hate it on sight. Arriving at the Disney-style entrance beyond a patchwork of ramshackle townships, I was prepared to sneer. But I didn't. In fact we had good fun, playing tennis, splashing around in swimming pools, walking in the hills and tracking elephant and giraffe in a game reserve. It was tacky in parts, notably in the gambling halls, but there were enough diversions outdoors for an amusing weekend. Stopping off again on my way west from Pretoria, I found it had grown. It was a lot bigger in fact, with the addition of a 'Lost City' supposed to represent a mythical African kingdom, replete with an outrageously lavish hotel, a golf course on which crocodiles added a new dimension to the term water hazard, and a maze of streams, lakes and waterfalls in the largest man-made jungle in the world. It was vulgar in concept and tasteful in detail. Amid the extravagant kitsch there was fine artwork and craftsmanship. And the jungle was amazing.

I have always liked forests, and in particular the tropical kinds with creepers and giant flowers and things that screech, and whirr and scurry among massive fallen trees that look like petrified dinosaurs. The jungle of the Sun King was not the real thing – it didn't have leopards and trees that pierce the sky – but it was pretty good. The publicity material said it covered 62 acres, with 1.5 million plants in twenty-two areas representing wet and dry climates. The three-layered rainforest had ebony, fluted milkwood and red beech, and the arid section had baobab trees that were hundreds of years old and weighed up to 75 tons. There were 300 species of palm from places like Central America and the Philippines, euphorbia from Saudi Arabia and camel thorn from the Kalahari, and *Aloe suzannae* from Madagascar that had flowers 5 metres long and filled the night with a wondrous scent. Fig trees had been planted to attract birds, and so far almost 200 species had set up home including sacred ibis, egyptian geese and paradise flycatchers. Eagles and herons controlled the rodent and reptile populations, and the waterways were teeming with 9,000 fish including barbel, tilapia and leatherback carp. Keeping this homespun web of life intact in what was naturally arid bush country was a panoply of irrigation stations, overhead misters, water sprinklers and fan-driven humidifiers. No wonder the monkeys felt at home. I saw a troop of them in the rainforest. I was sitting on a rock by a stream when they came swinging through the trees, chattering and chucking fruit at each other. They seemed unconcerned by my presence, and when they wandered off I was joined by a small bird with a long curved beak, which cocked its head and listened with interest to my pitiful attempts to mimic its melancholy whistle. I still couldn't make up my mind about this crazy place, but in the end I decided that if it was good enough for the birds and the monkeys it was good enough for me.

And on the seventh day the Sun King looked at his work and said it was good, and everybody could take the day off and play the slot machines. And so they took little plastic boxes filled with coins and sat before banks of flickering lights, rows of morons feeding coins into voracious machines with a mechanical precision that made you wonder if they were human. And when

King Sol saw the river of money flowing from the Great Hall of Automatons he was pleased, and ordained that another swathe of wilderness be transformed into forest, which was good news for the monkeys.

15

It was like the leopard used a tin opener on him

The old house beyond the rusty gate was empty. It had a forlorn air, as if it remembered the life that had gone out of it. Behind it, an obscure path wound through weeds and tall grasses to an outhouse with a thatched roof that had been a school for the local farming community.

Here plaster was flaking from the walls, ivy was creeping through broken windows and termite nests rose from the flagstone floor like stalagmites. Hornets were buzzing in the still air, trailing venomous stingers. The only sign that the room once echoed to the chatter and laughter of children was drawings scratched into the wall near the door, simple sketches of people with grinning faces and spiky hair. Kids' stuff from long ago. Outside, the heat shimmered on dry land covered with bush. If you took a few steps and halted, and listened to the drowsy concerto of birds and insects, you sensed an ancient peace. Then you looked towards the hills, and you knew there were leopards there, with amber eyes, dozing in the shade of thorn trees.

In the 1920s a young teacher contemplated this landscape, and later he wrote: 'There is no other place I know that is so heavy with atmosphere, so strangely and darkly impregnated with that stuff of life that bears the authentic stamp of South Africa.' Herman Charles Bosman had a way with words. A compelling storyteller, he left his teaching post to become a Kipling of southern Africa whose tales of rural Afrikaners survived him as amusing portraits of a way of life that has all but disappeared. A complex character, he served four years in prison after a shooting incident in which his stepbrother was killed, and then became an iconoclastic journalist with a taste for lampooning Johannesburg society. In the 1930s he lived in London, where he wrote for *The Sunday Citizen*, taunted the Mosleyites, flirted with Hitlerism, and slated T.S. Eliot. On the outbreak of war he returned to South Africa, where he wrote humorous essays and literary criticism until he died of a heart attack in 1951 at the age of forty-six. In his later years Bosman earned a reputation as an arch elitist, proclaiming his artistic and spiritual superiority over most of mankind. Happily he is best remembered for his tales of rural life that have become classics of South African literature.

It was the spirit of Bosman the aspiring writer and the little world he described that drew me to the Marico bushveld, the dusty hinterland near Botswana where he taught for six months and gathered the material for his stories. It lay along the N4 highway from Pretoria to the Kalahari, a semi-arid land of low hills, coarse grasses and acacia trees where cattle and game ranchers struggled to survive endemic droughts. It was a hard place where dust storms whipped by westerly gales blotted out the sun in spring before the rains came. But now it was late summer and there seemed to have been no shortage of water, because the countryside was green and the verges were bright with daisies and purple splashes of heliotrope. This was confirmed by an attendant in a petrol station in Groot Marico, a farming village snoozing in the afternoon heat. 'Ja, we had good rains this year. But three years before the *veld* was everything stones, nothing grass, only you saw stones.' The local information centre was a room in a bungalow in a side street that also served as the headquarters of a newly formed Herman Charles Bosman Literary Society.

There was not much on display yet, but among examples of his work there was a passage written near the farm school where he sketched his first stories: 'Sometimes, at night, when the world is very still, a soft wind comes sweeping across the *veld*. Then if you are outside, and listen very carefully, you can hear the story it has to tell. It is thoughtful, this little wind, and the tale it tells, as old as the world and as time-worn, has about it something that is yet new and sweet and strangely stirring. And this story is one that we all love to hear, for, steeped as it is in the fragrance of some romance of long ago, it awakens memories of far-off things – of trees that are dark in the moonlight, of crumbling garden walls, of star-dust and roses.' Even allowing for the flowery prose, I had to go and listen to that wind.

My first stop was a town called Zeerust, where a man who owned a hotel had been recommended to me. Friedrich Breytenbach was a big, shambling bear of a man with a crumpled, kindly face who was also a farmer and ran the only decent restaurant in town. He had been a stalwart of the far-right Conservative Party, which was difficult to reconcile with his amiable demeanour, but he had lost interest in politics. 'We're in a no-win situation,' he said. 'And there is nowhere else to go. There is no country that will open its arms to me, that will make me feel welcome. Where must I go?' So he stayed where he was, working long hours in a community he would probably never leave, and raising a brood of handsome children who were looking for ways of escape to the bright lights of Cape Town and overseas.

The heart of the Marico bushveld lay 50 miles north, he said. Most of the characters immortalised by Bosman had gone, but he would arrange for me to stay next day with a farmer who knew the area as well as anybody. In the meantime I should come and meet some guys in a place next to his restaurant. It was late in the evening when we arrived at the Las Vegas Casino

Palace, near the end of the main street, and the town was quiet. In the distance dogs were howling at the moon. Inside it was even quieter. The establishment consisted of a room that was empty save for slot machines ranged along one wall, a wooden bar and two men getting methodically drunk. The proprietor was Johnny, an itinerant Greek who travelled with the machines, set them up for a few weeks anywhere he thought he might make a few rands, then moved on. His companion was an elderly man with white hair who was introduced as Oom Jan, a retired big game hunter who lived somewhere in Botswana. A Hemingway character in a remote corner of Africa, Oom Jan had traded his guns for brandy, and bemoaned the passing of the days when the plains were thick with migrating herds of game.

I was given a warm welcome, a tumbler of brandy and Coke and my first lesson in bushcraft. There is only one way to get rid of a troop of troublesome baboons other than shooting them, Oom Jan said. What you do is catch one of them, paint him white, and set him loose. He goes back to the others, who take one look at him and flee in terror; he chases after them, and the lot of them keep going over the horizon. 'It works every time,' Oom Jan said. But Africa had changed. It had become civilised, and the days when a man could lose himself in the bush for weeks were gone. 'It's hard to go ape now. In the 1950s you could drive for three days in the Serengeti and not get past the herds of zebra and gazelle and wildebeest, with all the predators around them and the vultures above. In Zambia you can't find a white-eared cob any more. Around Lake Albert and Lake Edward in Uganda there were 40,000 hippos. Find one today and I'll kiss your ass on the steps of City Hall.' Now there were poachers using automatic rifles and lunatics who obliterated rhinos with rocket-propelled grenades to get at the ivory. Give Oom Jan a crack at these crazy buggers, and the vultures would be happy. Then there were the so-called experts who blundered around meddling with nature:

'Because some prick of a zoologist or an ecologist doesn't know what he's doing, you end up with too many bloody elephants destroying the bush.'

The slot machines blinked and flashed disconsolately at blank walls, and nobody came in to feed them. But the brandy flowed and, as the evening wore on, the stories became more extravagant. There had been a legendary Scotsman called John Hunter who had been hired to clear the 'white highlands' of Kenya of predators for settlers. He was reputed to have shot eighty lions in a single day, and to have rid the planet of 7,000 rhinos in his lifetime. It seemed to me this slaughter would have required a helicopter gunship, but I didn't mention this to Oom Jan. I left when Johnny started building a crooked wall of empty Coca-Cola cans. This was possibly the last time Oom Jan's stories were recorded, because a few months later he knocked back his last brandy and passed to, I hope, happier hunting grounds.

Friedrich's directions were fairly clear: take the main road heading north, go through the mountains, turn right on to a dirt road after the third village, follow a game farm fence and after some workers' cottages look out for a track to the farm of his friends Willie and Riana. There were no signs, but anybody in the area would put me right. Unsurprisingly I got lost soon after leaving the tarred road, but happily the first person I stopped to ask for directions was Riana, who had come looking for me. Life had changed in the Marico; there were fewer farms and people didn't socialise as much as they used to. But the land was much the same, rolling bush country criss-crossed by dirt roads, and in the midday heat you could easily picture one of Bosman's best known characters, a farmer who dozed off beneath a withaak tree and woke to find himself being inspected by a leopard.

My host Willie Delport was a cattle farmer who had seen plenty of leopards. He shot baboons on sight, because of the damage they wreaked to his tomato crops and his outhouses, but he always left a few for the leopards. 'If you get rid of all the baboons, the leopards will come after your calves,' he said. We were sitting on the *stoep* of his farmhouse, a light, airy place with polished wooden floors overlooking a garden bright with flowers and shaded by giant tamboti trees. Willie was a big man bulging from the traditional *boer* uniform of sweat-stained khaki shirt and shorts, with an impressive beard on a boyish face and an infectious giggle. Afrikaans was his mother tongue and he was fluent in five African languages, but he was sorry his English was rusty because he hadn't used it for a while. How long, exactly? He thought for a minute: *ja*, thirteen years.

The passage of time was not something that concerned Willie much. After being disappointed in love as a young man, he went into the bush with his cattle and his dogs and lived among Tswana people for six years. So he knew the Marico as well as any white man, and better than most. Riana was equally at home in the realm of the leopard and hyaena. She had been brought up on a farm, and when her family moved to Pretoria she cried to come back. 'You know all the people who moved from here, they long to come back. When you are walking in the bush, if you are tuned into nature, you see many things. I think it speaks to your soul.'

Society had changed. In the old days the farms were smaller and more numerous. It had been like a big family. People visited each other without making appointments, but now some folk seemed to be living for themselves. When Riana was a child there were big herds of kudu and springbok and impala, and her grandfather remembered lions and buffaloes in the hills. Now there were fences everywhere, and it was a shame the game couldn't trek for water in the dry seasons any more. But the spirit of the land was immutable. 'Communities change, but the *veld* stays the same. When you live here, every day the bush talks to you,' Riana said. And when the bush spoke, the people listened and learned. In Riana's garden there was a magnificent tamboti tree that Willie reckoned was 600 years old. After lunch, I noticed a lizard clinging motionless to its trunk. 'He'll stay like that all day,' Willie said. 'The old folk used to say if it was on the north side of the trunk, and it was facing north, it meant rain.' I looked at the unbroken blue of the sky and felt the hot, still air, and smiled at the quaint folklore. That night I was startled from sleep by a violent thunderstorm, accompanied by torrential rain that lasted till morning.

Like many country folk, Willie was a natural storyteller. Sitting on the *stoep*, watching the light softening over the hills in the late afternoon, I heard the kind of tales recorded by Bosman a generation before. 'People who come from the cities think it's easy to kill a leopard, but he is very shy,' Willie began one day. 'You think you will catch him, but he will catch you first.' He had been on the farm for about six months when a neighbour called to say he had caught 'a cat' that had been taking his calves, and he needed help. In these parts farmers used spring-loaded metal traps for predators, placing them around a recent kill, but they were not fixed to the ground because a leopard would chew off its leg to be free of it. Instead heavy chains were attached to the devices to make the animal easier to track. 'When we followed the trail we saw it was making a figure of eight, backtracking all the time. I had with me my dog Wolfie, who was a German shepherd. We were on open land, no bushes, when the dog stopped dead in front of us, growling. The next minute there was a big roar, the dog jumped back on the old man, and he fell on me, and we all fell down as the leopard jumped at us. But the chain got trapped between two rocks and jerked him back, and he lay in front of us, staring at us with his yellow eyes. In fact the chain was free now, but the leopard didn't know this and he just lay there, so I stood up slowly and shot him with my rifle.' That evening I went for a jog along a red dirt road winding through the hills, wondering if I was being observed from afar by amber eyes. I wanted very much to see a leopard in the wild one day, but not just at that moment. Instead I admired strings of little birds perched on telegraph wires like musical notes – here a crotchet, there a quaver – as if scoring the songs they were singing. As darkness fell they were joined by a chorus of frogs making plonking sounds, like stones dropping into water.

Often the telephone rang and Riana did not answer it. The reason was that they shared the line with other farms, each of which had its own number of rings. Thus the Delports, whose number was thirteen, were summoned by a local operator with one short and three long rings. This precluded privacy, but there were advantages. If telephones rang during the night many people would pick them up, assuming it was an emergency and that a neighbour might need help. The phone company wanted to instal an automatic exchange, but most people preferred things the way they were. Riana's grandfather had been the first to have a telephone in the area. When he received a message for neighbours, he stepped outside and signalled them with a mirror.

The best place to listen to Willie's stories was around a campfire in his backyard, with kudu *boerewors* sizzling on the grill and a Marico moon flitting above the jacarandas. An endless source of amusement was the antics of city people, particularly part-time hunters who came out at weekends to shoot game.

'I was working on another farm, cutting logs, when two guys from Joburg turned up and said they wanted to hunt kudu,' was how one story began. Willie told them it was the wrong time of day; the buck would be dozing in the shade and they should wait until evening. But they ignored his advice, and went into the hills. 'Next thing we heard a shot, and the guys came back and one of them said he'd shot a leopard on a *koppie*. This guy said he could shoot a kudu in the eye at 500 yards and he was sure he'd hit the leopard in the chest. I was not so sure, so I said wait here and I'll fetch my dogs, they know leopards. But when I got back they had gone on their own with a couple of little dogs from that farm, *stoepkakkers* (veranda shitters) these dogs were, they knew nothing about leopards.' Eventually there was a shot, then five in quick succession.

'Next thing one of the dogs came running back, he was going so fast he hit a banana tree and fell into the pond. Then the lame one came as fast on three legs as the other one on four. We knew then there was a problem, so I took my gun and my dogs and I went in the *bakkie* to look for them.'

What Willie found was the great marksman with most of his scalp hanging over his face, broken bones protruding from his cheek and forehead and deep gashes on his arms and body. 'It was like the leopard had used a tin opener on him, he was full of holes that guy,' Willie recalled. The man survived, partly thanks to Willie's rudimentary first aid with a torn shirt, and months later he returned on the advice of his therapist. 'He couldn't sleep for nightmares, and he wanted me to take him where he got attacked. He was very nervous, and when we got there he started shaking. Then I found his glasses – they were still hanging on a tree – and he started crying. After a while he said he felt better and the next time I saw him he was fine, except his head still looked chewed up.' As for the leopard, it had been wounded and Willie tracked it and shot it before nightfall.

Then there was the time Willie and a neighbour disturbed a leopard when they were dipping goats for ticks and it ran into the bush. Half an hour later it reappeared, bounding at full speed after a dog belonging to a farm worker. On the assumption that safety lay at home, the dog flew over a fence into a cattle *kraal* and headed for its master. Followed by the leopard. 'All hell broke loose,' Willie recalled. The cattle scattered, the farmer jumped into a water trough, Willie threw himself into a truck, and the owner of the dog lunged for his horse. Unfortunately the horse bolted, but not before the man had grabbed its tail, and the encounter concluded with the horse galloping into the bush, with the man hanging on, followed by the dog, followed by the leopard. Willie wasn't much help. 'I couldn't do anything, I was pissing myself with laughing.' Happily the leopard, disconcerted by the farce around him, lost interest and trotted back to the hills. Sitting by the dying embers of the fire, I could imagine the ghostly figure of young Bosman smiling at Willie's tales.

Deeper in the *veld* lay a hamlet called Nietverdiend, which meant 'undeserved', though nobody could remember why. It comprised a church, a school, a store and a handful of houses shimmering in a heat haze on the road to Botswana. If you blinked you would miss it, and if you didn't blink you might think you had imagined it. If you stopped and walked through it in the middle of the day when there was nobody around, you had an uneasy feeling you had wandered into a mirage. The dirt road heading out of it was real enough, and it led to a farm with a white metal sign with figures of a rabbit and a pair of trousers. It was the home of Deon and Tinka Haasbroek, whose name meant 'Rabbit Trousers'. Far from being abashed by his odd name, Deon displayed it on his fence. A sense of humour made life easier in these parts. His grandfather had owned the farm a few miles north where Bosman had taught, and now Deon rented it from his brother. But he kept his calves on his own land, because of the leopards that hunted around the old place. Deon didn't like to hunt leopards; if they could live together it was fine with him, but his calves were easy meat and if a leopard got a taste for them he had to shoot it.

I was expected, and invited in for tea and a chat about life in the Marico. Deon never knew his grandfather, but he remembered his grannie saying it used to take them three days by ox-wagon to get to Zeerust for supplies. She used to become sick travelling in the wagon, so most of the time she walked the 50 miles. Drought was always the biggest problem, and now the bush was taking over grazing land. 'When my father was a boy, he used to bring in the cows before he went to school. Then it was savannah, now it's all bush and you can't go into it even on horseback.' That meant more land for fewer cattle, thus fewer farms. But there was still room for buck, jackals, lynx and hyaena, and they all had their roles to play. 'I like the brown hyaena, it is the cleaner of the *veld*. It takes the after-birth of my cows.' His wife liked the kudu. After they were married they lived on his granddad's old farm, and one day Deon brought her a kudu calf abandoned by her mother. 'She slept in the bush near the house, and every morning at nine she would come for milk. You could stand and look for her, you knew she was coming, but you never saw her until suddenly she was there. Then one day she went off, and we never saw her again.'

The farming community was smaller, but it was still tightly knit, Tinka said. 'The reason we survive is because we help each other. You can have no secrets here, which makes us live honestly with each other.' But now they were facing a new threat. Reports of attacks on farms in the Free State and the Western Cape had created unease in the Marico, and last week they had attended a two-day course on security. Tinka said: 'I don't want my children to live in fear. I don't want to sleep with guns. But it's better here than in the cities. Life in our cities is terrible, they must lock everything up. It's as if their children are in cages.'

Some things had not changed. In South Africa white men owned the big farms, and black and coloured men and women worked on them. In the tribal areas families bought or rented smallholdings from the chiefs and shared common grazing land. That was the way it had been for generations, and that was the way it was likely to continue. The paternal relationship between boss and worker prevailed in the Marico as elsewhere, and much

depended on mutual trust. Deon said inter-family ties were strong.
A man on his farm had worked for his father and grandfather,
and he employed this man's son and grandson. He usually left
punishment for misdemeanours to his workers. 'They prefer to
settle matters themselves in their own way, with their own courts
on the farms. If a man who is guilty of a crime gets beaten, and
then he goes back to work, surely it is better than sending him
to prison?' I supposed the offender's view might depend on how
badly he was beaten. On another farm a youth who had been
caught stealing was sentenced by his peers to have all of his
fingers broken with a hammer.

Before leaving, I asked about Bosman. 'The old people didn't
like him much,' Deon said. 'Mostly what they read was the Bible,
which they regarded as true stories, and they couldn't understand
fiction, even if it was based on real life. Also my grannie said he
was difficult to live with, because he came from the city and he
liked all kinds of fancy food we didn't have here.'

My last stop was the old farm school, where I listened to the
wind that had told Bosman stories of long ago. But all I heard was
the creaking of the rusty gate and the distant drone of vehicles on
the highway to Botswana. The place still had a frontier feel to it
that was the essence of South Africa sensed by Bosman, but his
characters were long gone. I noticed the name of the farm was
Heimweeberg, which means Nostalgia Mountain.

Not everybody had left. Driving back to Zeerust, I passed a
wooden sign pointing up a dirt road to an empty horizon. It said:
'Cabbage 20 kms'.

'I said to one of these boys on one occasion, when he came
through a rather heavy fire: "You will get hit one of these
days, riding about like that when the shells are flying." "I
pedal so quick, sir, they'll never catch me!" he replied. These
boys didn't seem to mind the bullets one bit. They were ready

to carry out orders, though it meant risking their lives every time.'

Thus wrote Colonel Robert Baden-Powell, hero of the siege of Mafeking in the Anglo-Boer War, shining example of all that was best and pluckiest in Victorian Britain, and founder of a cadet corps in the beleaguered town that grew into the Boy Scout movement. The Boy's Own Adventure style of writing was typical of the man. His nonchalant, stiff-upper-lip telegrams were regarded as masterpieces of British understatement and courage under fire, for example: 'October 21, 1899. All well. Four hours of bombardment. One dog killed.' Baden-Powell loved every minute of it, and in later years progressively exaggerated the number of Boers involved from 5,000 to 12,000. When the 271-day siege was lifted by a relief force on 17 May 1900, the news was greeted with unprecedented jubilation in the streets of London.

In fact the Boers made only one serious attempt to capture Mafeking and maintained a fairly civilised siege, rarely fighting on Sundays and inflicting minimal casualties on the garrison of 800 men. This may have been because of the fact that the town, then capital of the British Protectorate of Bechuanaland, had no military importance whatever. When the soldiers left it reverted to a sleepy frontier town where nothing much happened until the 1970s, when a new city suddenly appeared in the *veld* beside it and was pronounced the capital of the 'independent' Republic of Bophutatswana. When this fatuous illusion eventually disappeared, the only noticeable effect on Mafeking was that its name had reverted to the Tswana spelling of Mafikeng, which means 'place of stones'. My guide book said: 'The history of Mafikeng is interesting, but you don't have to visit it to discover this. The present reality is mundane and hot.' Undeterred, I drove from Zeerust across a vast, bush-covered plain to see the place where our mustachioed hero beat the Boers with the help of brave lads rushing around doing good deeds under the misapprehension that they could cycle faster than bullets.

My first thought on reaching the town was to wonder how the Brits had defended it in the absence of hills or any other natural features. My next thought was: why bother? Mafikeng was a bland South African country town that had never possessed anything of note other than a railway station, a cattle market and one of the biggest creameries in the country. Time appeared to move slowly here. The lamp-posts were bedecked with posters for a political conference that had taken place six weeks before.

At least there was an entertaining museum, presided over by a little Welshman in a black yachting cap who had emigrated to Swaziland thirty years before. This incongruous character told me he had been trying to 'correct imbalances' in the exhibits, in accordance with the new order of things. This was apparent from a display in the entrance hall about Robben Island and its last famous prisoners, which had nothing to do with Mafikeng but was probably of more interest to local Tswanas than a dust-up between white soldiers at the turn of the century. Exhibits relating to the siege had been relegated to a side-room, but there was enough of interest to pass a couple of hours out of the midday heat. There were tattered remnants of the Union Jack that had flown above the British HQ at Dixon's Hotel, fragments of Boer shells, and a porcelain beer mug bearing the initials *BP* and the legend *The heroic defender of Mafeking*, followed by the maxim *Sit tight and shoot straight*. All jolly stirring stuff, I thought. Photographs showed Mafeking at the time as an untidy settlement of single-storey buildings, much like a frontier town in the American West, and Baden-Powell looking dignified in khaki tunic and the world's first Boy Scout hat.

There was also an account of 'the decisive role of black people without whose assistance the British garrison would have been defeated', a factor which our hero curiously omitted to mention in his pithy dispatches. Historians now tell us that as the siege dragged on African recruits became more active than whites in the defence of the town and the procurement of supplies, notably raiding the Boer lines and returning with cattle destined for the tables of the whites. On Christmas Day, 1899, ten weeks after the siege began, leading citizens joined Baden-Powell for a sumptuous dinner at Reisle's Hotel. Beginning with anchovy croutons and soup, they proceeded to oyster patties, calves tongue, poultry, nine varieties of joint, Christmas pudding, mince pies and Sandringham jellies. On the same day the local magistrate wrote that he was distressed by hungry natives leaning on his garden wall, staring at him and pleading for food. Our hero's response was that the toe of the boot should be applied to such grousers. He was more concerned with his young white acolytes: 'It is safe to say that there would have been no further development of the scout movement as we know it had there been no siege . . . the possibility of putting responsibility on to boys and treating them seriously was brought to the proof in Mafeking.'

I went to look for the site of Dixon's Hotel, the British headquarters, but it had become a furniture store overlooking a noisy street market. Baden-Powell's command post nearby was a clothes shop, and all that was besieging these erstwhile bastions of empire was a swarm of buses and trucks and blasts of African music from loudspeakers in the market. My good deed for the day was to get out of town.

16

She speaks to our ancestors and the rain comes

It is not easy to meet Modjadji V, the Rain Queen of the Lobedu, keeper of ancient secrets and necromancer supreme. For a start, tradition decrees that she lives unseen in a sacred forest high on a mountain, protected by an impenetrable wall of incantations and fearful spells. Even for chiefs, protocol requires more than a few days to arrange an audience with a legendary figure whose great-grandmother inspired Rider Haggard's *She*. But I had come a long way, so I tried anyway.

It was the legend of the Rain Queen that had drawn me to the valley of the Molototsi River, where the foothills of the Drakensberg Mountains tumble to the lowveld of the old Northern Transvaal. The story goes that in the sixteenth century a princess of the Karanga people in present-day Zimbabwe had a child as a result of an incestuous relationship with her brother. Fleeing the wrath of her father, she had the presence of mind to steal her tribe's magic rain-making medicines before heading south with a few retainers and finding refuge in a forest by the Molototsi.

Nothing much happened for about three centuries, until an eccentric scion of the princess announced that ancestral spirits had decreed he should murder his sons and found a female dynasty by impregnating his daughter. This done, he gave his daughter-bride the hereditary title of Modjadji, meaning Ruler of the Day, and entrusted her with the secret rain-making rituals of the Karanga. In a land where rainfall is erratic, the ability to control it by supernatural means – or at least to forecast it with remarkable accuracy – is widely regarded as big-time *juju*. In due course, Modjadji I and her successors became African Delphic Oracles whose mythical powers were revered by every chief within a radius of 2,000 miles. Even great martial tribes such as the Zulus and the Swazis paid them homage, and the land of Modjadji became known as loBedu, the Land of Offerings. The little tribe by the Molototsi was, so to speak, singing in the rain.

In the late nineteenth century a missionary by the name of Coillard reported that Modjadji's sanctuary lay in a wooded gorge. 'With the exception of a few privileged ancients none dare approach the sacred grove,' he wrote. 'No stranger is allowed to penetrate into the village of this chieftainess; it can only be seen from afar, perched upon the mountain side, like an eagle's eyre, on the edge of a black forest. She herself is invisible, so that certain individuals take it upon themselves to doubt her existence. Those best informed assert that Modjadji really exists, and they even add that she is immortal.' This proved subsequently not to be the case. When it became apparent that rain-making powers tended to diminish with old age and illness, the early queens graciously committed ritual suicide by sipping poison extracted from the brain and spinal cord of a crocodile. In his *Lost Trails of the Transvaal*, the historian T.V. Bulpin wrote: 'Just what manner of life was led by these secretive queens will never be known. Doubtless their strict seclusion had its pleasures, but in most respects they were martyrs to the rituals and legends which their own cunning had first fabricated.'

A helpful lady in the tourist office in Tzaneen, the main town in the region, said things had changed. 'I think you'll be

disappointed. They've built a modern house for her to receive
guests, and she just comes out and sits on a plastic seat. It's a
shame, really. They should have kept it all secret.' She thought
my prospects of an audience with Modjadji V in the next few
days were slight, but she would make the necessary contacts. In
the meantime, she suggested I have a chat with Jurgen Witt, the
curator of the local museum.

So I went looking for Herr Witt, and on the way I found a cure
for Aids. It was lying on a wooden table outside a fish and chip
shop, among a neat array of roots, twigs, powders and murky
liquids being sold by a young man with a dazed expression called
Philip. He claimed to be a *sangoma*, a traditional medicine man,
and with a bit of this and a dash of that he could banish everything
from malaria to constipation and impotence. The remedy for Aids
consisted of two bulbous roots and a dried leafy twig, immersed
in a litre of water and cooked for five minutes. A cup of this
liquid in the morning and another at night for ten days would
do the trick, and it cost only £3, which seemed remarkably good
value. Philip swore he had cured lots of men of Aids. 'Very
strong *muti*,' he said. Once on the road to recovery, his clients
could avail themselves of an ochre-coloured powder guaranteed
to restore their virility. A spoonful with porage and the average
man could satisfy five women a night, or the same woman five
times if he preferred, Philip assured me. At this point a smartly
dressed young black man with a mobile phone joined us, and I
asked his opinion of the aphrodisiac. 'Sure it works,' he said,
'even ten times a night.' Philip gave us a crooked grin.

Herr Witt had had an eventful life. As a young man he had fought
with a German anti-tank unit on the Russian front, and then had
been jailed in East Germany for anti-communist activities. On
escaping he fled to Sweden, where he worked as a lumberjack
and a bookseller, and tried prospecting for iron ore in the Arctic.

In Africa since 1952, he had developed an interest in archaeology, acquired a collection of Africana that filled the Tzaneen museum and been embraced by the Rain Queen as an honorary white brother. If he had lived a century before, Haggard would probably have written a book about this veteran adventurer, a tall, powerful figure with silver hair who looked as if he was still in good shape. If I had been a Russian tank driver, I would not have wanted him anywhere near me.

He confirmed that the court of Modjadji had lost some of its lustre. Officially she had become a Christian, and with the influences of Western religion and education her powers had diminished. 'Too many people demand to see her now, and I feel this does not serve a good purpose. It is degrading, and a further step downwards to the dissolution of this little kingdom. But she is still the spiritual leader, the divine queen.' You could tell Herr Witt cared, and you wished he could have met Modjadji's great-grannie. Pushing aside a sacred drum, he produced a map of the royal compound showing the *khoro*, or meeting place, in a stockade approached through a defile of tall wooden staves. This was where visitors were required to remove their shoes and approach the royal presence on bended knee, while clapping their hands and so on. I was then shown a photograph of the present queen, taken at her coronation in 1982 when she was about fifty. The Ruler of the Day appeared to be an ordinary woman with somewhat coarse features, sitting on a wooden throne and cloaked from head to foot in a leopard skin robe. It occurred to me that the fur would have looked much better on its original owner. Herr Witt was standing beside her, wearing smartly pressed shirt and shorts, along with one of her brothers, who was dressed in a scruffy track suit. 'She is not being paid the same respect as before,' Herr Witt said sadly. 'She becomes more and more of a show, like a wax figure of Madame Tussaud.'

The lady in the tourist office did not have encouraging news. The only courtier who could officially present me to Modjadji was absent on business, but she had arranged for a lesser minion to show me the royal compound in a couple of days' time, and maybe he could fix an audience. So I checked into a guest house on a fruit farm, and spent the next day exploring the surrounding highlands, which were known as the 'Land of the Silver Mist'. Actually it was more like the Land of the Grey Clouds and Lots of Rain, but the forests of bluegum and pine and tranquil lakes with rowing boats moored in the shallows were cool and fresh and a welcome relief from the heat and dust of the plains. I felt at home among the hills, meandering along quiet roads past signs for Glenshiel Country Lodge, a tea garden in a place called Cheerio and Stanford College, 'an independent English boarding school'. On visiting a plantation of exotic fruits, I learned that in 1672 W. Hughes, physician to Charles II, discovered avocados in Jamaica and enthused: 'It nourisheth and strengtheneth the body, corroborating the spirits and procuring lust exceedingly.' All of this was barely 30 miles from the realm of the Rain Queen, but it could have been another planet.

Herr Witt had given me explicit directions. I should head for a place called Duivelskloof (Devil's Ravine), follow a minor road along the banks of the Molototsi, look out for a dirt road by a petrol station in the valley and follow it for 5 kilometres into the mountains and with luck I would reach Modjadji's *kraal*. 'Not sure you'll make it in this weather without a four-wheel drive, though,' he added doubtfully. If the highlands around Tzaneen were reminiscent of Perthshire, the valley of the Molototsi lay in tribal Africa, a land of brooding mountains cloaked in dense vegetation, red dirt roads winding through hamlets of mud huts and thatched rondavels, and the air sweet with wild scents and woodsmoke. The track to Modjadji's village looked passable, despite two days of rain. I squelched up into the hills, past flocks of goats and barefoot children, and stopped halfway up to admire the view. From the patchwork of fields and villages far below, a murmur of voices and laughter drifted in the hot, still air. The forest echoed to the trilling and chuckling of birds. Everything was lush, humid and teeming with life. In the distance sullen clouds clung to the mountains like shrouds, but occasionally brilliant shafts of sunlight parted them like magic wands.

I announced my arrival in the royal village with a crescendo of whining, crunching and spattering as my car slewed at speed up a muddy bank and came to a shuddering halt by the gates of a municipal building where an old man was waiting to receive me. Derrick Mampeule was wearing shabby European clothes, but there was no mistaking the dignified bearing of a nobleman in the court of the Rain Queen. 'We were told to expect you,' he announced graciously. 'I will be your guide.' Before proceeding to the royal compound, he wished to show me the sacred cycad forest, which lay further up the mountain. Cycads are arboreal dinosaurs that have been around for 60 million years, and wandering among them on top of an African mountain is one of nature's great experiences. They begin life looking like monstrous pineapples, and gradually metamorphose into gigantic bananas with spiky leaves on top. They are the punk rockers of the tree world. This particular reserve had the biggest concentration of one species (*Encephalartos transvenosus*) on earth, and Derrick pointed out a path that dropped steeply among them into the heart of the forest. 'The way is too hard for me,' he said. 'I will wait for you here.'

It was like stepping back a long, long way in time. Within seconds I was enveloped in a moist green cocoon in which shafts of light played around fantastic shapes and shadows. Strange bird calls echoed across a deep valley, dimly visible in swirling mist. The only other sound was rain dripping from the forest canopy. This was Mother Africa in all her voluptuous beauty, and she was utterly enchanting. As two butterflies with midnight blue wings fluttered in front of me, I thought: Never mind Rain Queens, it was worth coming here just for this. The stony path continued to wind down the mountain, but I had no idea how far it was to the river that Derrick said lay at the bottom. He said it was 'very far', which could mean anything from a couple of miles to the coast of Mozambique. My knee was hurting from a stumble and it was oppressively hot, so I decided reluctantly to return. As I retraced my steps there was a sudden flapping sound. It could have been a woman hanging out sheets to dry in a distant village, but I prefer to think it was a pterodactyl startled by my approach.

In a clearing above the forest there was a small information centre, in which Modjadji V's coronation throne and leopard skin were displayed. The throne was a simple, high-backed wooden chair carved with the tribal symbol of a bush pig, and the robe was wonderfully soft. In general I prefer leopards to royal families, and I stroked the fur sadly. The centre also sold souvenirs. I bought a refrigerator door magnet in the shape of a rhinoceros bearing the legend 'Modjadji', and I could almost hear Herr Witt groaning.

Derrick was still hopeful. 'If you meet the queen you must take a present,' he said. This had not occurred to me, and this was not a great place to shop for royal gifts. Happily Derrick had the solution. 'A hundred rands would be okay,' he said. I felt the mystique beginning to evaporate. Then a big woman sprawling indolently at a bare desk in the municipal offices put an end to it. Only Mr Victor Mathekga had the authority to arrange an audience with Modjadji, she announced, and Mr Victor Mathekga was not here. End of story. But I could have a look at the *kraal* if I liked. So Derrick and I strolled across a clearing on the outskirts of the village to a narrow avenue of wooden staves leading to the royal stockade. I had been hoping for a few magnificently muscled praetorian guards with spears, but the only subjects of Her Majesty in evidence were youths in jeans and T-shirts lounging beneath a tree. Instead of tribal drums and incantations, rap music was blaring from a grocery store.

At the end of the defile lay the *khoro*, the sacred meeting place. Derrick dutifully removed his shoes but assured me I could keep mine on because it was muddy. Finally I was about to enter the inner sanctum where generations of Rain Queens had received ambassadors from the greatest tribes in Africa; this was where children had been sacrificed, and grisly rituals performed with the skins of previous queens, expertly removed after death; this was a place of myths and legends that had enthralled half a continent. What I saw was three barefoot urchins kicking a ball around a lamp-post in an otherwise empty clearing. Then from beyond the stockade I heard an unmistakable Texan drawl and a burst of gunfire. 'The court has television now,' Derrick said. As the heart of darkness, it left something to be desired.

But it was a friendly place. The court beyond the *khoro* comprised dozens of mud and brick huts and rondavels in a maze of muddy paths, each with a little orchard of fruit trees and people who smiled easily. '*Legai?*' they asked me politely, How are you? I learned to reply '*Rehona*', which means okay, and was rewarded with tours of simple dwellings in which food was stored in huge freezers and cooked over open fires on stone floors. The court of Modjadji, like much of rural Africa, was in a period of technological transition. Everybody seemed to be related to Derrick. He said the queen was his cousin. But then he said Victor the absent councillor was his brother, although they had different fathers. Introducing three women outside a hut, he said: 'This one is my sister, this one is the wife of my cousin, and this one is my cousin but she is my sister.'

I gave up on tribal genealogy, and asked him where the queen lived. 'Up there,' he said, pointing vaguely at the hill. I was tempted to stroll up and say hello, but Derrick was a courteous old man and I didn't want to get him into trouble with his extended family. So I asked him instead about the brick houses scattered among the traditional buildings. 'It is the new style. The young ones don't want to live in grass houses any more. They want to build like you people, because now they are educated.' And I bet they get their weather forecasts on TV, I thought gloomily.

But some of the old folk still kept the faith. On leaving, I asked Derrick if Modjadji still made rain. 'Yes, that is our belief. Just like you people pray to God for rain, she speaks to our ancestors and the rain comes.' I never got to see the Rain Queen. But her magic had gone, and I almost wished I had viewed her sanctuary only from afar, like the early missionaries. Then something struck me. As I entered Modjadji's realm, the skies had cleared after two days of rain. And as I drove back down the mountain her village disappeared in a torrential downpour. Pure coincidence, of course.

Heading towards the Limpopo, the northern boundary of South Africa, I came to a town named after a *voortrekker* leader who had died of malaria contracted on an epic journey to Portuguese East Africa in 1835–38. By the looks of it, Louis Trichardt had not missed much by leaving behind the settlement that bore his name. It had an interesting history as a lair of gun-runners and ivory traders, razed twice by neighbouring tribes who disapproved of such activities, but now it was a dreary place that seemed to have lost heart. In a coffee shop I met a white man who complained that the town was going to the dogs under a black administration. He said: 'Do you know the difference between a tourist and a racist in Louis Trichardt? Three months.' I had been considering staying the night, but decided to move on.

Driving east, I entered a land where ancestral spirits and python gods were fighting a losing battle against slot machines and fast food joints. It was called Venda, meaning 'Pleasant Land', and for centuries had been the home of a mystic tribe. Nobody knows for sure where the VhaVenda people came from, or when they first crossed the Limpopo. One day they were just there, with their myths and legends and pantheon of deities, which they distributed liberally in the rivers, lakes and forests of their new home. In the fastness of the Soutpansberg (Salt Pan Mountains), for centuries they repelled invaders and discouraged visitors, notably and probably wisely missionaries. It was not until 1898 that a Boer army of 4,000 men conquered Venda, at which point the locals had a word with their python god and a year later the Brits began to dismember the Boer Republics. With the exception of a bemusing episode of 'independence' under the apartheid bantustan system, the peaceable VhaVenda have been left pretty much to themselves since then.

I was aiming for a sacred lake whose waters came from the great sea that covered the earth before land was created. This was where the legendary python lived. Above it stood a forest where strangers ventured at the risk of angering creatures of the afterworld, in particular a white lion that guarded the burial grounds of chiefs. Neither seemed like a good place to spend the night, so I booked a room in the Venda Sun, a remote outpost of the empire of Sol the Sun King in the capital of the region, which was called Thohoyandou. It was named after a VhaVenda chief who mysteriously disappeared, and if the town suffered the same fate it would be no great loss.

It was the usual dismal collection of concrete boxes installed by South African architects whose idea of creativity was to put a potted palm in the parking lot. The Venda Sun, with all its brashness and seedy gambling halls, was bright and cheery and provided welcome comforts like a television channel featuring British football. It was mildly disconcerting to leave Old Trafford in the grip of winter, and stroll into the sweltering lobby of a hotel past a sign requesting clients to leave their guns at reception. The casino was small and raucous, packed with excited locals and chain-smoking Chinese with steadily diminishing piles of chips. I retreated to the pool for a swim by moonlight, to the befuddled amusement of a well-oiled crowd on the bar terrace. Then I found a sauna in a deserted gym. To my surprise it was switched on, so I lay down gratefully and switched off.

Mr Mashudu Dima was the man I wanted, the woman in the tourist office said. He was not only an experienced tour guide, he was an *inyanga*, a traditional healer, and he knew everything about the sacred lake and forest and the spirits that dwelled there. Unfortunately he was not working today, and nor was his telephone, but I could drive up to his house if I liked. This was easier said than done, as Mr Dima lived in a suburb in the hills where a muddy track made a valiant attempt to reach his home and gave up some way short of it. Abandoning my plucky little car in a ditch whence it had slewed, I was directed to a modern house where a young woman showed me in to meet her father.

Mr Dima was indeed the right man to guide me through the mystic world of the VhaVenda. His expertise had been called upon by no less than Mandela, who had invited him on visits to London and Berlin to explain the customs and traditions of his tribe. Mr Dima was a tall, slim figure with a neat salt and pepper beard and a professorial mien. He was fifty-eight years old, an articulate man with one foot in the spirit world and the other in the temporal, and equally at home in both. Sitting in his lounge surrounded by gadgets like remote-controlled TV and hi-fi, he explained why he did not eat fish. 'Anything that comes from water – fish, pythons, crocodiles – is taboo in our culture. If we take them out, the rivers will run dry. Even if we take insects from the water, there is no more rain. We must respect all things in the water.'

These were traditional beliefs that Mr Dima held to be an essential part of his culture, but they were not shared by the younger generation. He began discoursing on how life in Venda had changed: 'Before we were not sitting in houses like this. Then we were walking in the mountains, for 5 kilometres or even 10 kilometres in a day. When I was a child we never worried about having work because we had cattle, and we could plough, and there was plenty of food and we could eat fruit from the trees. Then they told us we must all live together in this place like this, and we must work like white men. In the old days we did not come home in the day to eat pap, but we stayed outside and ate the fruit from the trees, and we did not return until late in the afternoon. Young people nowadays do not know such food. When I was growing up, we ate meat only at Christmas or on special occasions. We mostly ate vegetables and salad, which is very healthy food. Now everybody is eating meat and getting sick.' Pointing to his trousers, he went on: 'Because you close up your body it cannot breathe. There is no air can get into my body. This is not living. Even we don't respect the chiefs any more. You can find them drinking beer in the shebeens. If they want to go to boogie, they go to boogie. What kind of chief is that? We had a king who was a young man, he went to the shebeens and he went with girls, and he ruled for only three years and then he was dead.'

Mr Dima said that traditional healers originally came from three tribes in Africa; the Masai, the Zulu and the VhaVenda. Now they were coming from all over the place, confidence tricksters with no powers or training who were debasing an ancient and noble profession. Worse, some of them were killing children for body parts for their bogus mumbo-jumbo. 'These people are not healers. It is simple. In our culture if you kill someone, the ancestors take away your healing powers. You are not a healer any more.' Almost as heinous in Mr Dima's view was the way these imposters obtained their medicines. 'We know the trees and the plants that cure sickness. But we take only one root from the west side of a tree and one root from the east side, because we know the tree must live. Now these people are taking all the roots, and the trees are dying.' He shook his head sadly, perplexed by the madness of the modern world. For a genuine *inyanga*, faith was vital. When I asked about the 'Aids cure' for sale in Tzaneen, he said: 'It is simple. If you believe these herbs can cure you then you will be well. But if you do not believe then you will stay sick.'

Mr Dima agreed to take me to the sacred burial grounds, but they lay deep in hill country, miles out of town, so we drove to the municipal offices to pick up a Land Rover. The vehicle was there, but the keys were not, and nobody knew where to find the man who had them. So we checked out a couple of garages, and an Afrikaner with a mobile telephone summoned his father who had a four-wheel-drive *bakkie*. The character who came to our rescue was a big, rotund man in khaki shirt and shorts, with knobbly tree-trunk legs rooted in huge boots. He had bushy eyebrows and an impressive white beard, and he was wearing a battered felt hat like an inverted flower pot. He looked like an outsized garden gnome. His name was Chris, and he had come equipped for our expedition with a crate of beer. I contributed pizza slices from a fast-food take-away, and Mr Dima said he was fine with his apples thank you.

They made an odd couple as we crammed into the cab of the *bakkie*, the bluff, hearty Afrikaner who called a spade a fucking shovel, and the quiet, thoughtful VhaVenda who never used one for fear of damaging root systems. As we were reversing out of the parking lot, we were blocked by a car driven by a black man who couldn't seem to make up his mind which way he was going. Eventually Chris stormed out and we heard him shouting: 'Take your car, and fuck off.' Mr Dima said quietly:

'He does not have good thoughts of black people.' I feared an uneasy atmosphere on the trip, but when Mr Dima began telling stories of the rivers and lakes Chris listened with interest. Soon the two of them were swopping tales and anecdotes in what was clearly a learning experience for both. Chris said he had been annoyed by a Vendan who had come to his house and, instead of knocking on the door, had sat outside, sounding a car horn. Mr Dima explained this was a courtesy. In Vendan culture you did not approach a man's home without being invited, so in the old days you stood outside and called him. Nowadays people used car horns, which admittedly was verging on bad manners. So what about the guy who came into the office of a friend of Chris's and sat in his best chair without being invited to? It is disrespectful to stand in the presence of a host, so the man sat down to show respect, Mr Dima said.

Chris mused on this for a while, then the subject turned to goats. He said if you hit a goat on the road and your car was damaged, nobody owned the goat. But if you put it in the back of your *bakkie*, a hundred Vendans would say where are you going with my goat? Mr Dima maintained a dignified silence, so I supposed it was true. One thing they agreed on was that the Indian community in South Africa was good for nothing. They had disproportionate power in government, and they sent their savings overseas. Chris said only one man in Africa knew how to deal with them. I knew what was coming, and turned to admire a buck cantering in the forest as he declared that the best thing that had happened was when Idi Amin took them all down to the docks and said to the rest of the world: Here's your fucking Indians, we don't want them any more.

Fortunately we were lurching along a muddy track through banks of cloud and mist towards the sacred Thathe Vondo forest, and the conversation turned to what lay ahead. It was where the bones of chiefs of the Thathe clan had been buried in wicker baskets since time began and were guarded for eternity by dreadful spirits. The ashes of others had been scattered on streams flowing into the lake below, which was called Fundudzi, the Lake of Homage. Among spectacular punishments one could expect for desecrating the forest was a plague of serpents. Residents of the lake included the *zwidutwane*, water sprites who were half creatures with one eye, one arm and one leg and who should be avoided by humans at all costs. This reminded Chris of a guy he once knew in Joburg.

Of a sudden we left a hillside scarred by commercial logging and entered dense woodland, past a wooden sign that said: 'Sacred Forest'. It did not say 'all ye who enter here abandon hope', but it warned visitors not to stray from the main path. This was hardly necessary, since it was enclosed by virtually impenetrable walls of giant hardwoods enveloped in tangled webs of ferns and lianas and creepers as thick as Chris's legs, which was saying something. We stopped by the biggest fig tree I had ever seen, and stepped into the wonderful, humid world of a cloud forest.

'This is the sacred place,' Mr Dima said. As usual he was speaking quietly, but his voice seemed to reverberate in the stillness of the forest. 'You are not allowed to pick flowers or take firewood. Whatever you see here is for the forest, it is not for you to take to your home. There is a monkey spirit, which can be dangerous. And there is a white lion here that protects the forest. You can hear him roar at midnight, but you cannot see him.' In fact I knew about the lion. The story goes that a chief called Nethathe had been a magician with the power to transform himself into animals to watch his people. Since lions were feared more than any other creature, his spirit naturally assumed this form to guard his burial place.

As Mr Dima was acquainting us with the forest dwellers of this world and the next, I caught glimpses of louries flashing crimson wing patches among the tree tops and heard the chatter of monkeys. But I searched in vain for the fabulous *Ndadzi*, the bird that flew on wings of thunder, flashing lightning from its eyes and bearing rain in its beak. One of its best tricks was dropping an egg at the foot of a tree, where it was instantly consumed by flames without leaving a trace of fire. Chris tried something similar, lighting his pipe with a match, which instantly flared out in the damp undergrowth, but it wasn't the same. I noticed Mr Dima carefully retrieved the spent match and put it in his pocket. Nearby was a magic waterfall, a shallow stream cascading over rocks, where we learned that Modjadji was not the only rain-maker around. 'If the waterfall makes a big noise we know there will be little rain,' Mr Dima explained. 'So we go to the chief's *kraal*, and his sister takes millet beer in a basket to the waterfall, and she pours it into the water and she talks to our ancestors and asks God to please give us rain so we can plant our mealies (sweetcorn). Then we have rain, and we have all our food, so every house must take one bag of mealies to the chief's *kraal* to say thank you, and then we eat them.'

An alternative favoured by the younger generation was to cruise down to the local fast-food store. They probably didn't listen to the stories of the spears, either. Traditionally the VhaVenda fought with bows and arrows. Spears were made not for war, but for remembering the ancestors. 'Each year in August when the leaves are pushing out, we take out the spears and count the ancestors for the children. We were not educated for writing names. So we take out the spears and say this is the spear of a certain man and we tell his story.' One of the reasons this custom was dying out was that the spears were disappearing from sacred sites near the lake, stolen by unauthorised visitors.

Piling back into the *bakkie*, we emerged from the forest onto a high ridge overlooking rondavels scattered in the bush. In the distance stood a towering wall of rock, and far below, enclosed by

steep hills, glittered the mystical blue waters of Lake Fundudzi. I
would have liked to walk along its shores, but Mr Dima said this
was forbidden without permission from the high priest of the lake
who lived on the other side of the mountain. Chris consoled me
with a parable about a herd of zebra led by a wild horse that could
be heard neighing in the wind but could never be seen. 'It's better
to imagine it than just see a horse eating grass in the *veld*. Just
like the lake. Better to look at it from here than go down and
see people washing clothes in it.' This was unusually lyrical for
Chris, and it was probably sound advice given the malevolent
presence of *zwidutwane* water spirits.

Mr Dima told us of an annual ceremony in which a child of
the chief was chosen to place an offering on a rock in the lake.
'A vine is tied to the child, who goes to the water. If the offering
is not accepted, the *zwidutwane* will cut the vine and the child
will be sucked down into the water. If the offering is accepted,
the child will walk on the water and then we blow reed pipes in
celebration.' I paused while jotting down the story at this point,
and looked at Mr Dima. 'I have seen this,' he said. I said this was
difficult to understand, and he replied: 'The culture of the black
people is different from the science of the white man.' Then I
recalled stories about a Palestinian Jew who walked on water
and rose from the dead, and wondered if the faith involved was
so different. I was still musing on this when Chris told us about
other scary local inhabitants. Once he had taken photographs from
a helicopter 600 feet above the lake, and he had been mystified by
what seemed to be scratches on the slides. On closer inspection,
they were partially submerged giant crocodiles. 'Big bastards,'
was how Chris described them.

Driving back to Thohoyandou, the conversation turned to
more prosaic matters. Mr Dima was despondent about the loss
of old traditions and disorder in tribal societies forced to adapt to
Western ways. 'Like the whole of Africa, we don't know what

we are doing now. Children don't respect our traditional ways any more. So how do we discipline them now? When they go to school they beat their teachers. They even carry guns. Everything is upside down.' Chris was more upbeat. A Jack of all trades, he had been thinking of trying something in eco-tourism and Mr Dima might be just the man to work with. 'We'll meet again,' he said when they parted and shook hands, which was something they would not have thought of doing before. When I dropped Mr Dima near his house, I watched him walking away, a dignified and slightly stooped figure picking his way carefully among the vegetable patches. There was something in him that invited respect and sadness. When he goes to the Sacred Forest for the last time, few will follow him with the same spirit.

Leaving Venda the next day, I took a high road that passed through a string of villages buzzing with colourful, relaxed groups of people who smiled a lot. I had time to enjoy my surroundings, because the road was an interesting obstacle course of cattle, goats, donkeys, the occasional concrete post, and little groups of people passing the time of day. Above me, eagles drifted across an azure sky. I liked Venda. The villages were scruffy to Western eyes, but the people were gentle and helpful, and the green hills and valleys they lived in were beautiful. It was on this leisurely drive through the Salt Pan Mountains that it occurred to me why I had not developed any particular fondness for South Africans during my sojourn as a journalist. The simple truth was that I hadn't got to know them.

Heading south, I came to a tearoom managed by a big friendly Venda woman. I asked her about spiritual customs, and she said: 'It is not like before. In the old days nobody would go to that forest, but now everybody goes and you don't hear the drums in the water any more. In the old days we had to bury our relatives in the mountains, but now we would rather do it near our homes.'

I said: 'So if they want to be buried in the mountains, they must walk there?'

'Yes,' she said, laughing, 'that is a very good idea.'

I hoped the distant rumble I heard was thunder.

17

You don't see the bodies lying around for long

There was a scuffling outside my tent. It had woken me from a fitful sleep with a start and a sense of danger. I lay still, listening to the unseen creature prowling on the other side of a deplorably flimsy barrier of brown canvas. Suddenly it snarled, the far wall of the tent snapped violently back and forth, and I let out a yell.

The call of the wild is something that is best heard from a safe distance. One can thrill happily to the roar of lions celebrating a kill from a sturdy stockade guarded by game wardens. One can observe with *sang-froid* a charging rhino from the upper branches of a stout tree. Listening fearfully to a feral beast losing its temper 3 feet away, when one is armed with only a fountain pen, is another matter. But this is what I had come to the Kruger National Park for.

'There is only one way to see the bush properly and that is to walk,' my guide Grant had said. 'Then you have to use all your skills to track the game and stay out of trouble. It's the only way to get a feel for the bush the way it was hundreds of years ago.' Accordingly we were in a camp by a river without so much as a 'no entry' sign between us and 146 species of wild creatures, many of them notoriously dangerous to man, prowling in the moonlight. I knew there were lions in the vicinity, because I had heard triumphal roars announcing a successful hunt. We had also seen the spoor of spotted hyaena, the undertakers of the savanna, which have been known to remove the faces of people sleeping in the bush. Thus when the walls of my tent began quaking I had vivid images of massive claws and bloody fangs ripping through the fabric and reducing me to digestible morsels.

Fortunately Grant was sleeping nearby, and the commotion brought him running. After a while, he said: 'Civet.'

'Sorry?'

'Just an old civet getting tangled up in the guy ropes.'

'Oh, right then.'

I consulted my field guide and learned that the African civet is a badger-like creature that preys on snakes and rodents. It is also partial to poultry, and will raid camp kitchens. My tent had been savaged by a badger, good grief.

I had come to the Kruger because it is one of the last places on earth where wild animals exist in anything like their natural state. The great herds and migrations are gone, but the incorporation of private reserves on the borders of the park have given its residents the freedom of a wilderness bigger than Wales. For the most part it is savanna bushveld, rolling plains covered with dull-coloured bush and relieved here and there by craggy *koppies*. It is a deceptive landscape, seemingly empty and yet teeming with life, echoing to the calls and murmurs of wildlife that predate the first Bushmen. Among bush willow, knob thorn and the great spreading marula are 'burn-outs', trees that have died of thirst, their bleached skeletons forming dramatic sculptures against the brilliant blue sky until they fall, devoured by termites or pushed over by elephants. The air is usually hot and dry and still, and when you lie down and gaze at the heavens you can almost sense the earth turning.

It is unwise to lie down anywhere in the vicinity of Cape buffalo, however. We discovered this on entering the park, when we encountered two massive bulls at a water hole. Fortunately we were in a jeep at the time and there was a high boundary fence between us. This did not prevent the beasts from glaring at us, snorting and giving every indication that they intended to charge through the fence and pulverise the jeep. The immense curving horns of the *Syncerus caffer* look like a handlebar moustache, which give their owners a vaguely comic look. This is entirely misleading, as buffalo are not noted for their sense of humour. They are justifiably among the 'Big Five' most dangerous mammals on earth. Fights between lion and buffalo have been known to last for two hours, and the lions do not always win. 'These are boys you don't want to meet in the bush on foot,' Grant said. 'They don't take kindly to strangers.' This was fairly obvious. After a while the bigger bull gave a final snort, flicked his tail, and trotted with his pal into the bush where they turned and regarded us defiantly like a couple of old buffers defending their cricket club from an assault by women's libbers.

At the other end of the zoological scale, I found out that cigarettes seriously damage the health of birds. Our party included half a dozen noisy Brazilian teenagers, who were smokers. When we arrived at camp Grant told them to shut up, and warned them not to throw away their fag ends because birds would eat them. The stubs swell to nine times their size in the birds' guts, so they no longer feel hungry and starve to death. 'Happens a lot round bush camps. But you don't see the bodies lying around for long, they're usually taken at night by hyaenas or cats.' By cats, he did not mean the fluffy kind that sit on windowsills.

When the first Portuguese navigators landed on the coast of Mozambique in 1497, they wisely gave this pestilent lowveld beyond the Limpopo a miss. It was a remote, mysterious land plagued by malaria and the dreaded tsetse fly, sparsely populated by nomadic tribes that had migrated south 800 years before. Few people who settled here survived. This was fine with the animals who roamed around happily until big white hunters turned up in the late nineteenth century and proceeded to decimate everything in sight. In an attempt to halt the slaughter Paul Kruger, then president of the Transvaal Republic, distinguished himself as one of the world's first ecologists by proclaiming a game reserve in part of the present park in 1898. This was about the time the Boers and the Brits became more interested in shooting each other than wild animals, so nothing much happened until after the war. The Brits then went ahead with the scheme and put in charge of it a peppery Scot by the name of Major James Stevenson-Hamilton, later Colonel, who 'commanded' the park from 1902 until 1946. Its legendary rangers in the early days included a Major A.A. Fraser, a giant of a man who drank large quantities of whisky, manifested total contempt for paperwork and on cold nights slept under his twenty-five dogs.

It is not as wild as it used to be, given that it has been invaded by tarred roads and permanent camps that accommodate thousands of visitors. The 'pathetic and dust-covered little wench', as Stevenson-Hamilton described the park in its early days, has become the *grande dame* of the South African tourist industry. But it is still possible to savour her untamed beauty far from the manicured lawns and souvenir shops of the tourist compounds, which is why I chose a walking expedition. We were based in one of the private reserves on the fringes of the park that had dropped its adjoining fences in 1994, having agreed to observe the Kruger's conservation policies. Our camp was a few tents on the banks of the Klaserie River, which I never saw because it was obscured by reeds so dense and tall that Grant said a herd of buffaloes could move through them without being seen. Bathing in the river was not encouraged.

As we arrived, a sweet smell of woodsmoke was wafting from the cooking area around a mighty jackalberry tree that was at least 100 feet high and looked as if it had been there for ever. The oven comprised two shallow holes in the earth, into which a big black cooking pot was placed on hot charcoals, with more hot coals heaped on top. This was the domain of Lettie, a Shangaan woman who spoke hardly any English and no Afrikaans. When she was not working, I would see her sitting on a little wooden seat at the back of her kitchen looking out at the bush. She would sit like that, hardly moving, for hours. Once I asked her through gestures what she was thinking about, and she just smiled. I sensed Mother Africa shrugging her shoulders at the white man again.

My own favourite spot for contemplating this wilderness was the lavatory, the one incongruous luxury of the camp, a flushing toilet screened on three sides by a wooden fence and open on the fourth to the river. From this fine perch, with the sun warm on my back and a gentle breeze sighing through the reeds, I could listen to the trilling of birds and watch for movement by the river. One day I was rewarded by the sight of two impala making their way delicately down the opposite bank and drinking their fill, oblivious to my presence. Rarely can a person have felt as content with his station in life and so at one with the beasts and the birds of the air.

Then Grant introduced me to the scorpion in the shower. It was quite a small scorpion, but it had taken residence in a hole in the ground at the entrance to the shower, which consisted of a suspended bucket with a spray tap beneath it. 'It's here most nights, so I tend to wear *takkies* when I take a shower,' Grant said. I like most animals, and I am happy to share the planet with those I do not like, but scorpions do not come into either category. Accordingly, at a propitious moment, I peed carefully and copiously into its nest and had the satisfaction of never seeing it again. I suspect I may have irretrievably damaged the web of life in this little corner of Africa, but I have no regrets. There are times when the survival instinct dictates no mercy.

Grant would not have approved, because he was of the new generation of *bwana* who has degrees in zoology and botany and has never shot anything living. In the bush he carried a Yugoslavian ZCZ .458 bolt-action rifle, but he had never used it. 'Most of the good guys have never fired a round,' he said. They relied on bushcraft, instinct and common sense to avoid trouble. They did not, for example, venture out at night on foot. Those who did tended to get eaten, or pay the ultimate price for disturbing a black mamba snake. In this respect, the lions had proved to be efficient border guards. The eastern edge of the park extended for almost 250 miles along the border with Mozambique, inviting incursions by illegal immigrants fleeing poverty and civil war. They usually jumped the fence and crossed at night to avoid the game wardens, Grant said. 'They move for a while then they sleep. If nobody is looking out, the lions take them. For a lion food is food. You walk across the park at night, you take the risk.'

So when we went hiking in the bush, we went early in the day before the heat frazzled everything and when the predators were digesting their nocturnal kills. In their absence, there was much to discover. On our first sortie we heard the raucous cries of baboons and learned it was possible to play with them from a safe distance. Every animal had a 'comfort zone', Grant explained, and if you entered it they felt threatened. In the case of baboons it was about 70 yards. If you stayed out of range and made exaggerated movements, they would mimic you. To prove the point, he faced a troop about 100 yards away and made a sweeping gesture with his right arm; we were treated to the sight of four baboons saluting us with elaborate courtesy.

Within a couple of hours we had discovered how to find water by following a particular bird at sunset (the double-breasted sandgrouse), catch venomous spiders with blades of grass, and get high by licking toxic frogs, which is a popular diversion among South American Indians. 'You have to know which frogs to lick and which not to lick, of course,'

Grant pointed out. We also inspected the faeces of a young giraffe.

'How d'you know it's young?' one of our party asked.

'Because they're close together. If they'd come from a greater height they'd be more spread out,' replied our Sherlock Holmes of the *veld*. Elementary, really.

Grant loved his job, and I could see why. Walking through the bush in the freshness of the morning, with dust on your boots and the spoor of big game all around you, is the best way to experience life in the wild. I was musing on harmony between man and nature when the latter intruded as a dark form flitting through the trees and a crescendo of hooves. It emerged in a clearing 100 yards away, shaking a massive horned head and making it abundantly clear he resented our presence on his territory. 'Just stand still,' Grant said unnecessarily. The wildebeest, or gnu, is an ungainly creature with the front of an ox, the rear of an antelope, and the tail of a horse. It is known for eccentric behaviour, including frantically shaking its head, bucking, running around in circles and rolling in the dust. This is thought to result from fly larva that wander up its nostrils and nibble on its brain. Evidently the maggots were bothering this fellow more than we were, because with a final angry toss of his head, he turned tail and disappeared in a cloud of dust.

Our next encounter was with a lone giraffe, loping along with a stately gait like a tall ship in a light swell. Docile appearances can be deceptive, however, as hunting lions have found to their dismay. Giraffe are the lion's most tricky prey, Grant informed us. 'It involves a lot of pride work, they circle it, then they sneak up on it and try to scare it so it slips. If that doesn't work they jump on its legs, but they've got to be careful of the hooves. One kick will break a lion's jaw and that's it – it dies of hunger.'

After all this excitement, our guide decided it was time for us to lie down and listen to the land. So we climbed a *koppie* and lay among rocks in the shade of Marula trees, and looked up at the sky and listened. At first there was nothing. Then, as our ears became attuned to the quietness, we began to hear a tidal wave of sound welling up from the plains, a multi-layered murmur of millions of bird calls that suggested a vast crowd of people chanting in the far distance. Then one of them came to call. It was a brown snake eagle, wheeling above us like a shark circling its prey, dropping to inspect us until we could see its bright eyes glinting in the sun. I was reminded of the name the Gaels gave to the white-tailed eagle that soared over the sea cliffs of Scotland, *Iolaire suil na-grein*, which means 'eagle with the sunlit eye'. A movement on the ground sent its African cousin veering away, but soon it was followed by a bateleur, an eagle with a curiously unsteady flight. With hardly any tail, it careens from side to side on canted wings like a nervous tightrope walker. Among these predatory dive bombers, swallows from Europe were darting around like fighter planes. Watching them you wondered at such little creatures travelling such great distances.

This was all very well, but the Brazilian kids wanted action. They wanted to see the big stuff, preferably at close quarters. This meant driving into the bush at dusk, when the carnivores became hungry and the herbivores became nervous. Before setting out I consulted *Signs of the Wild*, an excellent field guide by Mr Clive Walker, for a few pointers on what we might encounter. Lions being one of the big attractions of the Kruger, I read with interest that they have excellent sight, hearing, and sense of smell. On encountering a lion on foot, it is important to remain absolutely still and under no circumstances run. Details to look out for include the tail lashing up and down and the ears flattening, which indicate the beast is about to charge. It runs slowly at first and then more swiftly, somewhat crouched, with the head held low and the tail erect and stiff. 'In this situation it is very difficult to remain still,' Mr Walker concedes. 'One's inherent desire is to flee, but this carries with it the certainty of a permanent end to lion-watching.' It should be noted that the chances of shooting a charging lion are remote. The author offers no advice on what to do in such an extreme situation, although he notes helpfully that his trackers once halted a charging lioness by shouting at her. She apparently lost her nerve and braked about 5 yards from them. I made a mental note not to get out of the Land Rover.

The predator I most wanted to see was not the lion, which was a fairly common sight in the park, but the more elusive leopard. This svelte creature of the night has always fascinated me, and my desire to see one in the wild had been heightened by Willie's campfire stories in the Marico. According to the experts, *Panthera pardus* is solitary, secretive and mainly nocturnal. It is cunning, more silent than lions and an adept climber. The call is a coughing, rasping sound. Less easily seen on foot than any other carnivore, it is extremely dangerous when wounded, cornered or persistently disturbed (as the big white hunter from Joburg discovered in the Marico). It eats anything from fish to birds and dogs, but is particularly partial to baboon and will climb to the topmost branches of a tree in pursuit of one. I remembered reading that it is also a more efficient killer than the lion, dealing death swiftly by biting through the throat and neck. Any leopard that crossed my path could rest assured it would be treated with the utmost respect.

For a while nothing happened. An hour passed and all we saw was a little bird with turquoise wings that Grant identified as a lilac-breasted roller. I was getting bored driving around the seemingly empty wilderness, which was not nearly as much fun as feeling its grit beneath your boots. Then there was a blur of movement and four buffaloes appeared on a track ahead of us, and I was pleased to be in the Land Rover. They did what their species tend to do a lot, which was look fierce and glare at us. It was High Noon in the Kruger, and this path wasn't big enough for all of us. So we backed off and made a detour, which seemed to suit everybody. After that things happened quickly. A herd of wildebeest, startled by our approach, cantered across a clearing. Then zebra grazing ahead of us were alerted to our presence by nervous impala leaping into the bush like ballet dancers. Then something big and dark and heavy moved through a thicket close by, and came into a clearing and stood stock still.

The first thing to know about a white rhinoceros is that it is not white. It is in fact very dark and menacing-looking. The name comes from a mistranslation of the German word for 'wide', referring to its mouth. What strikes one most about meeting an animal like this in the wild for the first time is its oddness and its size. It is heart-stoppingly massive, exuding a raw power that is awesome. Even from the protection of a Land Rover, one regards this armour-plated battering ram with an evil spike at the business end with a touch of anxiety. When it got wind of us it trotted off into the bush.

Grant said to me: 'Got your camera?'

'Yes.'

'Let's go.'

He grabbed his rifle and jumped out, and without thinking I followed him in the direction the rhino had taken. It took me about ten seconds to realise what we were doing and to wish I had stayed in the vehicle. Let me admit here that I am no daredevil. The adrenalin-pumping big white hunter approach is not my style; I am not your bungee-jumping sort of chap. So tracking an unpredictable beast weighing several tons tends to make me uneasy. I wanted to ask pertinent questions about the behaviour of white rhinos, and in particular their attitude to men stalking them, but this was not the time for a zoology lesson. So I crept on, trying to banish from my mind the image of the horned one bursting from the bush in a murderous charge. Eventually I whispered: 'What do we do if it charges?'

'Stand still.'

Easy for him to say, him with the gun. Happily, from my point of view, the wind changed as we tried to circle the creature and it caught our scent and legged it. Back in the Land Rover, Grant said there had been nothing to worry about. White rhinos are fairly placid animals and less disposed to attack than their smaller but more belligerent black cousins. I flicked through Mr Walker's field guide, and learned that white rhinos can reach speeds of 25 m.p.h. when upset. In the event of a 'fast approach', he suggested getting behind a tree. This seemed more sensible than standing still and hoping for the best, and I filed the strategy for future use.

Soon afterwards, we came across a lone giraffe, and we regarded each other with curiosity. Of all of nature's odd creations, the giraffe is among the oddest. I felt as if we were being observed by a genial lighthouse.

As night fell, the air became soft and we heard a haunting bird call that Grant said was a fiery-necked nightjar. A young hyaena skulked alone through the bush, its red eyes glowing like coals, then a scrub hare hopped across the track and our guide said: 'Good lion food, easy to catch.' Birds of the night flew past on eerily silent wings, elongated and tapered to reduce sound so they could detect their insect prey. When the Southern Cross appeared like a ghostly kite, we learned how to use it to locate due south and to calculate the time. Grant reckoned it was indicating about 9 p.m., and he was twelve minutes out. We were lurching along a dry river bed, scanning the banks with a searchlight, when one of our party said she had seen something. We stopped and peered along the beam of light, but all we saw was trees. 'Nice tree,' I said. 'Yeah, show us another one,' another wit commented. Then, in the undergrowth, we saw the eyes: steady, unblinking, watching us. And they were amber. Grant lowered his binoculars and whispered: 'We've struck lucky. It's a leopard.'

We edged forward and stopped about 70 yards from the prone figure, which Grant identified as a female on the prowl for an evening meal. We regarded each other warily for a while, then she loped off into the bush. Grant guessed she was circling us, and sure enough a few minutes later we spotted her dark form slinking across our tracks. We turned and headed slowly back down the river bank. Rounding a bend, I found myself looking into the eyes of the leopard, which was crouching on a level with my head, barely 5 yards away. The first experience, wrote Robert Louis Stevenson, can never be repeated. The first love, the first sunrise, the first South Sea island, he recalled as 'memories apart that touch a virginity of sense'. Coming face to face with a hunting leopard, with nothing between you but fresh air, comes into the same category as one of the greatest thrills nature has to offer. Electrifying is a word that comes to mind.

Possibly because I was sitting in front of the open vehicle, she fixed her gaze on me and I found myself being mesmerised by limpid, dangerous, yellow eyes. Given the circumstances, I felt strangely at peace. So did the leopard, apparently, who was observing me with no sign of hostility. She seemed fairly relaxed, and I had an illusion that I could reach out and stroke that magnificent head and silky fur, that she would understand I admired her, and she would purr. Fortunately she dispelled this Dr Dolittle nonsense by yawning, exposing a fearsome set of incisors, and wandering off in search of dinner. The encounter had lasted five minutes. For a long time after she had gone the image of her was etched in the darkness. 'That's as good as it gets,' Grant said.

The fun wasn't over. A few minutes later Grant slammed on the brakes, stood up, and shouted to a girl sitting on the bonnet of the Land Rover to get her legs up. There was no mistaking the urgency in his voice. I peered ahead, but all I could see was a long stick near the front wheels. Then it began to move

in a sinuous, slithering manner. 'Black mamba,' Grant said, 'a
seriously unpleasant character'. In fact it is among the deadliest
snakes on the planet. Five millilitres of its venom will kill a
person, but to be on the safe side it usually injects more than
twice this amount. 'If it isn't treated quickly it can be a bit of
a problem,' Grant admitted. Cutting the wound and sucking out
the poison was a lot of nonsense – there goes another popular
myth – by the time you get your knife out, it is in the bloodstream
and gone. In the case of the mamba it was neurotoxic, meaning it
attacked the nervous system and induced coma within a couple
of hours. The good news was that you were then relieved of
the symptoms of severe throat pain, nausea, muscular agony
and extreme nervousness. The bad news was that you would
soon be dead. The other useful thing to know about mambas
is that they can grow up to 12 feet long, and rise one-third of
their body length to strike. Personally I cannot conceive of any
raison d'être for this abominable creature other than providing
material for horror stories. To hell with the web of life. I would
happily have driven over it.

Our final sighting was an African wildcat, squatting outside
a hare's burrow waiting for supper. It was tawny in colour and
looked like a house pet, which was not surprising because it
was descended from the cats of the ancient Egyptians who
domesticated the species around 4000 BC. Those still in the wild
were tasty morsels for leopards, so I passed on a friendly warning
about our earlier encounter and we headed back to camp.

The other big predator in the private reserves around Kruger is
man. Grant said conservation was expensive, and the smaller
game parks would struggle to survive on tourism. Foreigners
were willing to pay big money for game trophies, so they were
sold permits to shoot old animals or populous species like impala.
The proceeds were used to repair fences, employ game wardens,

dig water holes and maintain buildings and machinery. Grant said: 'If we've got an old lion that's likely to die or be killed in a few months, we figure it's better to get money for him from a trophy hunter that we can use to protect the next generation.' This seemed reasonable, but I still have problems sitting in a room surrounded by stuffed animals. I keep thinking they were killed by Neanderthals with high-powered rifles who risked little more than getting blood on their boots from the carcass. I once met an old Bushman in Namibia who had climbed into his cattle *kraal* with a spear and fought a lion that was attacking his livestock and killed it. He still bore the scars of the encounter on his back and arms. If he had thought of keeping it, that lion skin would have been a trophy to be proud of. Unlike the prey of big white hunters who probably never saw who fired the bullets that killed them.

Driving out of Kruger, I enjoyed a daydream of an old lion relaxing in his favourite armchair by the fire, spectacles balanced on his nose, pointing out to respectful cubs an array of hunters' heads on the walls of his study. 'That big chap with the whiskers gave us a bit of a fight,' I could hear the old man-eater saying.

18

Kaffirs lay on the ground like pumpkins . . .

Heading south, I came to the Land of the People of Heaven, which had seen more battles, treachery, pillage, and general mayhem than anywhere else in the country. Zulu means heaven and kwaZulu means place of the Zulu, and this is where the Boers and the Brits took it in turns in the nineteenth century to fight the greatest tribal army in Africa before turning their guns on each other. The result is a mosaic of historical sites extending into Natal with names that ring to the clash of musket and spear: Blood River, Isandlwana, Majuba, Ladysmith. More recently, the region maintained its reputation for blood-letting by staging a murderous conflict between Zulu and Xhosa in the first post-apartheid election campaign.

It was still not the safest place in the world, judging by a tourist brochure I picked up in Ladysmith. It advised visitors to avoid displaying valuables like jewellery and cameras, not to walk in deserted places or go out alone at night, and always to lock their car doors and keep the windows closed. Then they could relax and have a nice day. For such a perilous place, it seemed remarkably peaceful. Driving along a country road, I bravely kept the windows open to enjoy an endless vista of emerald hills, rolling grasslands and dark mesas that suggested a demented god had been going around slicing the tops off mountains. It seemed a land of plenty, with herds of fat cattle and goats, and handsome horses, and eagles swooping on meadows, and whitewashed rondavels with thatched roofs dotting the hillsides. All beneath an enormous sky in which puffs of brilliant white cloud hardly moved in the still air.

This was the land where a tall, brooding figure transformed an insignificant clan of farmers and herders into the most formidable fighting force on the continent and proceeded to conquer an area the size of Portugal. He was Shaka, a ruthless despot and inspired military tactician who taught the amaZulu (people of heaven) to fight in a way they had never done before. He scorned the traditional way of waging war, in which armies lined up about fifty paces apart and threw spears and insults at each other until one lot lost its nerve and ran away. Instead Shaka introduced the *iklwa*, the short stabbing spear, and the chest-and-horns attack formation in which the main body of an army advanced on the enemy while fast-moving companies of young men mauled its flanks. No more chucking spears and abuse from a distance; the bull's head of a Zulu army charged at speed and gored its foe at close quarters. When an *impi* of thousands of warriors was on the move, the earth trembled and so did anybody in its path.

At dawn on 16 December 1838, there was a substantial tremor when more than 10,000 Zulu warriors crossed the Ncome River in northern Natal and observed a Boer commando of 468 men drawn into a defensive *laager* of ox-wagons. What happened next convinced the Afrikaners they had a divine right to rule South Africa, and they started by renaming the Ncomo. Henceforth it was known as Bloedrivier, or Blood River.

The battlefield lies at the end of a dirt road that winds for more than 10 miles through hills east of Glencoe, a town with a name to conjure with in the anthology of massacres. It is a grassy plain bounded on one side by the river and on another by a *donga*, a deep cleft caused by soil erosion and overlooked by a low hill shaped like a saddle. At the entrance there was an unimpressive little museum with a dull presentation of Afrikaner history on information boards, and a few Zulu spears and shields for sale. Given the drama of the event, I had hoped for something more riveting than noticeboards and tacky souvenirs. But the Mecca of Afrikanerdom lay outside, where fifty-seven life-size replicas of ox-wagons cast in steel and bronze stood in the 'D' formation assumed by the Boer commando in 1838.

There was hardly anybody around as I strolled along a dirt track and through a meadow towards the wagons. Two German couples were buying wood carvings from Zulu youths tending cattle on the other side of a fence, but otherwise the *veld* was empty. When I stood in the middle of the *laager*, the only sound was of the wind sighing through long grasses by the river. Looking around the close formation of wagons, the parallels between the *voortrekkers* and the pioneers of the American West were compelling – gun and Bible against lance and spear, the firepower of incomers prevailing over the reckless bravery of natives, an inexorable conquest of fractious tribes. Except that this was no beleaguered wagon train of settlers fighting for their lives. It was a punitive expedition of well-armed men, spoiling for a fight to avenge the murder of a party of *trekkers* nine months before in the *kraal* of the Zulu chief, Dingane. Half-brother to Shaka, he had ensured a smooth transition of power a decade earlier by dispatching his sibling with a spear thrust. But when his army appeared on the banks of the Ncome, the white men were waiting for it.

As an early morning mist cleared, the Zulus charged in their bull-horn formation, and were decimated by musket fire and grapeshot. Three times they surged forward, and each time they were cut to shreds. 'Nothing remains in my memory except shouting and tumult and lamentations,' one of the Boers wrote later. 'We scarcely had time to throw a handful of powder in the gun and slip a bullet down the barrel, without a moment even to drive it home with the ramrod.' When the attack finally faltered, the Boer commander Andries Pretorius ordered horsemen out of the *laager* to pursue the Zulus. No prisoners were taken, and the battle became a massacre. Those who tried to hide in gulches or cross the swollen waters of the river were shot in droves. When the guns fell silent, more than 3,000 Zulu bodies were strewn around the wagons. Boer casualties amounted to three wounded. The Boer chaplain recalled: 'Kaffirs lay on the ground like pumpkins on a rich soil that has borne a large crop.' And the river had turned red.

I unhooked a chain on a gate in the perimeter fence and walked through a meadow to the river. The air was sweet with the scents of earth and grass, and drowsy with the drone of insects. The Zulu name for the river meant 'praiseworthy', because it was perennial and its banks were always green with tall grass. Now it was placid, a broad stream of muddy brown water meandering lazily around sandy shoals. Two herons were parked on one of the sandbanks, preening themselves. In the distant grasslands I could see the thatched roofs of Zulu *kraals*, and on the still air came the sounds of cattle lowing and a dog barking. Looking back at the *laager* from the banks of the river, it seemed dark and menacing. From the Zulu perspective it must have appeared small and vulnerable, until they came within range of its guns. I stood in the quietness and tried to imagine the cacophony of guns and war cries, the howls of pain and fear and the final terrible drumming of hooves. But time had dispelled the horror, and the wagons looked like an incongruous work of modern art left there by mistake.

Entering a time machine, I journeyed 20 miles and forty-one years forward to the scene of one of the most gallant defensive actions in British military history. On the afternoon of 22 January 1879 two Zulu regiments comprising more than 4,000 men attacked a mission station that the British had converted into a supply depot, with a garrison of 110 soldiers and thirty-four sick men in a makeshift hospital. The battle at Rorke's Drift lasted for twelve hours, and when the *impi* withdrew after being repeatedly repulsed it left behind 400 dead. British casualties were seventeen dead and ten wounded. Eleven Victoria Crosses were awarded, a record for a single action. I had long wanted to visit this place, after seeing the film *Zulu* in which Stanley Baker and Michael Caine portrayed classic *Boy's Own Adventure* heroes, valiant British soldiers in scarlet tunics standing shoulder to shoulder against hordes of murderous natives. A minor detail omitted from the film was that the Zulus were fighting because the British had invaded their land. It was an unprovoked incursion aimed at establishing British hegemony over southern Africa, and in particular control of its recently discovered diamond fields. Eleven days later, Zulu King Cetshwayo's part-time army of peasant farmers wiped out a major part of the central British column at a place called Isandlwana. It was a few hours after that when Zulu reserve units appeared at Rorke's Drift, 10 miles to the west.

Go and see Dave Rattray, friends advised, he'll tell you all you want to know about the battles. He ran a guest lodge in wooded hills above the Buffalo River, a few miles from the old mission station. The lodge was full but he put me up in an empty farmhouse nearby, and arranged for me to join a party he was taking to Rorke's Drift late that afternoon. In the meantime I browsed through his collection of guns and spears, and regimental insignia, and books with titles like *Hill of Destiny* and *Thank God We kept the Flag Flying*. I could hear the ragged crash of muskets already, but I hadn't seen anything yet. David was an adventurous spirit of Scottish descent who had clearly missed his vocation, which was acting. At the mission station he arranged his audience in a semi-circle before the stone buildings and proceeded to give a performance that Stanley Baker would have been proud of. 'Here they come, black as hell and thick as grass,' he cried, and we could see the mass of Zulus advancing with a low murmuring like a swarm of angry bees. 'You mark your target, my boy, you mark your target as it comes' he called, and we could see men of the 24th, the Warwickshire Regiment, sighting their Martini-Henry rifles behind barricades of cornmeal bags and biscuit tins.

The scene had altered little since the nineteenth century, when two stone buildings with thatched roofs stood on raised ground below a rocky hill. Before them lay a broad plain bounded by low hills, and at the foot of a slope to the east flowed the Buffalo River that marked the boundary between British Natal and Zululand. The church the soldiers had used as a store room and the missionary house they had converted into a hospital had been restored and given iron roofs, and there were a few more stone buildings in the grounds, but otherwise the station was much as it would have appeared to warriors of the elite *Undi* corps of the Zulu army when they tried to storm it. My first impression was that it was remarkably small. The positions of the British barricades were marked with white-painted stones, and were only a few paces apart. The hospital, where the sick helped by a few comrades fought desperately from room to room before abandoning it under covering fire, was a moderately sized cottage with a small veranda. My favourite story concerned the quick thinking of a Private Waters who, finding himself cut off in one of the rooms, hid in a closet where he found a black fur coat left behind by the missionary's wife. With commendable presence of mind, he wrapped himself in it and sneaked out and lay among the Zulu dead, where he remained undiscovered until the fighting was over.

David concluded his narrative with a dramatic flourish. Urging us to watch *Zulu* again, he said: 'If you get through the last scene when they read the roll-call with a dry eye, there is a hole in your soul.' By this time several women in the audience were dabbing their eyes, and the men had the stern expressions of old soldiers who knew about these things. On the way back to the lodge, David spoke of reconciliation. 'We can use these stories to soften attitudes towards each other. When you see a Zulu with his eyes welling with tears when he hears of the funeral of Fred Hitch (a hero of the battle), that's when we start winning.' I wondered if the man would be so moved if he knew how many of his ancestors Hitch had shot.

Next day I tried to find the headmaster of the local school who had the splendid name of Mr Zulu, but he was away for the weekend. So I went to the museum at the mission station and a girl who worked there said I could go home with her and meet her family. Richard Mbatha lived with his wife and five children in a house of baked mud and wood on the other side of the hill. The arrival of a foreigner driving into their yard behind an indignant chicken caused surprise, but I was greeted with smiles and invited in for tea. I complimented them on their home, which Richard had built in the European bungalow style. He said: 'It looks like a brick house, but it is made of mud and now it is old and it is cracking and soon it will fall down.' Then it would be time to build another one was his philosophical attitude. His wife was a plump, cheery woman who apologised for the house being dusty, and busied herself wiping a coffee table and producing her best china tea set. Then she left the men to talk, with chickens poking their heads through the open door.

Richard was a slightly built, soft-spoken man who had worked for ten years in a factory in Johannesburg but he had come home because of violence in the townships. 'It was too bad in Soweto, always fighting.' In the 1960s he earned the equivalent of four pounds a week, on which he had to live and provide for the family he had left behind. Now he worked in the local museum, which paid little better, but it was cheaper to live here. He had four cows that provided milk, but this year his mealie crop had failed because of lack of rain and they were expensive to buy. They could afford to eat meat once a month, otherwise they lived on mealies and porridge, and vegetables that grew around the house. If he had money for books and uniforms, he would send his children to school. That was his priority, and maybe one day it would be possible. He was glad apartheid was gone – he had hated the Pass Laws that treated him like a slave – but now there was no work. 'There is nothing to do,' he said with a shrug. I asked what he thought of the battle at the old mission, but he had little concern for foreign soldiers who had invaded his country long ago, no matter how brave they had been.

The defence of Rorke's Drift had been a side-show to the main event that had occurred earlier in the day at Isandlwana. It was there that 20,000 Zulus overwhelmed the camp of the main British column held by 1,700 men, about half of them native levies. It was a shattering defeat for the British commander Lord Chelmsford, who had led half of his force out of the camp hours earlier in a fruitless search for the Zulu army. Chelmsford unsurprisingly played down the disaster and made the most of Rorke's Drift, and the lavishing of medals on survivors of the latter had the desired effect of turning public indignation in Britain into grateful pride.

Isandlwana is dominated by a bastion of rock that broods over a flat plain extending for 12 miles. From my room across the Buffalo River, I could see it rising from a jumble of blue-grey mountains like a monstrous shark fin. On closer inspection it has the form of a sphinx, which by a curious coincidence was the emblem on the collars of the 24th (2nd Warwickshire) Regiment encamped beneath it, following its Egyptian campaign in the Napoleonic wars. But here the winged monster of Thebes has become a tombstone. Survivors said the hill seemed sinister, and spoke of premonitions of disaster. Most battlefields are cloaked in sorrow, but at Isandlwana the horror of what happened still stalks an eerie landscape. It whispers among scattered gravestones, and around the rock where a handful of soldiers made a hopeless last stand. Even in bright sunshine the hill casts a baleful presence. When the Zulus attacked the sky was dark with rain clouds, and as the battle reached a climax the gloom was deepened by a partial eclipse of the sun. It was a nightmare at noon.

'At Isandlwana I myself only killed one man. Dum! Dum! went his revolver as he was firing from right to left, and I came along beside him and stuck my assegai under his right arm, pushing it through his body until it came out between his ribs on the left side. As soon as he fell I pulled the assegai out and slit his stomach so that I knew that he would not shoot any more of my people.' Thus a Zulu veteran described a scene repeated more than a thousand times within less than two hours, during which the British force was massacred.

It was a Sunday when I went there, and the church in the local Zulu village was full of women, children and old men. Most of the young men had gone to the cities, summoned from their ancestral lands by a new economic order. At a visitors' centre I bought a ticket that allowed me to drive along a dirt road around the base of the hill to a parking area. The dun-coloured plain was littered with ugly memorials erected by war graves boards, memorial commissions, old comrades and relatives. Among them were cairns, poignant piles of stones with white paint flaking from them, marking the mass graves of British soldiers. On the southern shoulders of the hill was a grassy knoll where a Captain Younghusband and his company had formed up shoulder to shoulder and fought to the last man with bayonets. Their action was commemorated with a small, square-hewn stone that had been painted yellow and looked like an electricity junction box. Nobody counted the Zulu dead, or erected memorials to them.

Three black people were wandering around, and I asked them what they thought of the place. One of them, a Zulu from Durban, said: 'It's history. I have no feelings. It was a long time ago.' Did he think there should be a Zulu memorial? He shrugged his shoulders; he didn't care. I climbed the hill, past the site of Younghusband's last stand, up a rocky scree, and finally on to the head of the sphinx. From here I could see the entire battlefield, the plateau from which the *impi* had poured like a giant snake, and the tracks to the Buffalo River where fleeing remnants of the British force were butchered. Some visitors have written of being deeply moved by this scene. I felt depressed, and an urgent desire to get away from this dreadful place.

A footnote to this colonial blunder was written five months later on the banks of the Itshotshosi River, 20 miles north of Isandlwana, when a party of British scouts was attacked by fifty Zulus. Three soldiers were stabbed to death, including a young Frenchman who had received military training in England and been commissioned as a lieutenant. He was the Prince Imperial, Eugene Louis Joseph Napoleon Bonaparte, and he was the last of the dynasty. Thus the martial line that triumphed at Austerlitz and Jena and reduced most of Europe to subservience was ended in a skirmish in Africa by a Zulu spear. Queen Victoria was not amused, and her humour was not improved by the Bishop of Natal who had the temerity to suggest that Christians ought to spare a thought for Zulus who had died 'nobly and bravely' in repelling invaders. Disraeli offered a droll perspective: 'A very remarkable people, the Zulu. They defeat our generals, they convert our bishops, they have settled the fate of a great European dynasty.'

The next British military tunic I saw was adorned with a lacy black brassiere. It was in a corner of Stan's Pub, which was the great cultural attraction of Babanango, a dusty hamlet on the road south through Zululand to the Natal coast. Stan was an ex-Royal Marine who had served in Burma, emigrated from Surrey to South Africa for a bit of adventure, drifted around as a liquor salesman, and ended up in Babanango because the local hotel was the only business he could afford to buy. He was a jolly widower with a round face and splendid white whiskers who walked with difficulty on gammy legs and spoke with a Home Counties accent. His establishment was a single-storey building with an iron roof shaded by giant bluegum trees that had begun life as a doctor's house at the turn of the century. Now it had a snug little pub crammed with old hats, caps, statues, flags and all manner of whimsical nonsense, much of it adorned with ladies' underwear. 'We let them take their knickers off in the toilet, but the bras have to come off in here,' he explained. Above him was a sign that said: 'I'm not a dirty old man, I'm a sexy senior citizen'. When I walked in, the bar was bulging with half a dozen big Afrikaner miners, one of whom was wearing a baseball cap that said: 'Instant idiot – Just add alcohol'. I wondered if I had strolled into the Mad Hatter's Tea Party.

Stan disabused me of this notion by providing an excellent lunch of beer and curry, which I enjoyed *al fresco* beneath the bluegum trees in the placid company of two guard dogs the size of small ponies. On going back into the pub, I found the miners listening with interest to Stan's explanation why there were bullet holes in his windows. One was the result of a customer testing a second-hand rifle. He had sensibly aimed upwards at a high window, and hit it dead centre. The others were the work of two cops who reckoned after a few drinks they could shoot just as well, which they couldn't. A hotel inspector had ordered Stan to repair his broken windows, but Stan said they weren't broken, they just had holes in them. I left when one of the miners mentioned he had a shotgun in the back of his car.

Back in Zululand, the road meandered over great green hills

clothed in a ragged patchwork of pine forests as far as the eye could see. After a while the sweeping, empty landscape became monotonous, and the town of Melmoth did not offer much relief. A desultory huddle of brick and concrete boxes straggling up a hillside, it did not cheer the spirit. My guidebook recommended the Melmoth Inn, which was said to be basic but friendly. It might have been, but it was closed. I went into a bar next door, where a crowd of Zulu men were getting tanked up watching a football match on television. The hotel opens at six, the barman said. It was then four o'clock, and I badly needed a hot shower and coffee, so I asked if somebody could open it earlier. Sure, the barman said, just call this number, so I did, but it wasn't working. Wondering what to do next, I went to a bank machine to withdraw cash but it wasn't working. Nor was the next one I found. That settled it. Melmoth had no interest in my custom, so I left.

Then the mists came down. They swirled out of the forests, wreathing everything in a cold, grey blanket that transformed the highlands into a spooky world inhabited by shadowy figures that loomed out of the gloom and vanished with no trace of their passing. While driving slowly round a bend I noticed a human foot protruding from the grass verge. It was attached to a black man who appeared to be unconscious. Whether he was dead or just dead drunk was hard to say, and a bend on a foggy mountain road was not a good place to stop and find out. At the first opportunity I turned and headed back into town, where I had seen a couple of cops checking trucks at a roadblock. Yes, the young Afrikaner constable said, somebody had told them about the guy down the road and as soon as they had finished what they were doing they would check it out. So there was a man in imminent danger of being reduced to mincemeat by the first speeding combi-taxi that came along, and the cops were more concerned about writing a ticket for a truck with faulty lights.

Maybe bodies by the side of the road were commonplace up here, and maybe the cops were fed up with it. But I couldn't banish the suspicion that they would have checked out the body sooner if it had been white.

It was a relief when the mists parted to reveal a succession of emerald, knife-edge ridges slicing down to a plain far below, and a sign that promised a bed for the night. The receptionist at Shakaland was pleased to see me. Yes, she had a nice hut for me, and there was just time for a hot bath before dinner and the traditional dancing in the chief's *kraal*, and this young fellow with the assegai would take my bag and show me the way. My heart sank when the bell-boy appeared in full Zulu warrior regalia, which meant he was sporting a grin and not much else. This was not the kind of intrepid exploring I had in mind. The hotel was a 'village' of beehive huts originally created for a television series and now catering for American tourists who felt at home because it was like a Zulu Disneyland. But it was well laid out in wooded hills above a lake, and the Zulu staff had a genuine enthusiasm for singing and dancing and enacting rituals that conjured an illusion of reality. I suspended my critical faculties in a bath scented with oils, and reflected that life in Shaka's realm would have been tolerable with modern plumbing and supplies of cold beer.

After dinner the cooks and waitresses entertained the guests with a selection of African songs, which they performed with lots of smiles and clapping and swaying of plump bosoms and bottoms. You could tell they were enjoying themselves; they loved to sing and this was as good an excuse as any. Then a dance troupe appeared with flaming torches to escort us to the *kraal* for their show. As we were leaving, one of the Americans tripped over a tree-trunk stool in the darkness and went down like a ton of bricks. This was not funny. He was an elderly man and he could have been seriously injured. As people crowded round to help, there was a whack and a woman went sprawling over another stool. Then another went over backwards with a yell. Now it was starting to get funny. They were going down like ninepins in a slapstick comedy routine, and I failed to suppress a giggle. When the mayhem was over, the dancers gathered the survivors and shepherded us into a large hut where we were graciously welcomed by a huge fellow with an impressive belly and the leopard skin robe of a chief.

By the flickering light of the torches and the throbbing of drums, dozens of dancers jumped into action, leaping and whirling and kicking above their height in a dazzling display of acrobatics and choreography. Never mind that they were performing nightly for tourists, they were Zulu and this was Zulu dancing and it was great fun to clap and stamp your feet and stab your spear in unison to tribal rhythms that were in your blood. Dazed by the frenetic drumming and chanting, I tried to imagine the earth-shaking crescendo of a Zulu army jogging into battle, and I couldn't. It was a sound even the survivors of Isandlwana must have found impossible to describe. Next morning we were given demonstrations of spear-making and throwing. During the former, we learned that the name *iklwa* for the stabbing spear introduced by Shaka was onomatopoeic, being the sound that it made on entering and leaving its victim. During the latter, we learned not to annoy a Zulu armed with a throwing spear from anything less than 50 yards. It is a sobering sight to watch a man pick up a spear and nonchalantly chuck it 40 yards at a shield on top of a gateway high above the ground and pierce it dead centre. When you see his chum casually demolish a pile of bones from the same distance you get the point of Zulu martial arts.

Before leaving, I asked a guide whether Zulu life was changing. 'I can say yes, especially we young people who follow other traditions. It is only the old people, our fathers and mothers, who live by the old ways.' So how did he feel about that? 'I can say it is not a good thing. When people lose their culture, they are nowhere. But it is very difficult to go back now.' One problem was that traditional costumes had become expensive. In the old days you went out and speared an impala or a kudu for its skin and a few wildcats for their tails, but now all the animals were in game reserves and you had to buy the skins. 'This is cheaper,' he said, tugging at his polo shirt. 'I can say it is the same all over the world. In a few years all the people will have the same culture.' On this gloomy note, I headed for the hills.

There was a notice in the hotel seeking donations for a village school where more than a hundred children shared a classroom. It was not far, the receptionist told me, but the road was bad. This quickly became apparent when my car slid backwards down a deeply rutted track strewn with boulders and came to a crunching halt on a tree trunk. Third time proved lucky, and soon I was bouncing along a red dirt road winding up into green hills dotted with villages on the summits. The school at Ncemaneni was easy to find, because it was playtime and you could hear the children from the next hilltop. I arrived in the company of an old woman who had waved at me to stop and jumped into the car, cackling in excitement and bestowing regal waves on her friends.

The village was a mix of mud and brick dwellings dominated by the wooden huts of the school on top of the hill. On arrival I was surrounded by bright young faces and welcomed by one of the teachers, Miss Buthelezi. Things were not so bad now, she said, they had 265 pupils and the size of the classes was down to about fifty. They had no textbooks, so there was no library, and there were no toilets and not enough desks, but they learned the basics of English, science, geography, history and maths, and they had one of the world's great playgrounds. It was a grassy clearing overlooking a panorama of green mountains and forests and lakes, with not a surfaced road or high-rise building in sight, and the children seemed as free as the wind. Miss Buthelezi was

upbeat about life after apartheid. 'It goes badly for some people
who have no work, but mostly people are very happy with the
new way, because their children are getting education and they
have radios and televisions. In some areas there is even piped
water and electricity.' In Ncemaneni the women still fetched
water from a river and the men fuelled a generator with oil,
but this seemed to be okay with everybody because they were
sociable occasions on which affairs of the day were discussed in
a leisurely manner.

One subject in which the children excelled was dancing. They
had won every competition they had entered, up to the giddy
heights of provincial level, and were thus officially the best little
dancers in Zululand. Miss Buthelezi suggested I might like to see
a few routines, and the children and I thought this was a good
idea. One of the older boys struck up a beat with a big old drum,
and the performance began with six barefoot boys gyrating and
stamping their feet in a sinuous python-like movement. Then a
line of girls swayed in unison and sang of good harvests and
successful deer hunts. Beyond them, nature provided a dramatic
backdrop of dark clouds and curtains of rain sweeping across the
hills and a lake far below. On a terrace down the hill three men
and a woman working in a vegetable patch had downed tools
and were jigging to the drumbeat. Music is a communal affair
in rural areas. The finale was a war dance called *amahubo*, in
which an elder boy led the others in a routine of cheering and
chanting and slapping wrists. The image was of a smiling little
impi in khaki shorts keeping alive traditions of their ancestors on
the roof of the world. Shaka would have been proud of them.

19

He believed in the higher nature of things

At the battle of Spioenkop in Natal in 1900, a volunteer corps of stretcher bearers distinguished itself in evacuating British casualties under Boer artillery and rifle fire. Its leader was a man who was destined to cause a spot of bother himself for the British Empire. His name was 'Mohandas Karamchand Gandhi.

Gandhi arrived in Durban in 1893 as a twenty-four-year-old lawyer to take up a case on behalf of an Indian businessman. A week later he was ejected from a train at Pietermaritzburg because of the colour of his skin, and he spent a cold winter night in the station waiting room wondering what to do next. By sunrise he had decided to stay and campaign for civil rights for Indians in the British and Boer states of southern Africa. He remained for twenty-one years, during which he devised a strategy called *Satyagraha*, literally 'truth force', which the world came to know as non-violent resistance. The first Indians had been shipped to Natal from the slums of Madras and Calcutta in 1860 as indentured labour for sugar plantations. At first the 'coolies' were ideal immigrants. They were cheap, exploitable and illiterate, and posed no threat to white supremacy. Then around 1890 they were joined by traders and grocers from the state of Gujarat, and agitation for political rights began. Cometh the hour, cometh the man Gandhi.

At the last count there were more than 1 million people of
Indian descent in South Africa, most of them living in and around
Durban. It was there I was now headed, and in particular to a
settlement on the banks of a reedy stream 10 miles north of
the city where Gandhi nurtured socialist ideals that sustained
the Indian community through decades of racial discrimination.

Durban looked as if it was practising to be Joburg-on-Sea. The
beachfront was still putting on a brave face of high-rise hotels and
holiday apartments for tourists, but the city behind was crumbling
with neglect and decay. It was a familiar scenario of white, and in
this case Indian, businesses fleeing to the suburbs and leaving the
city centre to street traders by day and hookers, muggers and drug
dealers by night. Grand old colonial piles like the City Hall were
stranded in seedy streets like bewigged aristocrats surrounded
by republican rabble. My guide book referred to the downtown
area in terms like 'ghetto' and 'no longer safe'. Even Victoria
Street Market, once a riot of colours and aromas of Indian
fabrics and spices, just looked as if it was on the verge of
a riot. Township traders had moved in, pitching stalls on the
pavements, and the teeming streets and elevated walkways had
become more reminiscent of Kinshasa than Calcutta. It was not
a happy transformation.

I still enjoyed jogging along the seafront, past the tacky tower
blocks and fast food outlets, and swimming in the warm waters
of the Indian Ocean, trying not to think about the harbour round
the corner being the busiest in Africa. But after dark I was happy
to find that one of the best curry restaurants in town was situated
safely in the hotel next to mine.

Mr Rugbeer Kallideen was my contact. A retired school
principal, he was the secretary of a trust that looked after the
settlement founded by Gandhi in 1904. He lived like most
middle-class Indians in a pleasant suburb of tree-lined streets

in the hills around Durban, which is where we met. On the way to the settlement, he said it had changed in recent years. Inspired by the writings of Tolstoy and Ruskin, Gandhi had created a self-sufficient community based on truth, justice and equality, where about thirty families worked as market gardeners. He called it the Phoenix Settlement, and it was there he printed the *Indian Opinion*, a weekly newspaper reflecting the views of the Natal Indian Congress that he had founded ten years before. Gandhi returned to India in 1914, but two years later his son Manilal came back to manage the settlement and edit the newspaper, which he did until his death in the 1940s. Then in August 1985 mobs from a black squatter camp rampaged through Gandhi's sanctuary of peace, forcing out residents and burning and looting their homes. Within a year the site was covered with makeshift shacks, barely distinguishable from the township overlooking it from an adjacent hillside.

We halted on a low concrete bridge fording the stream by the settlement. People from the squatter shacks regarded us curiously, a rare Indian and an even rarer white face in a car with Cape Town licence plates on the border of a disputed shanty town. 'His vision was so big, you know,' Mr Kallideen was saying. 'He believed in the higher nature of things. He had great trust in the goodness of human nature. He read the Bible and the Koran, and he came to the conclusion that all religions are essentially the same, like rivers flowing in the same direction.' I looked at the muddy brook passing beneath us, and pictured the thin, determined figure wading across it to plant the seeds of a just society in an oppressive land. 'There was injustice at that time, there was discrimination, there was poverty,' Mr Kallideen went on. 'The plantation workers lived in poor conditions, with no schools or clinics. It was their plight he took up. He said you cannot do this alone. This was a nurturing ground for the anti-apartheid movement.'

There was nothing growing now except a sense of hopeless-
ness. Before us, a dirt road straggled wearily through clusters
of ramshackle dwellings, among them a vegetable stall adorned
with slogans that mocked Gandhian philosophy. 'Me against the
weld,' one proclaimed. 'Trust nobody,' another said. Where the
followers of *Satyagraha* had grown Indian vegetables and beans
and herbs, there was only tin shacks and mud and people hanging
around with nothing to do. Gandhi's house stood on a hillside
in the upper reaches of the settlement. He called it *Sarvodaya*,
meaning 'to liberate all'. The mobs of 1985 had liberated the
modest wooden building of its roof and walls, leaving only
concrete foundations and a brick chimney breast. The fireplace
where Gandhi plotted his strategy of passive resistance was
defaced with graffiti of the hard-line Pan Africanist Congress,
one of whose catchy election slogans had been 'One settler one
bullet'. This was supposed to refer to white rather than Indian
'settlers', but in Phoenix the effect was much the same. The house
of Gandhi's son Manilal had fared little better. Only part of it still
had a roof, but it had been taken over by a Xhosa family from
Transkei who had covered the broken windows with blue plastic
bags. The building where the *Indian Opinion* had been printed
was a gutted shell, its ruined walls enclosing a mess of garbage
and excrement. The place looked like a Lebanese village after
the Israeli Air Force had paid a visit.

But true to its name, the settlement was about to rise again.
The Indian community, supported by Durban city council and
the Indian government, had been granted permission to restore
part of the site as a national monument. The squatters had been
allocated land nearby, and landscaping work had already begun.
'We want to rebuild Gandhi's home exactly as it was, as a kind
of sanctuary,' Mr Kallideen said. There were plans for adult
education courses in the old printing building, and a museum
with items like Gandhi's spectacles and sandals. 'We would like

this to be a place where people can come and draw inspiration from Gandhi's philosophy that banished fear and hate.' As we were walking back to the car, we were approached by three black youths. One of them was drunk, and he lurched into Mr Kallideen and demanded money. My companion, small, elderly, bespectacled, looked vulnerable in that beery embrace and I felt anger rising and an inclination to react in an un-Gandhi like way. But Mr Kallideen managed to extricate himself calmly and we reached the car without trouble. 'We don't like to come here at weekends when they have been drinking,' he said.

The Indian community was in a curious position. During apartheid, it had adhered to Gandhian principles of self-help to build its own schools and maintain standards of education. It was thus articulate, relatively prosperous and influential because of generous representation in government as a reward for its contribution to the anti-apartheid struggle. But it was worried. 'There is a bit of pessimism,' Mr Kallideen said over tea at his home. 'People are becoming disillusioned. There is a serious education crisis, and there is a perception that under the whites security was better. There is fear of affirmative action, this business of allocating jobs on the basis of race rather than skills. Once you begin to put the wrong people in places of authority, confidence goes down. Although the economy is still strong, it must be looked after by the right people. What we are fearing is that it must not go the Africa way, you know. If there is fraud and stealing from government coffers, the whole country will be dragged down. Then the young people will leave.'

What had happened to the Phoenix Settlement had been a shock, and now Indian traders were being driven from central Durban by hawkers from the townships. They were beginning to feel marginalised, and beyond the pretty illusion of a rainbow lay the unspoken fear of what had happened in Uganda and Fiji. Yet Mr Kallideen remained sanguine. He took the broader view: the evils of apartheid had been abolished, the country had abundant natural and human resources, and it had a democratic government that represented all race groups. I asked what he thought Gandhi would make of the 'new' South Africa. 'If Gandhi came back today I think he would be happy. When he was here, he was always fighting the law. He was a revolutionary. What he fought for was justice, equality and harmony. And generally that is what he would see here now. Perhaps you could say that in spite of what happened at Phoenix, part of his life's work was fulfilled.'

Next day was Shiva's birthday, and Mr Kallideen suggested I ought to go to the Somtseu Road temple. Lord Shiva is the Creator, the Preserver and the Destroyer, and thus a very important character in the Hindi pantheon, whose birthday is celebrated with due reverence. The temple in Somtseu Road was one of the oldest in the country, having opened in 1901. It was a modest building on a busy road, along from the Safari Surf Shop and next door to Achary's Take-Away. The main temple was a cool and peaceful place with a blue domed roof and white marble floor, flanked by smaller shrines, each with its own altar. There were only a few worshippers paying their respects with gifts of fruit, milk and sweets, and the air was suffused with incense and the tinkling of bells. I liked it immediately.

A priest dressed in plain shirt and trousers said he was too busy to talk, but I was welcome to have a look around if I liked. The first thing I noticed about Shiva was that he had four arms. His skin also had a bluish tinge, and a lady explained this was because he had saved the ocean, which was poisoned, by drinking the toxin. Otherwise he seemed none the worse for it, because he was smiling and obviously in good spirits. I went into one of the vacant shrines and sat on a stool, and admired a display of ornate little divinities adorned with necklaces of orange and yellow marigolds, incense sticks and bowls of fragrant oils. On the walls were brightly coloured paintings of multi-limbed characters riding tigers, playing sitars, carrying water lilies, and generally enjoying themselves.

One effigy was swathed in richly embroidered cloth with, curiously, a cheap travel alarm clock beside it. I pondered this for a moment, wondering if the clock was supposed to wake the deity from slumber in another world, or if it was an obscure allusion to mortality. I gave up, and perused instead a framed poster entitled *Essence of Shri Bhagauad Gita*, which seemed to be a kind of Hindi *desiderata*. The gist of it was that we came into the world empty-handed and we would leave it the same way, so there wasn't much point in getting attached to material possessions en route: 'You think it is yours and you are deeply engrossed in it. This attachment is the cause of all your sorrow. In a moment you are a millionaire, in the next you are a poor man. Mine–Yours, Small–Big, Ours–Theirs. Remove this from your mind, then everything is yours and you are everybody's.' In accordance with this abstemious creed, the altar beneath it was crammed with cheap plastic junk. But it was colourful junk, and pleasing to the eye and the spirit. I reflected how much more cheerful this temple was than the dour Presbyterian churches I had known as a child, and the Catholic chapels with their bloody images of pain and suffering. Here the divinities were serene and smiling, and having a nice time. Being among them felt comforting and uplifting.

As I sat there, people would ring a bell at the entrance to the shrine and step in, and go through quiet rituals of offering gifts and prayers and lighting incense sticks. The spiritual air was occasionally disturbed by a telephone ringing beside the altar, which brought the priest to answer it and carry on a conversation while the faithful continued with their devotions. I liked this informal, easy-going approach. On leaving, when safely out of earshot of the temple, I softly sang Happy Birthday to Shiva.

Back in the lobby of my hotel, I overheard a white shop

assistant and her Indian colleague warning American tourists
not to wear jewellery or carry handbags in the streets. Later the
Indian girl told me: 'Everything is going down except crime.
Health, education, jobs, there is a lot to worry about.' There were
two schools of thought in the shop on how such problems could
have been averted. The white woman said her forefathers should
have shot all the blacks. The Indian said: 'I think we should have
educated them. If you deny people the chance to improve their
lives, what can you expect? Maybe in the time of my children and
their children we will come together, but maybe we will end up
like Nigeria.' I suggested that Shiva might sort things out. 'Yes,
of course, prayers are important,' she said. I thought maybe she
should pray for Gandhi to come back.

Pietermaritzburg, where Gandhi's path of non-violent resistance
began, once boasted some of the finest Victorian architecture
in Africa. It included a red-brick extravaganza of a city hall
with a 150-foot clock tower reputed to be the biggest all-brick
building in the southern hemisphere. Then the concrete box
builders moved in, and down came the handsome stone and iron
edifices, and the city founded by the *voortrekkers* became another
mish-mash of quaint Victorian relics dwarfed by multi-storey
rabbit hutches. It was at the height of its splendour, however,
when the night train from Durban to Charlestown stopped on 7
June 1893, and M.K. Gandhi alighted and spent an uncomfortable
but decisive sojourn in the station pondering his future.

It took the city a long time to recognise the historic significance
of this event, but it finally did so handsomely. A life-sized statue
of Gandhi was erected in Church Street, a pedestrian thoroughfare
thronged with street traders where I found it surveying multi-
racial crowds with benign approval. The bronze figure was not
the gawky young lawyer ejected from the train, but the more
familiar elder statesman in baggy loincloth, walking with the

aid of a bamboo cane and his right hand raised in a gesture of peace. It was a good memorial to a good man. On one side of a black marble plinth was a quote by Albert Einstein: 'Generations to come it may be, will scarcely believe that such a one as this ever in flesh and blood walked upon the earth.' On another side were inscribed Gandhi's words: 'Non-violence is not a cloistered virtue. It is no impossible ideal . . . it is the soul force within every human being . . . the path of true non-violence requires much more courage than violence.' I thought of my dad, a pacifist who had been a conscientious objector during the Second World War. He had died a few weeks before, and on reading Gandhi's philosophy I felt intense loss and pride.

Towards the western end of Church Street, the character of the city changed. The smart department stores were gone, and the street was seedy and mean and vaguely threatening. I walked quickly, keeping an eye out for muggers, which was probably unnecessary, but I felt vulnerable and you are never alone with paranoia. The railway station stood on a rise at the end of the street. It was perfect: a classic red-brick Victorian building with gables, wrought-iron work, a handsome old clock above the entrance and a coat of arms featuring the lion and the unicorn. The Flying Scotsman could have toot-tooted through at any moment. Inside it was just as romantic. The hall had flagstone floors, brass chandeliers suspended from a wooden ceiling and baggage trolleys that looked like props from *Brief Encounter*. There were also four plaques on the walls commemorating Gandhi's brief encounter with destiny in the waiting room. The most recent was inscribed with Gandhi's own recollection of the incident, written in 1939:

'. . . one experience that changed the course of my life. That fell to my lot seven days after I had arrived in South Africa. I had gone there on a purely mundane and selfish mission. I was just a boy returned from England, wanting to make some money. Suddenly the client who had taken me there asked me to go to Pretoria from Durban. It was not an easy journey. There was the railway journey as far as Charlestown and the coach to Johannesburg. On the train I had a first-class ticket, but not a bed ticket. At Pietermaritzburg when the beds were issued, the guard came and turned me out, and asked me to go into the van compartment. I would not go, and the train steamed away leaving me shivering in the cold. Now the creative experience comes there. I was afraid for my very life. I entered the dark waiting room. There was a white man in the room. I was afraid of him. What was my duty, I asked myself. Should I go back to India, or should I go forward, with God as my helper and face whatever was in store for me? I decided to stay and suffer. My active non-violence began from that date.'

The waiting room was still dark, and there was nobody in it because it was locked. I peered in, and imagined the diminutive figure wrestling with his conscience, now with his head in his hands, now pacing the room, and then at dawn striding out with a new sense of purpose. It was a powerful image.

I wandered on to the platform, where a long goods train was trundling past. Above was suspended an antique clock with four faces offering four versions of the time, none of them correct. The original ticket office windows were still there, with black iron bars set in wooden frames carved in neo-classical form, but tickets were now issued in a modern office off the central hall. There I found an Afrikaner who had worked as a clerk at the station for twenty-eight years, and he reckoned some things hadn't changed since Gandhi's day. 'There are fewer trains than there used to be, but I still get all races giving me problems. They want to know who else is in the compartment, and they say if you will put me in with one of those people I'm not getting on your train. I say I can't tell them who is on the train, I can only book them a seat and if they're not happy with the other passengers they must speak to the train manager.'

Some things had changed, however. If Gandhi had left the station on the day I was there, I think he would have been amused by an advertisement for Vaseline across the road. It pictured a smiling black family, with the legend 'Your skin. Your pride'.

20

This thing of Mandela is driving away the ancestors

My way lay south through Transkei, the traditional home of the Xhosa nation whose people have lived, hunted and fished in a land of rolling green hills between the Drakensberg mountains and the Indian Ocean for a thousand years.

Its capital, Umtata, had a curious beginning. After years of strife between tribes on opposite sides of the Mtata River, the chiefs hit on the extraordinary idea of inviting whites to settle along the banks of the river to act as a buffer between them. Chief Ngangehzwe of the Thembu tribe was the first to put the agreement into effect by granting land on the south bank to whites at an annual rent of six pounds, thereby planting the seeds of a settlement that grew to become the capital of an apartheid bantustan. Half a century later, in a small village nearby, the Thembu clan produced another fellow destined to have an important say in settling disputes. With remarkable foresight, his parents gave him the middle name Rolihlahla, which means 'troublemaker'. The rest of his name was Nelson Mandela.

On entering Transkei, I passed a sign that warned of stray cattle on the road – for 180 kilometres. Driving through rural tribal areas in South Africa is an interesting experience. The long ribbons of Tarmac are the principal arteries of economic and social intercourse, and accordingly they are teeming with life: cattle, sheep, goats, donkeys, people carrying firewood, people lugging suitcases, people strolling with umbrellas as sunshades, children walking to and from school, footballers, wedding parties, people inspecting broken-down vehicles, people passing the time of day with them and fleets of dilapidated trucks and buses and combi-taxis weaving among them and enveloping them in clouds of noxious black smoke. The roads are strewn with potholes deep enough to cripple a tank, sticks, stones, dead animals and, on one notable axle-crunching occasion, a railway sleeper. The goats usually get out of the way of vehicles and people do sometimes, but cattle do not. They stand stubbornly in the middle of the road, staring with bovine serenity as you brake and swerve to avoid them. The livestock, like the deepest potholes, tend to congregate sociably on blind corners and summits. All of this is of little concern to local drivers, who make full use of both sides of the road to negotiate obstacles without reducing speed. The evergreen hills sparkling with silver streams are beautiful, but take your eyes off the road for an instant to admire them and it is likely to be your last view of Earth.

I was happy to see the lights of Umtata appearing before nightfall transformed driving from being hazardous to insane. It was rush-hour African style, which is not so much bustle as bedlam. I fled the swirling crowds and gridlocked traffic paralysed by chaotic roadworks, and headed out of town to the tranquillity of a Holiday Inn on a hill overlooking a university campus. It was raining softly as I swam alone in the hotel pool. Mist was curling through trees and the land was blissfully free of homicidal cattle.

Next day I went into Umtata to visit the tourist office, but it was closed. So was the museum across the road. The town had that shabby, neglected appearance common to tribal homelands

abandoned by whites who had taken with them the resources
to maintain them. The only building worth looking at was
a neo-classical yellow gingerbread palace with marble pillars
and a green domed roof that used to house the parliament of
the 'independent' state of Transkei. In the post-apartheid era it
had a more modest role as the seat of the Kei district council. A
presidential commission had just reported that the administration
of Transkei and the province in which it lay was riddled with
corruption, which made the name of this building wonderfully
apt. It was called the Bunga.

My main destination in Transkei was the village of Qunu,
20 miles south of Umtata, where the most famous political
prisoner of the twentieth century spent a happy childhood tending
livestock and becoming adept in the rural art of stick-fighting. In
his book *Long Walk to Freedom*, Mandela recalled: 'It was in
the fields that I learned how to knock birds out of the sky with a
slingshot, to gather wild honey and fruits and edible roots, to drink
warm, sweet milk straight from the udder of a cow, to swim in the
clear, cold streams, and to catch fish with twine and sharpened
bits of wire . . . From these days I date my love of the *veld*, of
open spaces, the simple beauties of nature, the clean line of the
horizon.'

At first sight, not much had changed. Qunu was a straggle
of modest dwellings in a broad, green valley sweeping down
to a shallow river. There were Western-style houses among
the traditional rondavels, but each had its vegetable patch and
they were still connected by dirt paths worn by bare feet that
would have been familiar to Mandela in his youth. An obvious
addition was a little store and post office powered by solar panels
by the main road. Another was a complex of dark red brick on
the other side of the road, surrounded by a security fence and
embellished with two flagpoles. This was Mandela's new holiday
home, where he liked to come at Easter and Christmas and kick

off his shoes, and wander over his ancestral land, and remember the taste of wild honey.

On approaching the gates I was observed by a flock of sheep grazing by the fence, and in the distance by a lone horseman swathed in a woollen hat and a long coat and carrying an umbrella against rain gusting from the hills. A couple of local policemen in plain clothes emerged from the house and we had a chat about life in the village. People grew mealies and raised sheep, they said, and did traditional dancing and had circumcision feasts, and the women still collected water from the river and cooked the family meals in big black pots. I asked if it was much the same in Mandela's youth and the policemen said they didn't know, but they would go and fetch Mandela's brother who was in the house. This came as a surprise, because I had been under the impression that Mandela's three brothers were long dead.

However Morris Sitsheketshe Mandela was clearly alive. He was a small, slight figure wearing a scruffy anorak, checked trousers and boots with no laces. Beneath a battered trilby hat was a handsome face with high cheekbones and eyes sparkling with good humour, but he bore no resemblance whatever to his famous sibling. The relationship was lost in the translation of one of the policemen, and I was left to assume Morris and Nelson were united by the African extended family system, in which cousins are considered brothers. We strolled through the village to Morris's house, and on the way the policeman called Wilfred acted as interpreter. Morris was born in 1932, which made him fourteen years younger than Nelson. 'He says he was happy when they were children. They drank sour milk from the cow, and they ate the cow, without buying anything. You can't get sour milk today. They used to go to town with horses, now they take taxis. He say so. Then they wore blankets, now it is western clothes. They used to move freely, walk everywhere at night, now he is afraid to go out after dark, because there is a sort of high rate of killing people. Also there were a lot of ceremonies in those days, and there are not so many today.'

We were walking across a field past brightly painted rondavels, splashes of colour in a gloom of mist and low clouds. The house where Morris lived with his wife was a bungalow surrounded by mealie and pumpkin patches, a menagerie of geese, goats and donkeys and a pig in a pen. The beauty of Mandela's valley was unspoiled. There was a timeless air about the cattle grazing on unfenced hills, and women fetching water from the river, and children running barefoot through the grass. Mandela recalled Qunu as a village of women and children, and it was still the same because the men were working on distant farms or in the gold mines. Morris took me down a slope to where his parents and a sister were buried beneath anonymous gravel markings with no tombstones. At first this apparent lack of concern for the dead had puzzled me, until I learned that in Africa ancestors live on in spirit form and are available for consultation on daily affairs. So what happens to the bio-degradable shell they leave behind is of little consequence.

I was reminded of this by a young schoolteacher who lived in the village, called Bantu Habe. One of the big talking points was the recent arrival of electricity, he said, and opinion was divided. 'The young people like it, but some of the elders say this thing of Mandela is driving away the spirits of their ancestors. They believe that in their sleep they dream of their forefathers, who tell them when they must slaughter a cow, and so on. They think the electricity is keeping away the ancestors, who don't understand why the houses are so bright now.' There was a reluctance in Qunu to abandon old ways. When workmen came to supply piped water, the women said the river supplied all they needed. 'They want to keep their culture as it is,' Bantu said. 'The young people still like to go to church, and sing in music choirs, and play football in the fields. When you go to big towns like Soweto you get involved in spending a lot of money for breakfast, but here you just milk your cow. When you want to cook something, you just make a fire and put your pot on it. And on our land we can grow anything we need.'

The teacher seemed content to live with a foot in both worlds, but post-apartheid upheavals were sending tremors through the village. The government was not working like before, people said, pensions were not being paid, men were being laid off from the mines and school standards were falling. At Bantu's school there were books but no other equipment, which meant that lessons in subjects like science were only theory. He called it learning without understanding. 'I don't say apartheid was good, but children learned at that time because managerial levels were very high. Now the teachers are not working.'

But there was still space to live and raise a family, and grow mealies, and walk in the hills, and look at what Mandela called the clean line of the horizon. Bantu lived with his parents and three sisters and an indeterminate number of children in a cluster of rondavels and bungalows by an open field. As we sat outside we were observed with grave curiosity by a row of barefoot scamps, and examined by a small black pig foraging for food. Bantu's mum smiled a greeting as she crossed the yard with a pile of washing. It seemed a good place to be. As he walked with me to my car, Bantu turned and gestured to his home and its plot of land, which would accommodate dozens of people in an urban squatter camp. 'You can have a site like this for twenty rands and a bottle of brandy to the chief and it belongs to your family for ever. You see how nice it is to live here?'

Late that afternoon I went for a jog on the campus of the University of Transkei, among grim grey faculty buildings that looked like concrete spaceships. There was an athletics meeting taking place at the sports field, and I went to watch. Despite steady rain the stadium was packed with thousands of spectators cheering youngsters running with power and grace any club athlete in Britain would envy. Hardly any of them had shoes, but they ran like the wind.

Part of the problem, the black man at the next table explained, was favouritism. He taught deaf children in Umtata, and we had struck up a conversation over dinner in my hotel. His sister had applied for a post in civil administration, for which she had the necessary qualifications and experience. The job had gone to a man who had neither, because he had been an ANC 'comrade' who had been imprisoned during the anti-apartheid struggle. 'It's happening all over,' he said with a shrug. We talked about the economic gulf between black and white, and I asked why he thought Europeans had colonised Africa rather than the other way around. 'God is on your side,' he said.

Heading south next day, I passed Qunu again. The policemen had told me a cow was to be slaughtered that day for a gathering of chiefs, and I noticed cars parked at the presidential compound and briefly considered stopping. But it was raining heavily, and I decided to drive on. Next morning I read in a newspaper that the main man at the meeting had been Mandela, who had come to settle a dispute between the chiefs and local government officials. So I missed seeing Mandela in his home village, but I saw an image of him the way he used to be. It was a boy tending sheep by the river, huddled in a blanket over patched trousers. He looked as if he had been there for a thousand years, and in his back pocket was a slingshot.

The bad weather discouraged me from making a side-trip to the Wild Coast, a starkly beautiful 150-mile stretch of beaches and wind-blown dunes infamous among early mariners as a graveyard for ships plying the Cape route to the East. My guide book did its best to persuade me to visit Port St Johns. An idyllic little town at the mouth of the Umzimvubu River, it said. I could enjoy tropical vegetation, dramatic cliffs, great beaches and a relaxed atmosphere among a colony of artists and craftspeople, it said. But since I could barely see the bonnet of my car for rain I gave it a miss, which was just as well. That day fifteen people were killed in fighting near the town, sparked by the murder of the son of a headman, and troops had been called in to find a war party of 300 men in the bush. Elsewhere in Transkei that weekend, eleven people died violently. A newspaper report of one incident read as follows: 'A truck driver was killed by another motorist after a collision at Smith Junction, Engcobo. After the accident, the truck became stuck in the mud and the owner of the other vehicle, a *bakkie*, assisted him in pushing it. He then shot him.' As one does.

21

The Passing of the Great Person
of the River

East London loomed out of the mist and rain, a dreary port sprawling around the mouth of the Buffalo River. The first time I came here had been to report on the sinking of a cruise liner. A notable feature of the story was that its Greek captain took the unusual view that he could best direct rescue operations from shore, and jumped on the first helicopter that came along. Happily, a magnificent effort by South African rescue teams saved the other 570 people on board, including a conjurer who had assumed temporary command of the vessel.

The only attractive part of the city was visible from my hotel, a beach promenade leading to a wilderness of huge sand dunes. In driving rain and swirling sea mist, with waves crashing through the gloom, nature produced an impressive *son et lumière* of ghostly illusions that concluded with a dazzling rainbow over the sea.

East London is the home of the world's only surviving dodo egg. It is in the city museum, along with a stuffed Coelacanth, a fish that was supposed to have been extinct for 80 million years until a fisherman caught it to their mutual surprise in 1938. I was more interested in an exhibit in a museum 30 miles away in King William's Town, a pleasant *dorp* with fine Victorian buildings that ensured its place in history by serving as the capital of the nineteenth century colonial outpost of British Kaffraria. The Kaffrarian Museum, founded in 1884 by the local naturalist society, had acquired the world's biggest collection of African animals. Among its 25,000 stuffed lions, rhinos, zebras, snakes and so on was a large, grey creature with a blunt nose and a quizzical expression in her little eyes that made her look like an old woman smiling. In her brief lifetime she achieved a fame in South Africa and overseas rivalled only by the cartoon animals of Disney. This was a legendary character, whose popularity transcended boundaries of race, creed, and religion, and when she died a nation mourned. This was Huberta, the perambulating hippo.

Huberta's story began in a game reserve near St Lucia Bay on the Zululand coast in 1928. Hippos are by nature sedentary and sociable creatures that normally waddle around familiar stretches of river in herds, but Huberta was different. For some reason best known to herself she went walkabout, heading south along the coast on an epic solo expedition. When her journey ended three years later in a river south of East London, she had travelled more than 1,200 miles. Some experts believed she had been looking for a mate, others thought she was just inquisitive about the world. Whatever the reason, her Great Trek caught the public imagination. Radio bulletins and newspapers reported her progress to a bemused public, and in the cities, farms and tribal homelands she became a cult figure that embodied the free spirit of Africa.

The government, under the terms of British Commonwealth statutes, classified her as Royal Game, which meant she was protected by law. Zulu mystics believed she was a reincarnation of Shaka, a Xhosa tribe declared she was the spirit of a great chief who had returned to seek justice for his people, the Mpondo said she was the spirit of a famous witch doctor, and at a Hindu temple in Natal she was deified as 'Protector of the Poor'. One day she was seen ambling through a sugar plantation in northern Natal; months later she turned up on a golf course in Durban in the early morning, went for a stroll in a park, and stood for a while gazing into the windows of a pharmacy. Her next public appearance was in Port St Johns, where she was seen browsing on the village green by moonlight. On the night of Sunday 8 March 1931, the driver of a goods train heading to King William's Town spotted a hippo asleep on the rails. Assuming correctly it was Huberta, he halted, gently nudged her with the engine's cow-catcher, and she trotted sleepily off into the bush. Then six weeks later came terrible news.

It was reported that a hippo had been found shot dead in the Keiskama River, 20 miles south of King William's Town. Public concern turned to anger, questions were raised in parliament, and the police were ordered to investigate. On 25 April the *Cape Times* carried a multi-deck headline: Huberta's Death Deplored; General Indignation in Natal; Flags Flying at Half-mast. The *Natal Mercury* published a black-edged photograph of Huberta under the banner headline: Huberta Assassinated. In fact she had been shot by four Afrikaner farmers who said they were unable to read or write and were therefore unaware of her protected status. When Nicholaas Jacobus Marx, his two sons and his brother-in-law appeared in court a month later charged with what the *Cape Mercury* called 'the dastardly deed', the courtroom was overflowing with two hundred spectators. Mr A.G. Greer, assistant magistrate, dismissed the farmers' claims that they had never heard of Huberta, and said if he went by public opinion he would sentence them to death. Unfortunately the maximum penalty he could impose was £25 fines with an option of three months' hard labour.

The day after Huberta died, the director of the Kaffrarian Museum and his assistant drove to the river to arrange to have her remains transported to King William's Town. The museum was inundated with cards of sympathy and poetry, and the people of Pietermaritzburg sent a magnificent floral wreath. Donations poured in to have Huberta sent to London to be mounted, where the work was duly carried out by E. Gerrard and Sons, Naturalists and Furriers, of Camden Town, at a total cost of £59 19s 6d (including shipping). On her return she was exhibited at Durban Museum, where 20,000 people went to see her in a month. Now she had pride of place in the Kaffrarian Museum, the happy wanderer who became the Marco Polo of hippos. She was a generously proportioned creature, with a girth almost the equal of her length. It had taken eighteen oxen to haul her body out of the river, and the chain had broken. Yet there was a sense of a gentle good nature in this itinerant herbivore who died with a puzzled expression in her eyes. Mr Gerrard and his sons had done a good job. Huberta looked remarkably life-like, as if she was waiting patiently for the museum to close for the night to wander away and continue her travels.

In an adjacent gallery I was interested to learn that in Xhosa culture, ancestral spirits invest certain plants, animals and people with powers of divination, healing, song, dance and oratory. Thus there were sacred animals such as the leopard (the spotted one), the hedgehog (the bashful one) and the hippo. The Xhosa word for hippo could have been coined for Huberta: *imVubu*, which means Great Person of the River.

Continuing south in the spirit of Huberta, I chose a minor coastal road partly because I wanted to see a place called Bell. There are three towns and two rivers in the world that share my name, all of which also share my inclination to wander off the beaten track. This one was named after Charles Davidson Bell, the surveyor-general of the Cape in 1857 when the eastern frontier received an infusion of unlikely settlers. They were members of the King's German Legion, a regiment that had fought as part of the British Army during the Napoleonic Wars and had been mustered again for the Crimean War. Unfortunately the shooting in Russia stopped before the legionnaires arrived, so somebody had the bright idea of sending them instead to the frontier between white settlers and unruly Xhosa tribes in the Eastern Cape. It soon became apparent the soldiers were not ideal farmers, and many of them were shipped off to India. However life improved for those who remained in the new settlement of East London when the good ship *Lady Kennaway* arrived from London carrying 157 prospective brides from Dublin. They then prospered and multiplied, and British colonial mandarins ordained that more Germans be dispatched to the area. Which is where the outpost of Bell came in.

I expected to be disappointed, and I was. My name-place was a clutch of rural dwellings on a hillside off a dirt road that seemed to be populated by women, children and goats. It didn't even have a museum. An old man sitting by the side of the road told me: 'This place is Bell, sir. The white people have moved to Hamburg. Here Xhosa people.'

The reason whites had moved on was because the farming community bearing the noble name of Bell had been expropriated in the 1980s as part of the bantustan of Ciskei. The descendants of the German soldiers and farmers had also abandoned places like Breidbach, Braunschweig and Marienthal. And there were hardly any left in Hamburg. This relic of old Germany lay at the end of a dirt road that meandered for 12 miles through empty hills to the sea. It emerged from a fine mist like a mirage, a melancholy scattering of wooden clapboard houses on a headland above the broad mouth of the Keiskamma River. From its highest point there was a magnificent view of giant sand dunes besieged by a lumpy grey sea and flying spray, but there was hardly anybody to appreciate it. A woman in a house with a 'For Sale' sign outside said most of the properties were weekend holiday homes. Life had gone out of the community and it would be hard to bring it back, she said. I went for a walk by the shore and tried to imagine the place alive with German and Irish voices, but there was only the sound of the wind rattling window panes of empty houses.

Algoa Bay is a historic landing place. Bartolomeu Dias stepped ashore here in 1488 after his first voyage round the Cape, and it was here four centuries later that 4,000 British settlers arrived to populate and cultivate the eastern frontier of the Cape Colony and inadvertently sow the seeds of conflict with the Boers. If either party tried to walk ashore today, it would get flattened in minutes, because Algoa Bay is now dominated by a city with a split personality. On one level Port Elizabeth is an agreeable place, with charming old buildings and parks perched on hills above the sea. On a lower level it is a nightmare of high-speed motorways that strangle the foreshore in a tangled web of dirty concrete. This was the bright idea of urban planners in the 1960s, who obliterated the gracious Victorian face of the city and replaced it with a growling mask of expressways that cut it off from the sea. Personally I would like to see the imbeciles responsible strung up by the bollards.

Fortunately I was staying with friends on the upper level, beside a park with all sorts of interesting diversions. It had an open-air swimming pool and an art gallery, and cricket fields and botanical gardens, and a good racial mix of people jogging and playing football and rugby and loafing around having a good time. All cities should have a park like this. Exploring a 'Heritage Trail', I came to a bronze statue of a horse being given water by a British soldier. The memorial was erected by public subscription in 1905 to the equine casualties of the Anglo-Boer War, with a liberal donation from the Metropolitan Drinking Fountain and Cattle Trough Association of London. The inscription reads: 'The greatness of a nation consists not so much in the number of its people or the extent of its territory as in the extent and justice of its compassion.' It is a pity the warlords of Imperial Britain did not consider these sentiments before dispatching half a million men (and a lot of horses) to crush the Boer Republics and seize their goldfields.

There were more fine words on a stone pyramid in a grassy clearing overlooking the city. The memorial was raised to Elizabeth Frances Lady Donkin, wife of Sir Rufane Donkin, acting governor of the Cape, who died of fever in India in 1818 and in whose memory the settlement on Algoa Bay was named a couple of years later. 'She left an infant in his seventh month too young to know the irreparable loss he had sustained, and a husband whose heart is still wrung by undiminished grief.' I felt a pang of sadness at this echo of lost love, but soon I was cheered by another declaration of devotion on a sign by the door of a pretty Georgian cottage: 'In case of fire please rescue the dog'.

If I had not been staying with friends in Port Elizabeth I would have taken a room at the Edward Hotel, a splendid colonial pile of pink stucco walls, and ceiling fans spinning above the flagstone floors of a glass-roofed arcade, and waiters in red waistcoats wafting up and down mahogany staircases with silver tea services. It was the way Raffles used to be, before the grand old dame of Singapore was tarted up for rich tourists and lost her soul. Gilt was flaking from some of the mirrors, but the scent of old wood was genuine, curiously bringing back memories of school classrooms in Scotland built around the same time. The bar was a dark, richly carpeted room with a dozen old-fashioned pendulum clocks clucking like a brood of hens, and the dining room was a mish-mash of Edwardian panelled walls, candelabras reminiscent of a Saxon keep and tables with red and white checked cloths that suggested a French bistro, all presided over by a stern grandfather clock at the entrance. Thankfully a hotel chain that had acquired the establishment a few years before had refrained from ripping out its heart and replacing it with mock

Olde Worlde nonsense, and thus its guests and its ghosts were assured familiar surroundings. A haunting presence was hinted at in the hotel brochure, which referred to the 'untimely death' of a previous owner. In fact the man and his wife were murdered on New Year's Day in 1972 by an irate wine steward, and the extant manager said when things went wrong the ghosts were blamed. I spent happy hours reading and writing in the palm court over afternoon tea, occasionally glancing up when a waiter rattled a cup or dropped a spoon, but of the unfortunate couple and the homicidal *sommelier* there was no sign.

I had not come to Port Elizabeth for any particular reason, other than a notion to have a look at a township that bore the name of my hometown in Scotland. When I was a child Motherwell was an unlovely Lanarkshire steel town with five cinemas, a public baths that had surprisingly produced a clutch of Olympic swimmers and a football team that lost more often than not and that against all logic and realism I have continued to support. (The team is widely believed to be called Motherwell nil.) The town's South African namesake is not mentioned in guide books, nor does it appear on national road maps. I learned of it purely by chance, on reading in a newspaper that an amateur team called Motherwell United FC had been thumped 5-0 in a regional cup match. This sounded reassuringly familiar, so I decided to pay it a visit.

The township was established in 1984 on the banks of the Swartkop River as an overspill settlement for shanty towns around Port Elizabeth, populated largely by Xhosa people from Transkei and Ciskei who worked in factories that made cars, chocolates and pharmaceuticals. Nobody knew where the name Motherwell had come from. In 1891 the farmland on which it stood appeared on survey maps as U.6.52, and it was supposed that it had been bought and named at the turn of the century by a

Scottish family. At first sight it appeared to be marooned in a sea of brightly coloured plastic bags. There were thousands of them, possibly millions, fluttering on open land around the township. Most of them were blue, but there were also red, yellow and green ones. There were so many that I assumed they had some agricultural purpose, but this proved not to be the case. 'It is the wind,' one of my companions said. 'They get blown over the *veld* by the wind. Refuse collection isn't so good here.'

I was accompanied by two young reporters from a radio station who had agreed to act as guides and interpreters in exchange for interviewing me for my impressions. The first resident of Motherwell collared by this press pack was Matanzima Cosa, a man with an enormous belly who was herding cattle in the *veld*. He had worked in a car factory but he had been laid off, then he had bought these cattle from farmers moving to the area from Ciskei. He also had a plot of land on which he grew cabbage, carrots, potatoes and peas. His partner and their two children lived with relatives because his house was too small. In fact it was a one-room shack of iron and wood, and he fetched water from a communal tap in a wheelbarrow, but he had no complaints. 'This man says he is happy,' one of the reporters translated. 'He likes to be in Motherwell where he can live in a town and still walk with his cows in the *veld*. He says this is important to him.' It occurred to me there was a historical symmetry in this. Both Motherwells were towns that had been developed on farmland, and Matanzima had come full circle. I mentioned this thought to him, and he said he would very much like to see the farms in Scotland one day. I said he would be lucky to see them through the rain.

Every community has its activists, people who organise and cajole everybody else and generally get things done. Motherwell had Dr E. Mamisa Nxiweni, B.Sc. (Hons), a bright, articulate woman who ran a busy GP surgery and the local community development forum. She had also produced ten children and sent eight of them to university. 'Women form the backbone of this community,' she said. 'Most of the men in Motherwell have been retrenched by declining industries. They have been hit hard, so women have to make ends meet. Fortunately we women are more resourceful than men.' To prove the point, she took us to a new shopping centre, where women were selling fruit and vegetables in an open market. It had been financed by white businessmen, but it was staffed by locals and was clean and well managed. The hawkers were doing a good trade. 'We are trying to show the world, and the old regime in particular, that we as blacks can make it with a little help,' Mamisa said. And black empowerment was making things easier. 'We have local councillors now. So if we have problems we know at least we have someone to go to, and that person will listen to us. There is knowledge and information and access. People know they will be dealt with humanely.'

But there were chronic social problems stalking the matchbox houses, men who drank themselves into oblivion and others who infected children with HIV. The incidence of paedophilia had soared after rumours that men could rid themselves of HIV by having sex with infants. In her surgery Mamisa saw three children a week with symptoms of full-blown AIDS, and she reckoned there were probably many more. 'It all comes down to ignorance and low socio-economic levels. We hope we are going to improve as people become more aware. At least now we have a chance to improve.'

The sports stadium in the district, unimaginatively called NU2 (neighbour unit 2), was full of enthusiastic improvers. On remarkably lush grass playing fields, two high schools were competing at football and netball in a cacophony of cheering and squealing. Casting a critical eye over the proceedings, I noted two differences from the home of Motherwell FC in Scotland. The grandstand was smaller and the football was better.

22

You've got to be big enough to take it

From Port Elizabeth I had a choice. I could head west along what is known as the Garden Route, a narrow coastal plain with beautiful forests and lagoons and beaches, littered with tourist developments erected on the fast-buck-and-to-hell-with-the-environment principle. The most popular resort of Plettenberg Bay boasts a superb beach dominated by a hotel of breathtaking ugliness.

Alternatively I could strike inland to a vast semi-desert, a land of huge silence and shadows covering a third of South Africa and barely disturbed by man. The early Khoikhoi people who lived in this wilderness of sparse scrub and misty blue mountains called it Karoo, meaning 'hard' or 'dry'. A South African author recalling her childhood on a Karoo farm wrote: 'It is a country flooded by sun; lonely, sparse, wind-swept, treeless on the flats for many miles.' So I drove north.

It happened quickly. One minute I was peering through flickering wiper blades at an industrial suburb of Port Elizabeth, the next I was over a mountain pass and beholding a desolate plateau shimmering beneath a metallic blue sky. On the horizon puffy clouds hung motionless above mauve-blue mountains, as if reluctant to venture over the plains and risk instant evaporation. The only signs of life were the empty road snaking across the *veld*, and a lone iron-roofed farmhouse huddling close to the parched earth as if trying to escape the heat. I got out of the car and walked for a few steps, and listened to a silence that had reigned there since the Big Bang died away.

Thousands of years ago Bushmen listened to the silence and heard sounds, and tracked game that would ensure their survival until the coming of the Europeans. Then trails appeared in the desert, and the Bushmen saw the dying of their nomadic race in the ox-wagons of farmers who feared God before man. I was musing on this historical cavalcade when I became aware that I was being observed. On the crossbeam of a telegraph pole, a kestrel was watching me with interest. We could have been the only two lifeforms in the world, and I felt a corresponding glow of companionship until the bird spotted another lifeform of edible dimensions and took off in pursuit of it.

After the noise and bustle of a city, driving alone through this primal landscape with hot, dry air flowing through the open windows was balm to the soul. Yet it was a hard and unforgiving place. It was said that to survive in the Karoo you had to be a good Christian or build good dams. The other thing you could do was find a grassy spot in a horseshoe bend of the Sundays River, build a neat town of Cape Dutch and Victorian cottages, and sell coffee and *koeksisters* to the sheep farmers.

This is more or less what the founders of Graaff-Reinet did, thereby providing the Karoo with a 'capital' and the invaluable services of carpenters, blacksmiths, wagonwrights and saddlers. Through time their settlement in a cleft of the Sneeuberg range came to be known as the gem of the Karoo, and more pretentiously as the Athens of the Eastern Cape. When I arrived it was closed. Or at least it being Saturday afternoon, it had gone to sleep for the weekend. Its 220 listed buildings bearing national monument plaques were snoozing in the sun like an abandoned film set, a make-believe frontier town after the production crews had gone home. I stopped for a coffee in an old hotel, startling a receptionist who had nodded off with a *House & Garden* magazine open on her lap. When I sat on a creaky leather armchair, it cracked like a gunshot. After a while I got up and crept quietly out of this town of Rip van Winkles, careful not to disturb their slumber any further.

The de la Harpe family traces its roots to the valleys of Savoie in the fourteenth century. Five centuries later a South African branch was founded by one Jean-Charles of that ilk, a lieutenant-capitaine of the Regiment de Meuron in the service of the Dutch East India Company. These were adventurous times, and the name of de la Harpe soon came to be known in the farthest reaches of the Eastern Cape, notably in the foothills of the Bankberg range north of Graaff-Reinet. It was there, in a remote valley, that a descendant of the man from Savoie found a wife and a farm called The Glen and settled down to raise sheep. By the time I arrived via R.V. Winkletown, the farm had moved to a more accessible valley at the foot of a mountain and passed through four generations of the same family. Anthony de la Harpe and his wife Marion, a.k.a. Tweet, had been stockfarming for thirty years, surviving recurrent drought and the attentions of lynx, black-backed jackals and human predators. To supplement their income they were taking guests, which was where I came in as a bedraggled figure in a car streaked with dust and grit.

'It hasn't been easy at times,' Anthony said over a sundowner on his *stoep*. 'You've got to be big enough to take it. You can't just give in.' What you have to take is the threat of drought searing sparse grazing land, uncertain wool prices and the loss of stock. The Glen had just lost six lambs in a week to lynx, and in one night 120 sheep had been spirited from a neighbouring farm into a coloured township. 'It's not hunger, it's a business. It gets done at full moon when they can see the sheep, and at the end of the month when their clients have money. The police know who the culprits are, but the jails are so full the thieves do a few hours' community service then they're at it again.' It was a lot worse than it used to be, and it was getting worse all the time.

But they lived in a spacious house with airy rooms and comfortable old furniture that was cool in the heat of the day, and there was a swimming pool out back in a well-tended garden, and at night the sky was a black velvet canopy sparkling with hundreds of diamonds. Tweet said: 'Children here have a better sense of values than in the cities. They stay children longer, instead of becoming little materialists. We would hate to move to a city.' But many farmers had. In the early days father and son would farm together, but this was no longer economically viable. A century ago there were three farms where The Glen now stood, and since Anthony had been there the farming population had almost halved. Some of those who remained had turned to raising game for meat and trophy hunting. On one farm to the south, hired guns in helicopters killed 800 springbok every second year for meat markets, but the herd size remained fairly constant. 'Your game farmer is your best conservationist because his family's livelihood depends on it,' Anthony said. 'There is more game now than before.'

In the hope of seeing some of it, next morning I went for a walk. To be more precise, Anthony took me in a *bakkie* to the site of the old farmstead in the hills and gave me directions to a rocky gorge that would lead me back to his house in the valley. Some of the original buildings were still standing, and one of them was used periodically as a shearing shed, but the place had the melancholy air of an abandoned croft in the Scottish highlands, a memorial to a way of life that had disappeared. The scenery was similar, and for once so was the weather. Light rain was drizzling from grey skies, and I was glad when Anthony's dog Vicki, an amiable cross-breed of great dane and bull mastiff, decided to join me.

The trail was rough and indistinct, but the gorge was narrow and there was little chance of getting lost. Anyway, I supposed that if I strayed too far Vicki would get fed up and lope off home and all I had to do was follow her. This was before she scampered off in pursuit of a reluctant playmate, a kudu that clattered up a steep slope and disappeared among high crags. For a while nothing happened, then there was a flurry of activity as Vicki introduced herself to the local wildlife. First a couple of rock rabbits called *dassies* came hurtling down the slope, then there was a rush of wings and a flock of startled guinea fowl took to the air. A stream of loose stones indicated a larger animal scrabbling about somewhere above me, then a shadow flitted across a rock face and materialised as a black eagle. Once they were regarded as pests and shot on sight, but now they were farmers' friends because they preyed on *dassies* that devoured grazing land. As a result these golden-eyed dive-bombers were multiplying, which was bad news for the rabbits but good news for everybody else.

I was lost in admiration for the eagle when I became aware that something was happening to the sky. It was turning very dark very quickly. Enclosed by the gorge, I had not seen the storm looming, and now it was venting its full fury on the hills with hissing sheets of rain and cannonades of thunder. I decided to make for higher ground, away from thickets that might attract lightning. I was halfway up the slope when there was a crack and a blinding flash of light, followed immediately by a crash of sky-ripping thunder, and I fell down. On reflection, I am glad it was only later I learned that I was traversing a type of rock known to draw lightning. This particular bolt came to earth about a hundred yards away and I was torn between curiosity to inspect the flashpoint, and a compelling instinct to leg it sharpish. It was at this point that Vicki reappeared, and decided the matter by bounding for home.

As we emerged from the gorge the storm passed, the sun reappeared and the Karoo became fresh and sweet with the scents of vegetation. For a few moments before the last droplets evaporated it was positively sparkling, and there was a sense that the storm had unlocked life-giving secrets from a barren land. Barely two centuries before, this had been the domain of people who knew all about nature's secrets. The ravine I had passed through would have been a hunting ground for the Bushmen who ranged light-footed over the plains. Then the ox-wagons arrived and the San, deprived of their hunting lands, fought back and stole the livestock of the incomers. Then the hunters became the hunted, and in a single generation they were almost exterminated. Within thirty years of Graaff-Reinet being founded in 1786, almost 3,000 San were killed in the area. Through time the survivors merged with the pastoral Khoikhoi, and they drifted into the employment of the settlers who had taken their land.

As I neared the farmhouse I came to a borehole, with its metal windmill clanking and drawing water into a storage tank. The land was becoming dry again, and assuming its familiar harsh appearance, but here was an oasis signalling life and a will to survive. Sometimes they are like ghosts, these skeletal windmills in the arid wastes of South Africa, but often I was grateful to see them as signs of human companionship in landscapes that seemed to cry with loneliness.

Appearances can be deceptive, of course. Motorists on the national route N9 a few miles south of Anthony's farm are unlikely to notice a small wooden sign pointing up a dirt track to seemingly empty bushveld. However it was here, beyond a straggly thicket of thorn trees, that I joined members of the New Mountain Tennis Club for their annual general meeting, a picnic and a few sets of mixed doubles. A couple of dozen people had congregated at the clubhouse, mostly stock farmers discussing rainfall or the lack of it, women laying out plates of food and children investigating mysterious things beneath rocks. It is one of the few tennis associations in the world whose members welcome rain. The storm that had almost frazzled me had been particularly welcome. 'That corner of the farm has really perked up,' I heard a man telling his neighbour.

The minutes of the previous AGM were read by the outgoing chairman, an airline pilot who had just flown in from New York. This involved discussion about a workman who had been given a kudu. It was unclear whether the animal was payment for repairs to one of the courts, or for earlier work on a thatched roof damaged by monkeys. The pilot who had been flying an airliner across the Atlantic a few hours before said he would find out whether the club still owed the handyman a kudu.

It was a pleasant social occasion, but there was concern about how long the club, and more importantly the community that supported it, would survive. The youngsters didn't want to work on the farms any more and were drifting to the towns and cities, there was talk of the government appropriating land for those who didn't have any, and recently a farmer had been murdered in an adjacent district. Now a consortium was trying to buy seventeen farms for well over the market rate, and nobody knew who was behind the bidding or what they intended to do with the land. Some people thought the money was coming from Germany for an eco-tourism project, maybe a game reserve, and there were even rumours of snow machines being brought in for a ski resort in the mountains. Whatever the truth, it was bound to be bad news for the farming community. Tweet said: 'There are farmers who don't want to sell, even for these fancy prices, but they don't want to be left isolated.'

She and Anthony were resolved to stay, providing crime or land redistribution schemes didn't force them out. Anthony said: 'If we can be left to farm, if the prices of our produce remain stable, if there is security, then we'll carry on.' After four generations, a lot of ifs would decide whether they would be the last de la Harpes to farm in the Karoo.

It is not generally known that the planet Mars lies west of Graaff-Reinet. The dusty plain that stretches into infinity is known locally as the Valley of Desolation, but any experienced space traveller would instantly recognise it as the Red Planet. It is vast and featureless apart from low hills that look like freak waves in a dead calm ocean. The soil has a reddish tinge, and beneath the glare of a copper sun it has an almost metallic sheen. And it goes on forever, to an unbroken horizon that shows the curvature of the planet.

The best place to view this wasteland is from the summit of a mountain above Graaff-Reinet, which is reached by a switchback road that seems to be in constant danger of falling off cliffs. Where the road ends, a path leads to nothingness. One minute you are on firm ground, among rocks and scrawny bushes, and the next there is nothing but space. You are now on the edge of a gut-churning precipice, surrounded by pinnacles of dolerite carved by wind and rain into images of monstrous broken teeth embedded in the valley floor. When I arrived, an elderly English tourist was standing on the extreme edge of a rock shelf projecting over this abyss, posing for photographs being taken by his nervous wife. I have never understood why people do this. I suspect it indicates a lack of imagination. A stumble, or a moderate gust of wind, and the woman could have been a winner of the World Press Photo Award. As I stood in silence an unseen eagle cried, and its call echoed in that awesome canyon as if all the eagles in Africa were there.

The road that skirts the southern edge of the Valley of Desolation leads to a town called Aberdeen, which was named after the Scottish birthplace of the Reverend Andrew Murray, minister at Graaff-Reinet in 1855. It is a Victorian toytown preserved by the dry desert air, with residents who appear not much younger and less well preserved. Its claim to fame is a church steeple more than 150 feet high that is reputed to be the tallest in the country, and at the latest reckoning leaning 457 millimetres out of plumb. But Pisa can relax. The Leaning Tower of Aberdeen is not a serious rival, and after a few beers most locals think it is straight anyway. I found a guest house that looked like a museum, filled with heavy furniture and lace curtains, and sat on a veranda and watched the world go by. This took about two minutes. Then I ordered a lunch of burger and chips, which was a mistake because it was seriously bad and induced a queasiness that made the church steeple waver.

South of Aberdeen lies arguably the most barren tract of the Karoo. It is hard to comprehend the immensity and the severity of this expanse of sparse scrub and bush, where sheep farms are the size of small countries. If we are visited by space invaders, I hope they land here. A quick look round should convince them Earth is incapable of supporting life and they will zoom off and try somewhere else. The *trekboers* were made of sterner stuff, of course. Standing by the side of the road, surveying this pitiless land of heat and dust, I wondered at the determination of the pioneers who traversed it in their jawbone wagons without the least idea of how enormous it was or what lay on the other side of it. I suspect this is where the expression *hou noord en fok voort* was coined.

Maybe they were just trying to get away from Willowmore. I found it in a fold of hills that marked the southern edge of the Karoo, a drab little *dorp* clinging precariously to life for reasons best known to itself. I stopped at a café and asked a woman who served me coffee what people did in town. 'Nothing,' she said. 'There is nothing to do here. There is a timber mill, or they do nothing.' She was right. On my way through I passed a few stores, a church, a sad-looking hotel and people doing nothing. It came as no surprise to learn that Willowmore's water came from a borehole on a farm called Wanhoop, which means despair.

I headed west towards the Groot Swartberge, the Great Black Mountains that stood between the Karoo and the temperate coastal belt of the Western Cape. From a distance they looked like a formidable barrier, a great dark wall shrouded in storm clouds, and on closer inspection in driving wind and rain they were positively creepy. There was a way through them, a serpentine road through a gorge of demented sandstone that crossed a stream thirty times in 8 miles and vice versa in times of floods. There were signs warning of falling rocks, and in the riverbed there were boulders the size of houses. It was not a place to be in bad weather and I was glad to be out of it.

On the other side lay a landscape that Tolkien could have created, a long, narrow valley crowded with cone-shaped hills, an army of misty silhouettes marching towards the setting sun on a great adventure. There was something else in the valley. I was warned by a sign that said 'wind', but by then it was unnecessary because I was struggling to keep the car from being blown off the road by great unseen fists battering at the windows. Evidently the valley was a natural wind tunnel with a lunatic at the controls.

By the time I reached the town of Prince Albert, I was a weary man. I was fatigued by the heat and glare of the desert, and cowed by the dark mountains, and I felt small and lonely. I ached for cheerful company and a few simple comforts – a hot bath, good food in an old-fashioned dining room, a quiet drink in a pleasant pub, that sort of thing – and Prince Albert and its Swartberg Hotel provided the lot. The town was a sleepy huddle of Victorian and Cape Dutch cottages on the edge of the Karoo, and the hotel on its main street was a lovely old place with sash windows, polished wooden floors, oil paintings and candlelight reflecting in gilt mirrors. According to the tourist board, it was worth two stars.

As I settled into a steaming tub with a glass of wine, I awarded
it a galaxy.

The other thing the hotel had was haunted paintings. I have
explored spooky castles, houses and even ships, but ghostly
paintings was something new. It was partly the prospect of
discovering a kindred spirit of Dorian Gray that had brought me
here. One of the spectral works was hanging near the reception,
a large canvas of Delville Wood in France, where the South
African Infantry Brigade was torn to shreds in 1916. It was a
winter scene, with the lone figure of a woman carrying firewood
towards a row of houses on a slight rise, leaving footprints in the
snow. The story was that the footprints of soldiers appeared at
night, and in the morning they were gone. I dined beneath the
other haunted picture, which was one of a pair depicting similar
scenes. In the first, a young woman in a white robe was gazing
at a pool fringed with reeds, and in the other an older woman was
standing on a path by the same pool. She was supposed to be the
same woman, and in between Acts I and II she had murdered her
lover and thrown his body into the water. Occasionally the foul
deed was betrayed by the pool in the second painting turning
blood-red and the woman's face becoming old and haggard.

The hotel manager was sceptical. He had been there for a year
and he had never seen ghostly footprints at Delville Wood, or
the murderess stricken by old age. He had seen the pond turning
red, but he attributed this to a trick of light at certain times of
day. I peered at the woman in white for a while and there was
no doubt she had a curious expression, as if the painting had
been tampered with. In the absence of evidence to the contrary,
I dubbed her Miss Gray.

'Your room is haunted as well,' the barman said. 'Rooms 6
and 8, supposed to be some old man wanders about. Never seen
him myself, though.' The odd apparition would not have been
surprising, given that the hotel had seen some wild shenanigans

during a short-lived gold rush in 1890. But there were no cold draughts or rattling chains in my room, and I settled gratefully into bed to watch a murder mystery on television. Every traveller has idiosyncrasies. One of mine is never to engage a chain lock on a hotel bedroom door, in case of fire. It was thus with some surprise that I noticed, as I switched off the light, that the chain was in the locked position. I suppose the other occupant of the room was not concerned about fire.

23

He left to look for a better life, but he didn't find one

The road to Hell is paved with gravel and sand, and it winds for a very long way among mountains that look as if they are screaming. It is a Lilliputian track in a world of geological monsters with grotesque faces, and it comes as no surprise when it ends in a hair-raising plunge down an almost vertical cliff. Dante would have recognised it immediately.

When the road was built in 1962, it was hailed as a lifeline for a reclusive farming community that had been living happily in a 'lost' valley in the Great Black Mountains for more than a century. Instead it was a death-knell. Within thirty years everybody had gone, and the place they called Hell was left to the baboons and leopards, and ghosts of the past.

The real name of the valley is Gamkaskloof, which means Ravine of the Lions. It earned its nickname in the 1940s from a livestock inspector who had to trek 15 miles over the mountains to examine its cattle and goats. 'It's hell to get to,' he pronounced, and the name stuck. Not everybody was happy with the epithet, notably the Gamkaskloofers. When one of them found an income tax return waiting for him at the post office in the nearest town, addressed to 'The Hell', he scrawled across the envelope: 'First find out whether people in Hell also pay income tax' and returned it to the postbox. The incident was typical of the generations of Afrikaner farmers who lived about as far from the madding crowd's ignoble strife as it was possible to get without leaving the planet. When the only way in or out of your neighbourhood of 6,000-foot mountains was a tortuous cliff path known as *die leer* (the ladder), you tended to be an independent sort.

Tales of this remote Shangri-la had drawn me here, but when I saw the dark ramparts of the Groot Swartberge I quailed. To reach the valley I would have to drive 6 miles up a gravel road of hairpin bends and dizzying drops to the summit of one of the most daunting mountain passes in the country, and then traverse the massif for more than 20 miles on a dirt road that dropped 2,000 feet in its last 2 miles. And then come back the same way. Watching a storm crackling over the mountains, I surmised that venturing up there alone would not be much fun, and therefore would be best avoided. Once the decision had been made I felt light of heart, and I was happily contemplating another evening in Prince Albert when a man in a pub said: 'So you're interested in Hell. I know just the guys who can take you there.' There are times when you wish people were not so helpful.

Marius van Wyk, a burly ex-soldier and steelworker, knew the road to the valley. So did his pal Dries Marais, a cheerful young truck driver, because he had been raised there. And it just so happened they had begun organising tours to it. 'It's not a good road to drive alone, and we can tell you stories about the place,' Dries said, which sounded encouraging. Next morning they turned up in a battered minibus with supplies of beer and *boerewors* and assurances of fine weather, and we headed hopefully for the hills. The main gate to Hell is a cleft in the mountains that leads to a ravine enclosed by towering walls of sandstone. It is a natural cathedral with a congregation of weird rock formations that leer at travellers with twisted faces, as if frozen in the agony of their creation. This is where, on a grassy bank above a stream, young people from Gamkaskloof and Prince Albert used to get together for picnics and dances. Gazing up at the thin sliver of sky, I reflected that the acoustics for the accordions and fiddles must have been wonderful, and it was a pity the locals couldn't muster a symphony orchestra. Beethoven's Ninth swelling through that canyon would have been mind-blowing. Dries said: 'When you come into Gamkaskloof I don't think you will believe there was staying there white people. I don't think there is anywhere on earth like Gamkaskloof.' I believed him.

The road over the Swartberg Pass that lay before us, or rather above us, was designed by Thomas Bain, a master civil engineer of the nineteenth century who with his father Andrew built most of the early mountain roads and passes linking the Cape with the interior. He personally carved out twenty-two passes and fathered thirteen children, which made him something of a legend in his lifetime. This road took more than three years to build with a work force of 200 convicts wielding pickaxes, spades, sledgehammers and gunpowder. Big boulders were removed by the ingenious method of heating them with fire and then dousing them with cold water, causing them to split. The construction cost £14,500, not including the upkeep of the convicts, who devoured one ox and sixteen sheep a day. At the time Bain warned that the road would be steep. In fact the gradient is 1:8 in places, and if it had snow it would make a zippy downhill ski course. When the *Oudtshoorn Courant* reported on 16 September 1886 that the road was open it warned that the government took no responsibility for people falling off it. A century on, it looks as dramatic as it did when the first ox-wagons and horse-carts crawled over it. On the steepest sections it is bounded by a low dry-stone wall, which is all that prevents careless motorists from becoming skydivers. Near the summit (5,172 feet), there is a view of a slope on which the wreck of a vehicle is impaled on rocks far below. 'Some cars went over here,' Dries said. 'The people didn't come out alive.'

As an afterthought, he added: 'This is nothing. Wait till you see the road to Gamkaskloof.' I couldn't wait.

It stretched for ever, a narrow ribbon of white snaking through a wilderness that seemed to be the roof of the world. It took an engineer called O'Reilly and eight labourers two years to complete its 23 miles from the Swartberg Pass to the valley, and almost immediately the community it was intended to serve began to disintegrate. They had wanted the road to take their produce to market and bring in supplies, and to reach medical help. But gradually the children left for higher education and jobs, and they were followed by the old and sick. In 1991 the last farmer sold out to a nature conservation trust, and the valley became silent.

As we scrunched along the gravel road, Dries talked about Hell in the old days. There had been about 120 people in twenty families in the valley before the road came. The Cordiers were the rough family: 'The old man, when he sent the boys to bring in the sheep, if they didn't move fast enough he would get his gun and shoot around them.' It was one of the Cordiers, Oom Karel, who was evacuated by the one-legged flying doctor after being bitten by a donkey. Telephones had arrived with the road in 1962, so they were able to call Dr Coetzee in Prince Albert when old Karel received a bad bite. Manie Coetzee was an ex-fighter pilot whose military career ended when he lost a leg in a crash, so he bought himself a Tiger Moth. He was the only man crazy enough to fly into Gamkaskloof. When he landed and announced that Karel would have to go to hospital, his patient took one look at the plane and said he would rather die of the donkey bite. So Manie threatened him with a huge syringe, and Karel got on the plane and his friends and relatives crowded round and he bade them a solemn farewell. And when he got back they had a big party.

Dries's driving was as interesting as his stories. He had a habit of turning round to explain something, and he liked to take his hands off the wheel to make gestures, usually when we were inches from the edge of an abyss. When the minibus conked out a couple of times, requiring strenuous banging at something with a screwdriver, I was happy to get out and sit in the sun and not worry about falling off a cliff.

The first view of Gamkaskloof is from a high saddle. One minute you are grinding up a steep slope towards a ridge, the next there is nothing ahead but the sky. Then you look down and far below is a narrow green valley enclosed by stone-coloured mountains, and you wonder how on earth anybody found it. The first human footprints were left by Bushmen, probably tracking game by the Gamka (Lion) River that intersects the valley. Legend has it the first white man to see it was a farmer whose livestock had strayed up the river. All that is known for sure is that the first farmer to settle in Gamkaskloof was Petrus Swanepoel, who came with his family and his stock in 1830. He was followed by other Afrikaners fed up with British administrators and their tax collectors in the Cape. They simply moved in and closed the door on the rest of the world behind them. When Boer commandos fleeing the British blundered into the valley at the turn of the century, they found people with long hair living in mud huts, speaking High Dutch, wearing goatskins and only vaguely aware that there was a war going on. Dries said: 'My father said they never worried about what happened outside Gamkaskloof. They just lived from day to day.'

The valley was more of a gash than a glen, 12 miles long and only a few hundred yards wide, but in contrast with the barren heights it was lush with a profusion of mimosa, wild olive and milkwood trees. From above it looked like a big green snake slithering through the mountains. I was glad of the clear skies and sunshine, which made the helter-skelter descent only slightly terrifying. It was like driving down the Leaning Tower of Pisa, only from twenty times the height. Local custom decreed that if two vehicles should meet on the single track road, the ascending one should reverse. I had already decided that in this event I would get out and walk for a while.

Happily there was nobody else around, save for a lone baboon who regarded us with polite interest as we reached the valley and slewed along a sandy track through encroaching vegetation. Dries was happy. 'You can't believe why people call this place the Hell. I will come here every day if I can. It's so peaceful, you can forget everything.' I saw what he meant. The ground rose steeply on either side, but the atmosphere was comforting rather than claustrophobic. The sense was of being in a haven, a place of peace and safety, hidden and protected by the mountains. You felt you could come to no harm here, and that the presence of good neighbours lingered. 'Everyone here was a good Christian, really deep down,' Dries said. 'They did everything together. When a man wanted to build a house, everybody came and helped him till it was finished.' It was easy to imagine farmers pottering around the whitewashed cottages scattered along the valley, and harvesting wheat and fruit among retinues of cattle, goats and donkeys. Wooden trestle tables still lay in overgrown gardens where figs and raisins had been dried for carrying over the mountains by donkeys to be traded for salt, sugar and tools. The donkeys accomplished these treks in a happy daze, having been fed on local marijuana that was reputed to give them strength.

The air was hot and heavy with the buzzing of insects and bird calls, and when we left the minibus the sound of our feet on the bare earth was loud. At one house we were greeted effusively by a ginger cat that was remarkably sleek and well fed. 'There are mice here,' Marius explained. There was also the rusting black hulk of the first motor car, which came to the valley in 1958, four years before the road, in an epic journey assisted by teams of happy donkeys. Nature had bestowed a bouquet on this achievement by rooting wild flowers in the engine block. More

than a dozen cottages of unbaked brick and straw thatch still stood
in shady meadows whose Afrikaner names translated as Middle
Place, End Place and Old Place. Some had been preserved by
their former owners and were available for overnight stays. The
key to the house of Dries's Aunt Annetjie was beneath a stone
by the door, near where fresh spring water bubbled into an old
steel sink. Like the other houses it was a simple dwelling with
solid wooden furniture, patchwork quilts on the beds and checked
curtains in the windows – a Hansel and Gretel village beneath
an African sky. At night, by the light of candles and paraffin
lamps and wood-burning stoves, it must have been the last word
in cosiness.

'If you want to have the feeling of Gamkaskloof you must
stay a week here,' Dries said. Even a few hours gave a good
insight when you were sitting on the *stoep* of Dries's grandfather's house, in the shade of an enormous pepper tree, with
boerewors sizzling over an open fire. Marius said: 'My grandfather used to say it was so hot here in the summer you could cook
eggs on the rocks.' Dries said: 'It is like the sun stands still.' In
fact it was like everything was standing still: time, the mountains,
the world, and the effect was a feeling of utter contentment. Rip
van Winkle could have been dozing beneath a milkwood tree.

Dries's father had courted his mother by riding nearly ten
miles each way between their homes every day. In those days
the men would hunt buck in the mountains, and catch fish in
the river with nets, and drink beer made from wild honey that
made them tipsy for a week every time they drank water. Then
they visited each other and told stories, because there were no
telephones or radios or televisions, and no desire for them. 'I
wish I could live here in the time it was full of people,' Dries
said. He was three years old when his family packed up, gave
their house to old man Cordier, and left the valley. 'My father
doesn't want to come here any more. He is unhappy because

he left to look for a better life outside, and he didn't find one.' This did not surprise me. Driving back over the mountains, I had the thought that they put on their most fearsome faces to deter intruders. For the truth was that far from being Hell, the Ravine of the Lions was a little Garden of Eden.

Dries arranged for me to visit his parents next day. They lived in a small house in a quiet street in Prince Albert, wondering why they were there. They knew why they had left the valley – same reasons as everybody else, times had changed, the children wanted regular jobs, and the old folk wanted to be near a doctor. But they had lost a way of life that no modern comforts could replace. They missed the peace and quiet, they said, there was never any crime in the valley, and the only danger was from leopards taking the stock. People used to walk for miles to visit each other, now they couldn't be bothered to get in their cars and drive for five minutes to say hello.

Piet Marais was a craggy-faced old man with kindly eyes and big, rough hands. He was shy with strangers, and when I asked if I could take a photograph he reached instinctively for his wife's hand and held it as they posed without expression. Listening to Piet's stories translated by Dries, it occurred to me he had much in common with the original San inhabitants of the valley – an intimate understanding of the land they lived in, acquired over generations, and a deep sense of loss at being parted from it. Every day was a good day, Piet said. The best days were in the planting season when they ploughed together. They never missed anything, there were always people coming and going and bringing them news. Nobody had any money because there was no need for it. If you wanted tools or anything else you couldn't grow, you took your extra corn and fruit and honey to town and traded. The raisins of Gamkaskloof were the best you could find anywhere. The baboons were always a problem – they wrecked everything and there were so many of them the leopards

couldn't eat them all – so the farmers shot them and took the ears
and tails as proof to Prince Albert where the council gave them
money that they used to buy provisions. Apartheid? There were
two coloured families who worked on the farms for a share of
the produce. People worked together all day and then they went
to their own homes; it didn't feel like apartheid. In the end they
had left like everybody else because they thought they could have
a better life outside the valley, and they found out too late they
were wrong.

Dries said: 'Even if they didn't leave Gamkaskloof, with all
the new technology today like satellite television it wouldn't be
Gamkaskloof any more. The children wouldn't work like they
did in those days on the land.' On leaving, I asked the old man
from Hell if he thought it could ever be revived. He said no, it
was finished, and there was immense sadness in his eyes.

This hard land had a habit of producing special characters. I
found another a few miles from Prince Albert, on a derelict
farm that appeared suddenly on a bend in the desert road. It was
like a picturesque mirage, with gaunt windmills clanking among
outbuildings with flaking façades and the ground gradually
reverting to bush. The most striking feature was a low wall by
the road that sparkled and flashed in the sun, being imbedded with
fragments of coloured glass bottles, shards of pottery, batteries,
bicycle reflectors and an old torch. Beside it lay a bizarre display
of odds and bobs: crude toys and ornaments fashioned from tin
cans, bottles, bits of wood and coloured plastic. It was a scene
the stoned donkeys of Gamkaskloof could have dreamed up.

The designer of the Brightest Wall in the World and its panoply
of creative junk was a tall, slim character who carried himself
with dignity despite being draped in a coat, trousers and hat of
multi-coloured cotton patchwork. He looked like a harlequin.
His skin was as black as midnight and he spoke English in

measured, cultured tones. By way of introduction, he leaned down to a concoction of tin cans and toothbrushes and said: 'This is number twenty-two thousand, two hundred and six.'

His name was Jan Schoeman and he had been raised in the nearby town of Klaarstroom, but he was a travelling man and magazines had dubbed him 'The Patchman of the Karoo'. When the mood took him, he loaded a ramshackle rickshaw with his goods and chattels and trekked from wherever he was to somewhere else. He had been born 'on the road', the son of an itinerant labourer, and he thought he was about eighty years old. For a long time people had called him Outa, an affectionate Afrikaans term for an elderly black man. He began his travels when apartheidniks evicted him from his home in Prince Albert. 'Because of the skin they threw me out,' he said in a voice that intimated wonder rather than anger. He was a gentle, courteous man and his motto was: Make the best of life. Now he was heading for Namibia, which was 400 miles across the moonscapes of the Northern Cape, but he had been hit by winter storms and he was resting up on this abandoned farm for a while. He would resume his journey when he had fixed his rickshaw, which he called the locomotive. It stood lop-sidedly beneath a thorn tree, a sorry sight with a broken wheel and warped planking. 'Then I will go to Namibia and maybe I will end my story there,' he said. Maybe he would build a little house with two rooms, and walls like the one he had made here with clay and coloured bottles.

There was no doubt Outa was a bit loopy. He knew who the British prime minister was, because he had written to him with a few philosophical suggestions, and he was puzzled that he had received no reply. Perhaps I could call the gentleman when I returned to London and remind him that Outa was waiting to hear from him. In the meantime I went for a wander around the farm buildings, and he resumed his position beneath a thorn tree, hammering at pieces of junk and whistling a jaunty tune. These were the only sounds, along with the whirling of tin windmills that Outa had made and the banging of his frying pan against a post in the wind. Occasionally a car would stop and the people would look at Outa's work and chat with him, and he would say 'go well' and they would leave with bemused smiles. They were travellers like him, he said, only they went a little faster. When it was time for me to leave, I asked what lay ahead for him, and he said: 'Every morning I say Outa your body tell you that you are no longer sweet sixteen. I have become like an old ox. I must not wait for death in my old age. He must meet me on the road.' I hoped death would have a long way to travel.

The most interesting European settlements in South Africa are those founded by pioneers who left their own distinctive stamps, from the grandiose to the whimsical. A fine example of the latter is Matjiesfontein, a Victorian hamlet masquerading as a town in a particularly desolate stretch of the Karoo. It has one street with a post office, a pub, a coffee shop, a few quaint old houses, a railway station and a hotel that was a military hospital during the Anglo-Boer War and where the Union Flag still flies bravely from castellated ramparts. Around the corner are a church, a court house and a police station, none of which serves its original purpose any more. Once a day a red London double-decker bus potters along the street and back again, thus providing the citizenry and visitors with the social highlight of the day. Where the unpaved street ends, a dirt track wanders hopefully towards a range of barren hills that look as if they were left over after God made Afghanistan. In fact all of this was created by a young Scotsman who left a waterlogged ship at the Cape in 1876 with five pounds in his pocket and no idea what to do next.

What nineteen-year-old Jimmy Logan did next was get a job as a porter with the infant Cape Colonial railways. Within three years he was stationmaster at Cape Town, and a year later he was appointed superintendent of a stretch of line on the main route north to the Kimberley diamond fields. Logan noticed two things about his new situation fairly quickly: one was a constant stream of hungry and thirsty travellers, and the other was that the dry desert air had cured his weak chest. So he quit the railway, acquired the refreshment room concession at Matjiesfontein, and proceeded to develop the obscure station into an internationally renowned health spa patronised by the great and good of Victorian society. A succession of Cape Governors were guests of 'the Laird of Matjiesfontein', along with Cecil Rhodes, Randolph Churchill and the Sultan of Zanzibar. In Logan's resort they found an oasis of thousands of newly planted deciduous fruit trees, irrigated from the country's first artesian well. Matjiesfontein was the first village in South Africa to have electricity, and its main street was fashionably adorned with lamp-posts imported from London. During the Anglo-Boer War it was a British command post, with 10,000 soldiers billeted in the surrounding *veld*. Logan patriotically recruited his own mounted corps for the war, and equipped them at his own expense.

When he died in 1920, his creation faded with him, and when a highway by-passed it thirty years later it sank gently into oblivion. Happily it was acquired by a Cape hotelier, who had made considerable progress in restoring it by the time I arrived late one afternoon in a cloud of dust. The Lord Milner Hotel had character, specifically an old and musty character wearing a shabby genteel costume. The beds were lumpy, the linen smelled ancient and the food was mediocre, but who cares. My friend Connie had motored up from Cape Town to join me, and we strolled into the *veld* and found a bully beef tin from the Boer War, and played an imaginative set of tennis on a court that had seen better days but not since the turn of the century, and luxuriated in twin baths with enormous brass taps, and gazed starstruck at

the brilliant night sky of the Karoo. There was also a steam
locomotive on a disused railway siding to admire, and views of
the mountains and the desert from a large wooden veranda that
was like the promenade deck of an ocean liner. Next morning a
woman from Johannesburg was complaining loudly about things
in her room that were not working, notably the staff. She had
entirely missed the point.

If there was a point to Matjiesfontein, it was to be found in
the railway station, which had been converted into a museum
and endowed with a wondrous private collection of memorabilia.
Steps led down through a wooden floor into a warren of rooms
crammed with an eclectic mish-mash from Victorian houses,
ships, battlefields and railway stations. There was also a page's
uniform from the Court of Louis XIII. My favourite item was a
chamber pot with a ceramic eye on the bottom, and a legend in
elaborate script: 'If you promise to keep me clean, I won't tell
what I have seen.' It was a wrench leaving Matjiesfontein and
returning to the real world.

Logan and his wife were buried in a cemetery near the
railway line. Logan was a keen cricketer, and nearby lay one
of his heroes, George Lohmann of Surrey, who died in 1901
at the age of thirty-six. In this wilderness far from the cricket
fields of England stood a headstone with a stirring eulogy:
'This monument was erected by the Surrey County Cricket
Club and friends in South Africa in memory of one of the
greatest all-round cricketers the world has ever seen. A bowler
of infinite variety, a splendid field, and a resolute batsman.
He did brilliant service for Surrey from 1884 to 1896 as well
as for the players and for England. His whole heart was in
cricket and he played the game from start to finish. Ill health
alone compelled him to retire from the cricket field while still
in his prime.'

Logan's grave was marked by a granite cross with Celtic

designs that merely stated when he had been born and when he had died. But most days a fitting requiem echoed through the flinty hills beyond the railway track, in the lonely hoot of the Trans Karoo Express.

24

I like my life. I will die here.

Then I headed south out of the desert and drove over two mountain ranges to watch a huge yellow moon rising from an aquamarine sea. It was a full moon, and soon it was glowing like a Chinese lantern and casting a silver trail on the darkening water. In the distance, a long sweep of sand dunes with wild grasses like tufts of sparse hair glowed pink and then were tinged with gold. On a headland above a bay a cluster of fishermen's cottages with thatched roofs added perspective to a scene that had attracted artists since the turn of the century.

It was the fishing community that had drawn me to this windswept coast near the southern tip of Africa, and the story of a shipwreck that had been the beginning of it. In May 1815, the British government troop ship HMS *Arniston* ran into heavy weather off the Cape on a voyage home from Ceylon. After days of battling gale-force winds that had ripped away most of her sails, she struck the Agulhas Reef and sank within hours, taking with her 372 men, women and children. Only a carpenter's mate and five sailors made it to shore, where they survived on shellfish until they were found by a farmer's son two weeks later.

Within five years fishermen had established a settlement near the site of the wreck which they called Kassiesbaai, meaning bay of the *kassies* or cases washed ashore from vessels impaled on the reefs. They prospered on the shoals of yellowtail and Cape salmon, and in due course acquired the land that was held in trust by their fishermen's union. For generations they lived happily in their stone cottages by the sea that sustained them, until one day they discovered they had a problem. The problem was that they were coloured, and the bureaucrats of apartheid had decreed that Kassiesbaai was much too nice a place for such people, so they were to be removed lock, stock and fish barrel to shacks in a dreary township along the coast. This was one of the rare occasions on which a white community stood up for their coloured neighbours and told the apartheidniks to bugger off and leave the fishermen alone. Happily the liberals won the day, and the community outlasted the idiots who had tried to destroy it. A few years later the entire village was proclaimed a national monument. The white folk had settled on the other side of the bay, in a place they called Waenhuiskrans (Coach House Cliff) after an enormous sea cave nearby. Later it came to be known as Arniston, although officially it retained its Afrikaans name, with the result that the bay came confusingly to shelter two communities with three names. By the time I arrived they had settled into a comfortable post-apartheid coexistence, with the coloured fishermen clinging to their old way of life on the headland and the whites making a good living from renting their homes to holiday-makers.

One of places where the two communities mingled was Bob Harman's store in Arniston. 'Go and see Bob,' people said when I asked about gaining an introduction to the fishermen. He knows everybody, they said. Mr Harman was a businessman who had moved to Arniston a few years before, with a view to winding down and doing a bit of fishing. But he couldn't let alone so he bought a run-down grocery shop and turned it into a thriving general store that sold everything from washing powder to fishing nets and funny hats, then he transformed the place next door into the most popular restaurant in the village, and in response to public demand he built up a bed & breakfast and holiday homes business. He liked to keep busy, did Bob. I found him on a dais at the back of the store, behind an old desk awash with papers and fish hooks, discussing rugby and fishing with a couple of regular customers. 'Old Samuel is the man you want,' he said. 'Lived here all his life, knows the village and the fishing better than anybody.' So Bob made a phone call, and I went with my Afrikaner friend as translator to meet Samuel Marthinus, doyen of the fishermen of Kassiesbaai and their lay preacher.

It was a Saturday morning, and half a dozen brightly painted fishing boats were drawn up on the shore, their nightly work over. As we walked up a sandy rise towards the cottages, a boy sitting on a wall with three girls said (in Afrikaans): 'Would you like us to sing for you?' They sang a shanty, of men rowing through big swells, and pulling nets heavy with fish, and women gathering on shore to help bring in the catch; and their thin, lilting voices blended with the sigh of the sea beyond them in a melody that was timeless. None of them asked for anything, but we gave them each a coin, feeling uncomfortable and wishing we had sweets or fruit to give instead.

Samuel was waiting for us. He was lounging barefoot by his doorway with a newspaper, a big man with a ready smile and a physique men half his age would envy. He was sixty-eight years old and had fathered nine children, and when I asked how many people lived in his house he had to think. Seven, he reckoned, including grandchildren. It was a cosy place with low ceilings, adorned with pictures of his family, his boat and Jesus. Three of his sons worked on the boat, a 25-foot motor vessel of fibre-glass and wood, which was called *Nicolene* after a son Nico and daughter Julene. When he was a boy the boats had sails and the men had to row them out of the bay, he said, now things were easier, but not much. It was still a hard life, and it was getting tougher.

The problem for the community of around 800 people was that there were fewer fish. A current from Durban still brought the yellowtail and red romans down the coast, and the summer south-easters still warmed the water and made the fish lazy and easy to catch. But Japanese and Russian trawlers were gobbling up the shoals on the 45-mile and 75-mile banks, and sometimes at night they raided inside the fishing limits, leaving less for the line fishermen in their small boats who rarely ventured more than a dozen miles from shore. Often they had to sail far up the coast in search of the fish that once teemed in the shallows off the village. The economics were easily explained: 'There are more people and less fish, so we will become poorer and life will be harder. Even the younger generation, if they can't fish there is no other work here.' But there were always sharks at the beginning of summer: 'That is the time for catching them, especially the white death, that's the one that eats people. We see a lot of them and we are not allowed to catch them any more, but if we get a lot of money we will kill them. The people from North Africa like to eat them.'

This did not deter children from swimming in the bay as they had always done, although for a while the beach had been reserved for whites. Sam remembered the day when white officials announced coloureds were not allowed to play there any more, and how white children used to beat them if they did. 'Now our children can go and lie there like big fat seals,' he said with a laugh. The ebb and flow of race relations bemused the fishermen, but barriers were coming down for their children, who were more relaxed about mixing with whites than their elders. Of apartheid, Sam said: 'As a Christian I have forgiven, but there is still a little something in my heart that scratches.'

At this point Frank Swart dropped by. Frank was secretary of the Fishermen's Union and a draughtsman who designed houses and extensions of whitewashed stone and thatch in the village, in accordance with regulations of the monuments council. He agreed times were hard, with some households having virtually no income in winter. The government had promised a community centre, a clinic, a library and a rugby field, but none had materialised. 'When we asked for just a little to extend our craft shop and open a coffee shop they said they couldn't help us.' Frank said it was because the government had no money, but Sam suspected race was part of it. 'They don't want to help us because there are not many black people here,' he said. The union had launched a public appeal for funds to build holiday cottages and a coffee shop, but it was overshadowed by plans by an investments company to build almost 200 houses on the dunes next to the village. Most people were opposed to the development because it would ruin the beauty of the coast, but some said maybe it would provide badly needed jobs. Sam thought there must be other ways for the community to survive without a new town with tarred roads and street lights on its doorstep. Kassiesbaai had got on well for more than a century without either, he said.

Despite the problems, it was a good place to live. Sam said: 'I feel free here. There is no trouble, and I am not afraid of anyone. I leave my door open all day, and if it is hot at night I leave my windows open. These things you cannot buy even if you live in a castle.' I asked him what was the best thing about life in the village. 'The most beautiful thing is when you see a fisherman coming in with a boat full of fish, and he is smiling and everybody is happy, and the women come to the harbour and share in the happiness because there is food for their families.' Sitting by the open door, watching barefoot urchins playing in the sandy street, I imagined a Cornish fishing village of the last century. The sun was hotter and the skins were darker, but I guessed the ethos was much the same.

Into this reverie stepped a character who could have fitted into either scene, because he had been born to the sea. Sam's son Nico was a handsome man with a deep chest and broad shoulders, dark haired and easy-going, and like his father he padded around in shorts and bare feet. Some of the guys his age had left to look for work, he said, but city life was not for him. He liked to be his own man, and that is what he was when he went fishing on his father's boat. 'It's a free life,' he said. 'You can do what you like. You're your own boss. I like my life. I will die here.' The bright lights of Cape Town and Durban held no attractions for a fisherman whose village had received electricity only three years before. 'It's too rushed in the cities. It's nice and quiet here. Just in winter when the wind blows and the boats can't go out, that time becomes heavy. But no, I will never leave.' In a restless world Nico was anchored to an old way of life, and it was good to know that on summer nights a boat would put out from Kassiesbaai for the fishing grounds for at least one more generation. As we rose to leave, Sam apologised with a splendid fisherman's idiom for not speaking English. 'I can catch the English with my eyes and ears, but I can't throw it out with my mouth,' he said.

Next day we came back through the village after a walk along the shore, and our faces were known and people wished us good day. It was a fine morning and a breeze was stirring the sparse grass around the cottages and capering with lines of washing. Doors and windows were open, and people were doing odd jobs around their houses and stopping to chat with neighbours, and children were running over the sand dunes. I found myself envying them. There was a communal warmth and security I remembered from childhood in a street of tenements in Lanarkshire, which I had lost somewhere along the way. Sam had said: 'When somebody dies, the whole community is heart-sore.' People were worried about making it through the winter when the fishing stopped, the union was falling into debt, and some of the youngsters were getting into drugs. But they were holding together. There was a real sense of community, and when things got bad there was always somebody to share the load. There were worse places to live.

The door to Sam's church in a converted cottage was open and we looked in. The morning service of the Assembly of God was over and there was nobody around, but two guitars and a banjo were lying beside a small altar. Light was streaming through the open windows on timber beams and rows of wooden benches, and the sigh of the sea was so distinct it was like being inside a seashell. By the door, a sticker celebrated a recent arrival: 'I love electricity'.

A group of tourists was expected that morning, so the craft shop was open. It was a hut where two women served tea and home-made cakes, and sold knitwear, model boats and patchwork dolls made in the village. I bought a stone painted with a scene of whitewashed cottages and fishing boats that still brings the sun and the sea into my home in dark northern winters. One of the women said most families supplemented their incomes with odd jobs. Some of the women worked as cleaners in the local hotel and a military base along the coast, and in winter some of the men earned good money by going out with the big Atlantic trawlers from a port near Cape Town. Not every man in the village earned his living from fish, but before you did anything here you had to learn to be a fisherman, to have something to fall back on. When I mentioned we had met the pastor, she told us a story about the first man to have been converted in Sam's church. She remembered it was a day of mist and fine rain, and when the service was over the man had left a hand-written message for the congregation. It was: 'Take it step by step and God will put the miles together.'

That evening I watched the last rays of the sun casting a soft light that seemed to make the ocean translucent. A lone youth was swimming steadily across the bay with matchstick brown arms, cutting through the water like a little seal. For once the sea was calm, and an old man on the shore said when the moon came up the fishing would be good.

The bodies washed ashore from the *Arniston* were buried in groups of ten in the dunes north of Kassiesbaai, and goods salvaged from the wreck were offered for sale by public auction two months later. This was not an unusual occurrence along this stormy coast, which lay on Europe's trading route to the East Indies. In a museum a few miles inland, at a nondescript farming town called Bredarsdorp, I saw a map marked with 120 red and white circles. Each denoted a shipwreck on a 45-mile stretch of local coastline, which gave the area a notoriety comparable with the skeleton coast of Namibia. A helpful lady in the museum explained that vessels kept sinking in the old days because of uncharted reefs far out to sea, magnetic disturbances that affected compass bearings and storms driven from the Cape by south-easters. Spontaneous combustion was also a problem on coal-carriers, she added interestingly. A typical tale of misfortune involved *Nostra Signora de los Milagros*, a Portuguese East Indiaman blown on to rocks off Cape Agulhas on 16 April 1686. A Siamese delegation on its way to the court of Louis XIV managed to struggle ashore, but during the trek to Cape Town hunger took its toll and the mandarins were compelled to eat their shoes. Only a few gaunt survivors reached Table Bay a month later, thus proving there is little nutritional value in footwear.

The shipwreck museum at Bredarsdorp was full of such lore, as well as bits and bobs from ships that went down: flags and anchors, a 12-pounder canon, coins and crockery, and advertisements from the *Cape Argus* for auctions of salvaged merchandise. In the 1870s the citizens of Cape Town were invited to bid for coffee, wine and brandy from the steamer *Celt*, 2,000 hogshead staves and ten ploughs from the schooner *Minnie*, and nine bales of straw hats from the barque *Elizabeth A. Oliver*. Museums should be places that fire the imagination, and this little collection succeeded admirably with its star attraction. In a high-ceilinged room towered monumental images of Norwegian kings, English knights and Flemish noblemen, gazing at distant horizons with the stern bravado they displayed on the bows of ships battering through black south-easters. Looking up at the figureheads you could hear the high-pitched shriek of gales, and see huge waves advancing and feel the tremor of them slamming into wooden hulls. All the romance and danger of roaming the high seas in tall ships was there, incongruously, in a side street in a sleepy little *dorp* 15 miles from the sea.

25

The most southerly fish in Africa

The southern tip of Africa lies at the end of a country road that runs as straight as an arrow across flat scrubland and then winds around a rocky coast to a red and white lighthouse that was modestly modelled on the Pharos of Alexandria, one of the Seven Wonders of the Ancient World. Given the stream of ships that came to grief in the area before the light was built in the 1840s, it is a wonder nobody thought of it before. This is Cape Agulhas, the dreaded Cape of Needles, so called by sixteenth-century Portuguese navigators who observed on passing the point that their compass needles showed no declination between true and magnetic north. For many of them, unfortunately, this interesting discovery came too late.

The village that grew up on this rugged shore began life in the 1930s as a holiday resort for local farmers, and has all the appeal one would expect from a place founded by people whose idea of a good time was to drive a few miles from the farm and look at the sea and worry about the stock back home. Its claim to fame is announced on a sign by a petrol station that says 'Welcome to Agulhas, the Southernmost Town in Africa'. There are other signs proclaiming the most southerly café in Africa, and the most southerly bed & breakfast in Africa, and I found myself musing on whether an enterprising lady might one day advertise her services as the last hooker before Antarctica. The lighthouse is, of course, a museum (the most southerly in Africa), while still fulfilling its original purpose. It was built with public donations and contributions from Calcutta, Bombay, Madras, St Helena and London, and when completed it projected a light of 4,500 candlepower with oil derived from sheeptail fat. It now shines more brightly, but this mini Pharos at the wrong end of Africa still looks odd. The architect who considered its fake entrance resembled the Temple of Isis was a man of great vision.

The geographical southern extremity of the continent is marked by a stone cairn that stands on the rocky shore at a latitude of 34°, 49′ 58″ south. It is adorned with a plaque and arrows pointing out that you are 6,135 kilometres from the South Pole, 13,882 kilometres from the North Pole, 147 kilometres east-south-east of Cape Point and 9,797 kilometres from London if anyone is interested. When I arrived a middle-aged man from the Midlands of England, wearing a red baseball cap and not much else, was prancing about on top of the cairn and giving a good impression of a baboon. He was also trying to film himself with a video camera. I presumed it had something to do with the magnetic disturbances.

Of more interest was that this was officially where the icy currents of the South Atlantic collided with the warm waters of the Indian Ocean. If there was a titanic clash of tides going on, a battle for supremacy between two of the greatest bodies of water on Earth, it was not apparent. Beneath blue skies the sea was deceptively calm, breaking with a regular rhythm against dark, craggy rocks streaked with lichen. When the ape-man of the cairn and his chums had left, I sat alone listening to the wind and the waves and gazing at this graveyard of ancient mariners on the edge of the world. The first Europeans who passed this way had little idea of what they might discover in the continent that loomed to port, and none whatever of the frozen wastes that lay to the south. It was vaguely disturbing to contemplate that beyond the horizon lay nothing but the tumult of the Roaring Forties and the loneliness of Antarctica.

If Dias returned today, I fear he would be disappointed. The first human habitation he would encounter in Africa is a red-brick bungalow with an iron roof near the cairn, bearing signs in English and Afrikaans saying 'Private Property'. This is probably an improvement on the natives who chucked stones at him when he first arrived, but not much. Turning my back on the entire continent, I ventured a few steps beyond the cairn towards the sea. There I bathed my feet in a tidal pool and watched little brown fish flitting in the clear water, musing that they were unquestionably the most southerly fish in Africa.

My journey was almost complete, but there was one more place I wanted to visit. In the early hours of 26 February 1852, a British frigate carrying reinforcements for the Eighth Frontier War in the eastern Cape struck a sunken reef about a mile off a point whose notoriety was well established. It was called Danger Point. HMS *Birkenhead*, 1,900 tons, was powered by steam-driven paddles as well as sail, and she was one of the first of Her Majesty's iron-hulled warships. But she was ripped open by the rocks, and about a hundred soldiers sleeping on the lower deck were immediately drowned. What happened next was a drama that established the maritime tradition of 'women and children first', known to seafarers as the Birkenhead Drill.

Danger Point is reached by a dirt road that snakes across a bleak, flat peninsula towards a raised headland dominated by a lighthouse. There was nobody around when I parked in the lee of the slope, and the sounds of an agitated sea carried around the promontory that blocked it from view. From the crest, the view was unnerving. Even on a calm day, Atlantic swells surged and crashed with impotent fury against the barely submerged rocks that had claimed the *Birkenhead*. It was hard to imagine how anyone could survive a shipwreck in such treacherous waters, but all seven women and thirteen children aboard had reached safety because of an act of extraordinary heroism. Only three of the eight lifeboats could be launched, and the women and children were helped into them along with as many men as they could take. Then came the general order to abandon ship. At this point the officer commanding the troops, Lieutenant-Colonel Alexander Seton, drew his sword and ordered the men mustered on deck not to jump for fear of swamping the lifeboats that were struggling to get away. The men duly stood fast, even when the ship broke in two and her funnel and main mast crashed onto the deck. Within twenty minutes of striking the reef, *Birkenhead* plunged. Dozens of men were rescued by a schooner, and others managed to swim ashore, but 445 soldiers and sailors perished, including Seton and the ship's captain, Robert Salmond. An official account said 'great numbers were taken by sharks'.

Standing on the headland, I tried to picture the disaster. But the reef was baring its teeth at an empty sea, and only the wind seemed to remember with a mournful note through the wires of a radio mast.

After six months on the road, I was barely an hour's drive from my starting point. My journey had begun in the southern spring and now it was autumn, and a mellowness had settled on the land after the cycle of fruitfulness and harvesting. I felt it too as I drove towards the sunset, a sense of having come full circle and of labours rewarded. In my travels I had caught glimpses and echoes of the old Africa, and seen the transition to a new order that raised hopes and fears. The wind of change forecast by Harold Macmillan in 1960 had blown away racial oppression that had endured for three centuries. But incompetence and corruption in government were threatening the fabric of freedom, and there was unease even among those who had most to gain from the 'Rainbow Nation'.

The euphoria of majority rule had evaporated, and Tutu's vision of a multi-racial Utopia remained an ideal. The cycles of optimism and despair were short, and there were concerns that time was running out. It seemed that the country in search of an identity was handicapped by a split personality: on the one hand it had a wealth of natural resources, the best infrastructure in Africa, and people with entrepreneurial skills to harness them; on the other its cities were decaying, the shanty towns were mushrooming, and chronic violence was spiralling out of control. There was a joke about whites fleeing crime-ridden neighbourhoods of Johannesburg and Durban for the relative security of Cape Town. The joke was that it was like running to the top deck of the *Titanic*.

So thousands were jumping into lifeboats bound for Australia and Europe. They looked at the rest of Africa and saw an economic disaster, a black hole devouring energy and resources, and they were afraid their country was going the same way. The government was struggling to deal with the legacies not only of apartheid, but of centuries of colonialism. Its task was to realise the aspirations of the black majority and dispel the anxieties of other races; to raise basic living standards, curb violent crime, and stem the emigration of white professionals the country could ill afford to lose. The essence of the problem was expressed by a newspaper editor: 'People are worried that public administration and law and order are breaking down. It is vital we get it right before we go over the edge.' For the majority of black and coloured people, there were no life-boats to Europe or Australia. They were trapped by poverty as firmly as ever, and they had to endure horrific violence in their communities without the protection of electrified fencing and armed security guards, or even the semblance of an efficient police force. For them the race against time was becoming critical.

So was Tutu's rainbow merely a pretty illusion? After months of listening to South Africans discussing their future, I suspected it was. But I tended to be optimistic that this exuberant assortment of races and tribes would work out a *modus vivendi*, on the grounds that the crooks and the crazies were vastly outnumbered by decent people determined to rub along with each other as best they could, because there was no other way.

There was no other way from the summit of the last mountain pass on my journey but down, on a switchback road to the coastal plain around Cape Town. On one side, the jagged ramparts of the Hottentots Holland mountains were glowing crimson in the setting sun, and on the other the broad curve of False Bay swept towards a familiar sight. High above the sprawl of human settlement, aloof yet benign, stood the silhouette of Table Mountain. It was like a sign saying welcome home.

Epilogue

A few weeks after I had written the last chapter of this book, a 14-year-old boy squeezed through the burglar bars of a house in the Woodstock area of Cape Town. It was the dead of night, but he had been heard.

A woman cradling an infant daughter awoke her partner, who went to investigate. Bleary with sleep, the man confronted the intruder, a knife flashed, and he was fatally stabbed through the heart. The youth was arrested in the neighbourhood two days later, still wearing clothes stained by the blood of his victim.

The blood belonged to John Rubython, to whom this book is dedicated. John was a courageous photo-journalist whose work memorably exposed the lunacy of apartheid. It seemed absurd that he should be killed by one of the township urchins whose cause he had championed.

I wrote a brief appreciation of his life which was published in South African newspapers. In it, I pointed out that a measure of a civilised society is the extent to which it safeguards its people from violent criminals in their midst, and it was clear South Africa was failing the test. In anger, I concluded: 'So farewell, John old pal. The society you fought so hard to achieve doesn't deserve you.'

The funny thing is that I know John would not have agreed. He would have shaken his head at yet another senseless death, then he would have found something positive to restore his faith in humanity, and continued riding hopefully on South Africa's emotional roller-coaster. Along with millions of others with nowhere else to go.

LONG WALK TO FREEDOM

Nelson Mandela

The riveting memoirs of the outstanding moral and political leader of our time, *Long Walk to Freedom* brilliantly re-creates the drama of the experiences that helped shape Nelson Mandela's destiny. Emotive, compelling and uplifting, *Long Walk to Freedom* is the exhilarating story of an epic life; a story of hardship, resilience and ultimate triumph told with the clarity and eloquence of a born leader.

'Burns with the luminosity of faith in the invincible nature of human hope and dignity . . . Unforgettable'
André Brink

'It is the style, so typical of the man, which marks this marvellous book as a truly personal work . . . Superb'
Gerald Kaufman

'A truly stunning account of his extraordinary life . . . A vivid testimony to an unusual mixture of courage, persistence, tolerance, and forgiveness'
Sir David Steel

'One of the most extraordinary political tales of the 20th century and well worth the investment for anyone truly interested in the genesis of greatness'
Patti Waldmeir in the *Financial Times*

'An epic of struggle and learning and growing, it tells of a man whose idealism and hope have inspired a world prone to cynicism . . . [it] should be compulsory reading'
Mary Benson in the *Daily Telegraph*

Abacus
0 349 10653 3

FROST ON MY MOUSTACHE

The Arctic Exploits of a Lord and a Loafer

Tim Moore

'Made me laugh out loud in public, like an escaped psychopath'
Observer

In 1856, the swashbuckling aristocrat Lord Dufferin sailed
to Iceland and the Arctic Circle, an adventure that became a
bestselling travelogue. A century and a half later, soft suburbanite
Tim Moore tried to recreate the celebrated journey with a similar
degree of pluck, dignity, and stiff upper lip.

Whilst Dufferin's battle with icebergs and the elements is a tale
of derring-do, Moore's struggle against seasickness, a clan of
Brummie Vikings and terrifying hallucinations involving Nerys
Hughes is all too plainly one of derring-don't. As Moore says,
'Dufferin seems the personification of Kipling's "If". I'm more
of a "But . . ." man myself.'

'A joy' Vic Reeves

'Book of the year' *Spectator*

'A contender for Bill Bryson's crown as king of comic travels'
Sunday Times

'One of the funniest travelogues you will ever read' *Express*

Abacus Travel
0 349 111405

OUR LADY OF THE SEWERS

And Other Adventures in Deep Spain

Paul Richardson

'He knows stuff about Spain we fly-by-nights can only guess at'
Guardian

Paul Richardson's mission – 'to sieve out the ancient, perverse
and eccentric from the new, nice and normal' – took him from
coastal plain to mountainous peak. It also took him, often by
surprise, from ritual pig-killings to wood-chopping competitions,
from an alchemist who eats stone, to pilgrimages in the name of
obscure Virgins, his journey into deep Spain is captivating, often
hilarious – and always highly illuminating.

'Richardson writes vividly about some of the wilder characters he
meets . . . read *Our Lady of the Sewers* if you want a glimpse of
the surviving truth behind tour-operator clichés, and for a view of
Spain that is becoming ever harder to find'
Sunday Times

'Puckish, witty, casually erudite . . . delivers acute and sharply
observed portraits of both people and places'
TLS

'Fascinating . . . The really amazing thing about Spain is
that it continues to stimulate people into writing books as
interesting as this'
Independent on Sunday

Abacus Travel
0 349 10857 9

Now you can order superb titles directly from Abacus

☐ Travels in the White Man's Grave	Donald MacIntosh	£9.99
☐ Long Walk to Freedom	Nelson Mandela	£10.99
☐ Our Lady of the Sewers	Paul Richardson	£7.99
☐ Ciao Asmara	Justin Hill	£10.99

Please allow for postage and packing: **Free UK delivery.**
Europe; add 25% of retail price; Rest of World; 45% of retail price.

To order any of the above or any other Abacus titles, please call our credit card orderline or fill in this coupon and send/fax it to:

Abacus, P.O. Box 121, Kettering, Northants NN14 4ZQ
Tel: 01832 737527   Fax: 01832 733076
Email: aspenhouse@FSBDial.co.uk

☐ I enclose a UK bank cheque made payable to Abacus for £ ....

☐ Please charge £.............. to my Access, Visa, Delta, Switch Card No.

▢▢▢▢▢▢▢▢▢▢▢▢▢▢▢▢▢▢▢

Expiry Date ▢▢▢▢ Switch Issue No. ▢▢

NAME (Block letters please) ....

ADDRESS ....

....

....

Postcode ....Telephone ....

Signature ....

Please allow 28 days for delivery within the UK. Offer subject to price and availability.

Please do not send any further mailings from companies carefully selected by Abacus ▢